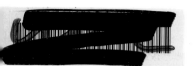

D1570459

Contemporary Questions Surrounding the Constitutional Amending Process

CONTEMPORARY QUESTIONS SURROUNDING THE CONSTITUTIONAL AMENDING PROCESS

John R. Vile

PRAEGER

Westport, Connecticut
London

Library of Congress Cataloging-in-Publication Data

Vile, John R.
    Contemporary questions surrounding the constitutional amending
process / John R. Vile.
        p.   cm.
    Includes bibliographical references and index.
    ISBN 0–275–94541–3 (alk. paper)
        1. United States—Constitutional law—Amendments.   2. United
    States—Constitutional history.   I. Title.
    KF4555.V56   1993
    342.73′03—dc20
    [347.3023]   92–41606

British Library Cataloguing in Publication Data is available.

Library of Congress Catalog Card Number: 92–41606
ISBN: 0–275–94541–3

First published in 1993

Praeger Publishers, 88 Post Road West, Westport, CT 06881
An imprint of Greenwood Publishing Group, Inc.

Printed in the United States of America

The paper used in this book complies with the
Permanent Paper Standard issued by the National
Information Standards Organization (Z39.48–1984).

10 9 8 7 6 5 4 3 2 1

Copyright Acknowledgments

The author and publisher gratefully acknowledge permission to reprint from the
following articles:

John R. Vile. "Legally Amending the United States Constitution: The
Exclusivity of Article V's Mechanisms." Adopted from 21 *Cumberland Law
Review* 271–307 (1990–1991) by permission. © 1991 by CUMBERLAND LAW
REVIEW.

John R. Vile. "Limitations on the Constitutional Amending Process,"
Constitutional Commentary 2 (Summer 1985), 373–88.

To Willard and Norma Scofield

Contents

Preface

I have been fascinated by the constitutional amending process and by associated mechanisms for constitutional change for more than a dozen years. Moreover, I firmly believe that an understanding of these topics involves far more than a mere tallying of amendment votes and an explication of their context. Rather, I think that the subject of constitutional change deserves the same kind of attention that has been devoted to such topics as representation, federalism, judicial review, executive leadership, and the like.

In a number of previous books, I have attempted to widen the existing field of study. My first book, *Rewriting the United States Constitution* (Praeger, 1991), outlines some forty plus proposals that have been introduced from Reconstruction to the present to remake the U.S. Constitution. I followed this book with a look at major American statesmen and theorists who have discussed the amending process in philosophical terms (*The Constitutional Amending Process in American Political Thought*, Praeger, 1992). I have also written a supplemental book on the U.S. Constitution in which I emphasize the importance that amendments have had in American constitutional development (*A Companion to the United States Constitution and Its Amendments*, Praeger, 1993), and, almost simultaneously with this book, I am editing a volume of readings (*The Theory and Practice of Constitutional Change in America, A Collection of Original Source Materials*, 1993) designed to show that discussions of the processes of constitutional change have been a permanent staple of political thought.

None of the books that I have authored to date addressed modern amending controversies in depth, although I have from time to time engaged in a number of such debates in the forum of law and political science reviews.

This book addresses such controversies in a systematic fashion which focuses, where possible, on the intentions of the Framers of Article V and on the history and the lessons of experience of the operation of this process.

To this end, I have organized this book around five basic themes, or questions, that encompass most issues of modern debate; they follow an initial chapter which details the history of the amending process in America. The importance of the questions I have chosen should be apparent; the labels used to designate them are, however, somewhat arbitrary and overlapping.

The first question is that of justiciability. Specifically, which branch of government should have the ultimate say over issues involving the amending process? Should it be the legislative or judicial branch? This may seem a peculiar place to start an inquiry but it is quite important. If Congress should make amending decisions alone, they might be far different than if they are to be subject to subsequent judicial review. Moreover, there are conflicting legal precedents in this area as to what role the judicial branch should play.

Deciding on an arbiter does not, of course, necessarily indicate what approaches this arbiter should take. The second question that I address in this book is accordingly the question of standards. Specifically, I focus on what rules are most appropriately applied to procedural issues surrounding the amending process. While some might argue for ad hoc case-by-case decision making, the primary debate is between those who favor a formalistic approach and those who stress contemporary consensus. Again, there are justifications for both approaches in existing case law, and there has been sharp controversy over such issues as whether Congress was justified in extending the ratification time for the Equal Rights Amendment, whether states have the right to rescind ratifications of pending amendments, and whether the belated ratifications of the Congressional Pay Raise amendment have been valid.

One of the most fascinating set of procedural questions has centered on the untried Article V convention mechanism, with the fundamental question being one of safety. In Chapter 4, I accordingly address the third question of whether there are adequate rules and enforceable limits on such Article V conventions and, if so, who is responsible for enforcing them. This matter is perhaps the most contentious area of current debate, and it is important to address this issue beforehand rather than in the middle of a partisan political controversy.

Focus on the formal amending process might, of course, be misplaced if there are means of changing the Constitution outside of Article V. In dealing with the fourth question of exclusivity, I address claims that the Constitution can be amended in such fashion. Such assertions range from relatively mild claims for judicial review to stronger allegations that the line between constitutional interpretation and constitutional amendment is impossible to draw to claims like Bruce Ackerman's that an informal process of "structural amendment" has developed. These claims are addressed in Chapter 5. Chapter 6 continues the focus on the question of exclusivity by examining the arguments of Akil Reed Amar that there are ways to propose and ratify constitutional amendments outside of Article V mechanisms.

In subsequently focusing on the fifth question of limitations, I address claims that there are implicit restraints on the substance of constitutional amendments that may be offered. Arguments first raised by John C. Calhoun, later by early-twentieth-century conservatives, and then by more liberal scholars such as Walter Murphy and others hypothesizing such reservations have been recently applied to the flag-burning controversy. I address both general and specific claims in this chapter, ending this book with what this and other controversies teach about the relationship between the amending process and the idea of government by the people.

While this book is shaped by the questions it addresses, it is also influenced by the scholars it engages in dialogue. There are literally hundreds of articles on the amending process, some born of partisan controversy and others of a more general nature. While I have attempted to be relatively generous in footnote attributions to participants in current debates, this book does not focus on all participants equally. I have found that a number of participants in modern controversies have addressed problems from a larger theoretical perspective. By and large these individuals have published in respected journals; most have written multiple articles and/or books on the subject. Among them are Walter Dellinger, Walter Murphy, Akil Reed Amar, Sanford Levinson, Grover Rees III, Charles Black, William Van Alstyne, Paul Weber and Barbara Perry, Laurence Tribe, Douglas Linder, and Bruce Ackerman.

I have learned a great deal from all of these writers as well as from many others, but, in a number of cases, I also have sharp disagreements to express. These views are recorded here not with a view to stir personal animosities but with the higher objective of pursuing truth and stimulating still further debate. Perhaps more than most, I have discovered that my own views are best sharpened by consideration of the views of others. I hope that all who read this book find their own thinking about the amending process clarified and that they are challenged to engage in still further thinking and dialogue about this fascinating subject.

Acknowledgments

As much as any other work I have written, this book builds on research and writing that I have done in connection with earlier books, articles, and essays that I have written, a few of which are cited on the copyright acknowledgments page. During my years of research on the constitutional amending process, I have accumulated numerous debts to teachers, colleagues, editors, and others who have stimulated and refined my thinking. I have acknowledged many of these individuals by name in previous works.

Again, I owe special thanks to the Research Committee at Middle Tennessee State University which awarded me a grant during which I was able to make some headway on this and other projects. More generally, I owe thanks to the supportive administrators, colleagues, and students at this institution who have encouraged me in my work. Our interlibrary loan librarians, Betty McFall and Peggy Colflesh, have been especially helpful in locating obscure journal articles and helping me to track down articles listed in the latest issues of the *Index to Legal Periodicals*. My wife Linda and my daughters Virginia and Rebekah have again made the usual sacrifices necessitated by a husband and father whose scholarly obsessions have often left them with special burdens which they have cheerfully shouldered. My friends and the members of the MTSU Political Science Department, too, have allowed me the leisure to pursue my thoughts and have patiently endured my explanations of obscure points of law. I also wish to thank my helpful editors at Praeger, James Dunton, Richard Sillett, and Clare Wulker.

I dedicate this book to a special uncle and aunt who, while serving much of their lives as missionaries to Zaire, have also been especially generous to and supportive of my family and me.

Contemporary Questions Surrounding the Constitutional Amending Process

Chapter 1

The Origins and History of the Constitutional Amending Process in America

One of the glories of the United States of America is its claim to live under a written constitution, thereby formalizing James Harrington's wise maxim that government should be an "empire of laws and not of men,"[1] while departing from the British model of parliamentary sovereignty.[2] As bicentennial celebrations of the United States Constitution in the last decade have indicated, this Constitution is now the world's oldest. It has also served as a prototype for many newly emerging democracies.[3]

Although some individuals have asserted that the U.S. Constitution is a perfect document,[4] such claims do not ring true to those who know its history and origins.[5] Although many hoped and prayed for divine blessings on their work, the fifty-five delegates to the Constitutional Convention of 1787 did not go to a mountaintop to receive authoritative commands but rather spent a long, hot summer forging a series of compromises that would lead to "a more perfect Union."[6] Some of their solutions have remained relatively permanent, but others were clearly inadequate and have since been revised.

ANTECEDENTS TO ARTICLE V

A clear indication that the American Framers recognized the inadequacy and contingency of their own work while expressing faith in the wisdom of their posterity[7] is revealed by Article V of the Constitution which provides for formal constitutional change.[8] This provision was not a complete novelty in that an amending process had been developed in rudimentary form in a number of the charters that were issued in the mid-Atlantic region, beginning in the 1680s, by William Penn.[9] In proclaiming independence,

Thomas Jefferson had asserted the peoples' right "to alter or abolish" their existing government.[10] So too, a number of the revolutionary state constitutions, recognizing that the failure of the British Constitution to accommodate legal change had been an important factor leading to the American Revolution, provided for constitutional change.[11] Some provided for amendment by extraordinary legislative action, some utilized the uniquely American mechanism of a constitutional convention,[12] and still others used a council of censors.[13]

Article V was a particularly giant step beyond the mechanism in the first continental government, the Articles of Confederation. On the order of the treaty that this agreement resembled and in accord with the doctrine of state sovereignty it embodied,[14] the Articles required complete state unanimity for any amendments proposed by Congress.[15] No amendments were adopted through this mechanism which proved so ineffective that it had to be ignored when delegates assembled to write a new constitution.[16] Its authors realized that they needed to provide greater flexibility if their document were to avoid a similar fate.

THE ARTICLE V AMENDING PROCESS

What emerged from the convention was a process designed neither to be so easy that amendments would lose their distinction from ordinary laws nor so difficult that the process would be ignored or lead to rebellion. Thus noting that "the plan now to be formed will certainly be defective, as the Confederation has been found on trial to be," George Mason observed that amendments would be needed and that "it will be better to provide for them, in an easy, regular and Constitutional way than to trust to chance and violence."[17] The amending mechanism was also clearly designed, consistent with the federal nature of the Constitution, to provide an important role for the states and to encourage widespread national support. Thus, in defending the amending process, James Madison noted that

The mode preferred by the convention seems to be stamped with every mark of propriety. It guards equally against that extreme facility, which would render the Constitution too mutable; and that extreme difficulty, which might perpetuate its discovered faults. It, moreover, equally enables the general and the State governments to originate the amendment of errors, as they may be pointed out by the experience on one side, or on the other.[18]

This new process involved two steps. First, two-thirds of both houses of Congress would propose amendments. Second, these would subsequently be ratified, at congressional discretion, by three-fourths of the state legislatures or by conventions in three-fourths of the states. If Congress proved unresponsive to national needs, amendments could be proposed in a convention that Congress would be obligated to call after receiving petitions from two-thirds of the state legislatures. While providing an amending process, the American Framers rejected pleas such as those of Thomas Jefferson for periodically scheduled changes in the fundamental law;[19] in practice, however, some states would come fairly close to such a model.[20]

The national amending process contained two explicit limits: One preserved the compromise by which slave importation could continue for another twenty years. The second guaranteed that states would not be deprived of their equal suffrage in the U.S. Senate without their consent.

Consistent with eighteenth-century notions of constitutional elegance, the language of Article V is sparse. This has left a number of important issues in doubt. Nowhere perhaps are questions more pronounced than in the matter of the still unused constitutional convention mechanism. These ambiguities have not, however, prevented the amending process from serving at some critical times in American history as the alternative to revolution that it was intended to be.

THE BILL OF RIGHTS

The new process received an early test as a result of the Federalist/Anti-Federalist debate over ratification of the Constitution.[21] A key objection of Anti-Federalist opponents of the Constitution, a reservation shared by some of its friends,[22] was that the new constitution did not have a bill of rights specifically delimiting the powers of the national government over the civil rights and liberties of its citizens. Although Federalists initially argued that a bill of rights was unnecessary and might (if certain rights were inadvertently omitted) even prove dangerous,[23] constitutional proponents eventually agreed to support a bill of rights as a means of reassuring the public and of heading off the possibility of another convention which would perpetuate national uncertainties and possibly undo the work of the first convention.[24]

When, true to his word, James Madison sought to introduce the Bill of Rights into the First Congress, however, he encountered many arguments for delay. Perhaps the most compelling argument was that it was foolish to amend a document whose weaknesses had not yet been demonstrated in actual practice.[25] Madison's persistence was nonetheless rewarded, and ten of twelve amendments which were proposed to the state legislatures were ratified in 1791.[26] These amendments, particularly the first eight, are perhaps the most revered part of the U.S. Constitution.[27] Formulated largely from prior provisions in state bills of rights as well as from proposals which had been submitted by the states as they ratified the Constitution,[28] key provisions of the Bill of Rights provide protections for such freedoms as speech, religion, and assembly as well as guaranteeing due process rights for those accused of, or on trial for, crimes.[29]

The Ninth and Tenth Amendments deal less with individual rights than with the states and the principles organizing the new government. The Ninth Amendment, rediscovered in a number of cases in recent years[30] and the subject of great contemporary interest,[31] indicated that the listing of rights in the Constitution was not intended to void rights already protected by the states. Likewise, the Tenth Amendment indicated that powers not granted to the national government were reserved to the states.[32]

The two amendments proposed by Congress but not ratified by the states dealt neither with individual rights nor with reserved rights and powers but rather were designed to patch up matters of detail within the Constitution itself. The first, which would have quickly been made obsolete by population growth, changed the ratios for representation in the U.S. House of Representatives so as to guarantee at least one representative for every 30,000 residents until that body had 100 members or more. The second provided that a congressional pay raise would not go into effect until the meeting of the next Congress.[33] Neither these, nor any of the other ten amendments, were proposed with time limits, no such limits having been mentioned or required in Article V.

THE ELEVENTH AND TWELFTH AMENDMENTS

The Eleventh Amendment was proposed in 1794 and ratified in 1798.[34] This amendment provided that the judicial power would not extend to cases against a state by citizens of other states or nations, thus effectively giving states sovereign immunity in such cases. This amendment overturned the Supreme Court's decision which had accepted such jurisdiction in *Chisholm v. Georgia* (1793).[35]

It may well have been understood from the beginning that one of the purposes of the amending process would be to reverse judicial opinions contrary to the popular understanding or desires as to how the Constitution would be interpreted, but this author, at least, has not seen a clear statement to this effect prior to the adoption of the Eleventh Amendment. Moreover, this complex relationship between judicial review and constitutional amendment which developed during the Marshall Court[36] does not appear to be fully worked out until Alexis de Tocqueville's *Democracy in America*.[37] It is interesting that the Court itself was called upon to rule upon the ratification of the Eleventh Amendment in *Hollingsworth v. Virginia* (1798) and that, in upholding the constitutionality of this amendment, it decided that a president's signature was not a requisite for its ratification.[38]

It seems clear that the amending process established itself relatively early as an admired constitutional mechanism and as a reason for constitutional loyalty. In few places was the role of Article V clearer than in Washington's Farewell Address where he admonished that

The Government... containing within itself a provision for its own amendment, has a just claim to your confidence and your support. Respect for its authority, compliance with its laws, acquiescence in its measures, are duties enjoined by the fundamental maxims of true liberty. The basis of our political system is the right of the people to make and to alter their constitution of government. But the constitution which at any time exists till changed by an explicit and authentic act of the whole people is sacredly obligatory upon all.[39]

Like the Eleventh, the Twelfth Amendment dealt with a matter of constitutional detail, a glitch that revealed itself in the electoral college when Thomas Jefferson and Aaron Burr, in effect running as a party ticket, received an equal number of votes.[40] The Twelfth Amendment provided that electors would now cast separate votes for president and vice-president.[41] This constitutional repair has not eliminated the possibility that a president, especially in a three-way race, can be elected without a majority of the popular vote, but more drastic changes in the electoral college (including direct popular vote) have yet to be implemented, and the current system that embraces federalism by representing states as states continues to have its defenders.[42]

THE NINETEENTH CENTURY AND AMENDMENTS THIRTEEN THROUGH FIFTEEN

The early nineteenth century also witnessed the proposal of another constitutional amendment designated the Reed Amendment (after its sponsor, Maryland Senator Philip Reed) which would have prohibited individuals from accepting titles of nobility. Ratified by twelve states, the amendment was actually included as part of the Constitution in a number of contemporary printings of the document; in 1874 Congress passed a law effectively extending the prohibition of this amendment to U.S. diplomats.[43] Another amendment that failed to be ratified was the so-called Corwin Amendment proposed just before the Civil War as part of the Crittenden Compromise in a last-ditch effort to avoid conflict by guaranteeing slave-holding states that the nation would not interfere with the institution of slavery.[44]

As the Civil War broke, earlier expressions of faith in Article V as an adequate safety-valve began to give way to criticism that the mechanism was too difficult.[45] At least one constitutional scholar, Philadelphian Sidney George Fisher, proposed that Congress be able to make such changes, much along the order of the British Constitution, where parliamentary sovereignty prevailed.[46] In adopting the Confederate Constitution, the Southern states, in a mechanism never used during the war, provided that amendments would be proposed by conventions called at the request of three states and subsequently ratified by two-thirds of them.[47] Southern secession and claims of sovereignty by constitutional conventions in Kansas, Illinois, and other states created anxiety and renewed thought about the constitutional convention mechanism.[48] Many states would, of course, revise their constitutions during the Civil War and Reconstruction periods.

The amending process in the Constitution of 1787 showed that it was not dead when three amendments were ratified shortly after the Civil War.[49] While the Corwin Amendment had sought permanent guarantees for slavery, the Thirteenth Amendment abolished such involuntary servitude except as punishment for crime; this amendment extended Lincoln's Emancipation Proclamation which had been justified as a war measure and applied only behind enemy lines.[50] The Fourteenth Amendment overturned the notorious *Dred Scott* decision of 1857[51] by bestowing citizenship upon all persons born or naturalized in the United States and by granting protections against state deprivations of their privileges and immunities, their right to due process, and their right to equal protection of the laws.[52]

It was not altogether clear, however, just how much the authors of this amendment, who themselves appear to have pursued conflicting objectives, intended to interfere with existing state prerogatives, and one consequence was that the Supreme Court read these guarantees much more narrowly than some of the amendment's supporters had hoped.[53] The *Slaughterhouse* cases thus offered a very cramped reading of the privileges and immunities clause.[54] The Civil Rights cases of 1883 overturned the Civil Rights Act of 1875 which had prohibited discrimination in places of public accommodation; the Court ruled that the equal protection clause applied only to state, and not to private, action.[55] *Plessy v. Ferguson* subsequently permitted state-mandated segregation (so-called Jim Crow laws), as long as separate facilities were equal.[56]

The Fourteenth Amendment was, however, rediscovered and reborn in the 1950s with the Court's reversal of the *Plessy* decision in *Brown v. Board of Education*.[57] Subsequently, the equal protection clause was extended to classifications other than race,[58] and the due process clause increasingly became the vehicle by which the Supreme Court came to apply guarantees, once thought only to limit the national government, to the states as well.[59] The enforcement clause of the Fourteenth Amendment was also discovered in the latter half of the twentieth century as a means of augmenting and justifying congressional powers against discrimination.[60]

Reflecting the nature of the times in which it was proposed, the ratification of the Fourteenth Amendment became a highly charged issue. One problem was that it was unclear whether the seceding states, whose representatives were not then seated in Congress, should be counted in assessing the number of states needed to ratify.[61] Moreover, a number of states attempted to rescind their ratifications of the amendment, an action about which the Constitution was silent.[62] The secretary of state, William Seward, then responsible for certifying whether amendments were adopted or not, summarized the situation for Congress. He counted twenty-three loyal Union

states as ratifying plus six Southern states; Ohio and New Jersey had voted
rescissions; if their votes were counted, the number of total ratifications
(29) was one more than the three-fourths required. The issue was further
complicated by the fact that Georgia, which was not on Seward's list, sent
a telegram indicating that it, too, had ratified. Congress subsequently promulgated the amendment.[63] Because additional Southern states ratified as
a condition to readmission to Congress,[64] however, and because the Constitution made no specific provision for such congressional promulgation,
it was not altogether clear that such promulgation ultimately made any
difference.[65] Only one other amendment (the Twenty-Seventh) has been so
promulgated by Congress.

Although Section 2 of the Fourteenth Amendment had provided that
states that denied the right to vote would have their representation reduced,
this clearly was not enough to guarantee that the franchise would be extended to newly freed blacks. The elimination of such racial discrimination
was the goal of the Fifteenth Amendment, a goal hindered well into the
1960s by such mechanisms and subterfuges as literacy tests, difficult reg-
istration procedures, grandfather clauses, all white primaries,[66] gerryman-
dering,[67] physical intimidation, poll taxes, and so forth.[68]

THE PROGRESSIVE ERA AMENDMENTS

No amendments were adopted from 1870 to 1913, although judicial interpretations certainly accommodated the Constitution to changing times in
less obvious ways.[69] Amid a chorus of critiques—most by leaders of the
progressive movement—suggesting that the amending process was unduly
rigid and undemocratic, however, the process once again showed itself
capable of responding to deeply felt national needs.[70] The Sixteenth Amendment,[71] ratified in 1913, overturned the Supreme Court's much maligned
opinion reversing earlier precedents[72] and voiding the national income tax[73]
under authority of one of the vaguest sections of the Constitution of 1787.[74]
In the same year, the Constitution was significantly democratized when the
Seventeenth Amendment provided that U.S. senators would now be chosen
by popular election.[75] Many state legislatures had already begun to accept
the popular choice in making their selections, and other senators were prod-
ded into joining the necessary two-thirds majority by state threats to call a
constitutional convention under Article V.[76]

The Eighteenth Amendment, ratified in 1919 and later repealed by the
Twenty-First Amendment shortly after Franklin D. Roosevelt's election,[77]
provided for national prohibition of alcohol.[78] Never before had sumptuary
legislation been incorporated into the supreme law of the land. Apart perhaps from the Fifteenth Amendment, never did an amendment meet with
such sustained resistance. While the Twenty-First Amendment left states
with the option of limiting the sale and consumption of alcohol within their

jurisdictions, consensus had developed that, on the national level at least, the power of constitutional remedies was limited. This limit was not imposed, as some contemporary commentators had hoped, by persuading the Supreme Court to void the substance of amendments, but by convincing representatives to repeal it.[79]

Other court challenges to the Eighteenth Amendment did prove important. In *Hawke v. Smith* (No. 1), the Court overturned a state constitutional provision mandating state approval of amendments by referenda.[80] In *The National Prohibition Cases,* the Supreme Court rejected claims that the subject matter of the amendment was outside congressional authority while ruling that the two-thirds majority referred to in Article V was two-thirds of a quorum rather than of the full congressional membership.[81] In *Dillon v. Gloss,* the Supreme Court decided that amendments became effective, not when certified by the secretary of state, but when ratified by the last state.[82] Moreover, while accepting the seven-year time limit which had been incorporated into the text of this amendment (the first ever to be so included), the Supreme Court also declared that ratifications must follow sufficiently near upon amending proposals to reflect a contemporary consensus. In *Leser v. Garnett,* the Supreme Court rejected claims that the Nineteenth Amendment was an invasion of the reserved powers of the states and of the state of Maryland's own constitution, declaring that the state's ratifying power "is a federal function derived from the Federal Constitution; and it transcends any limitations sought to be imposed by the people of a State."[83] In *United States v. Sprague,* the Court subsequently decided that Congress was vested with complete discretion in determining whether amendments were ratified by state legislatures or by state conventions.[84]

The Twenty-First Amendment which repealed the Eighteenth was the only one ever to be ratified, not by state legislatures (then dominated by rural interests where dry forces were strong) but by special conventions called within the states.[85] Over some contemporary protests, these conventions turned out not to be true deliberative bodies but rather registered up or down votes, not very much different from state referendums.

The failure of the Eighteenth Amendment was matched by the success of the Nineteenth Amendment which extended the right to vote to women, some of whom had been battling for this privilege since before the Civil War.[86] Suits challenging the constitutionality of this amendment were quickly dismissed, and no subterfuges similar to those that had followed upon the Fifteenth Amendment were adopted to bypass it.[87]

FROM THE PROGRESSIVE ERA TO THE TWENTY-SIXTH AMENDMENT

A proposed amendment that would have given the national government the authority to regulate child labor[88] would also have overturned Supreme

Court decisions in *Hammer v. Dagenhart*[89] and *Bailey v. Drexel Furniture Company*.[90] Following the example of the Nineteenth Amendment rather than the Eighteenth, this amendment was reported to the states without any time limit. When states continued to ratify thirteen years after this amendment was proposed, the matter came to the Supreme Court. Despite the decisions that the Court had earlier made to clarify problems in this area, the Court now declared in *Coleman v. Miller* that the timeliness of state ratifications was a "political question" for congressional determination.[91] The amendment never received the necessary number of ratifications, however, and, practically, the amendment became moot when, in the aftermath of its "switch in time that saved nine," the Supreme Court overruled its earlier decisions questioning congressional power over child labor under the commerce clause.[92]

Amendments from the Progressive Era to the present have dealt with a variety of matters. The Twentieth Amendment, ratified in 1933, shortened the terms of lame duck officeholders by moving presidential and congressional inauguration dates forward. The Twenty-Second Amendment, partly motivated by partisanship,[93] reinstated the informal rule that had governed to the election of Franklin Delano Roosevelt limiting a president to two full terms in office.[94]

Three amendments were ratified in the 1960s. The Twenty-Third Amendment, like the Twelfth, modified the electoral college, this time extending electoral votes to the District of Columbia which had been previously excluded because it was not a state. The Twenty-Fourth Amendment eliminated the poll tax in national elections, an action later extended by the courts to the states via the equal protection clause of the Fourteenth Amendment.[95] The Twenty-Fifth Amendment was designed to deal with the issue of presidential disability.[96]

There was a popular but unsuccessful movement from the 1930s through the early 1950s to limit Congress to a maximum tax on incomes of 25 percent.[97] Also much discussed in the 1950s was the so-called Bricker Amendment that would have limited the power of the president to enter into executive agreements with other nations, bypassing constitutional treaty-making provisos.[98] Quite popular in the 1960s was a proposal led by Senator Everett Dirksen of Illinois to call a constitutional convention to reverse the Supreme Court's reapportionment decisions.[99] This call apparently came but a single state call short of the necessary two-thirds and, along with a series of proposals by the Council of State Governors,[100] stimulated considerable debate about the constitutional convention mechanism in law journals of the day.[101]

The Twenty-Sixth Amendment, like a number of previous amendments, expanded the national suffrage, this time extending the right to vote to those eighteen years and older. Prior to this last amendment, the Supreme

Court had limited the scope of a provision in the Voting Rights Act of 1970—which attempted to accomplish this goal by legislation—only to national elections.[102]

RECENT AMENDING CONTROVERSIES

In the last two decades, two amendments have been proposed by Congress but not ratified by the states. The first and most controversial was the proposed Equal Rights Amendment that would have incorporated protections for gender in the Constitution. Initially received quite warmly, ratifications of this amendment stalled at thirty-five states, three short of the three-fourths majority needed. Ironically, arguments against the amendment ranged from claims that it would undercut family structures and traditional values to claims that the amendment was no longer needed in light of more progressive decisions in the area of gender by the Supreme Court.[103]

As the deadline for ratification of the Equal Rights Amendment approached, some began to notice that the ratification deadline for this amendment was not included within the text of the amendment where it would presumably be self-enforcing, but in the congressional authorizing resolution that accompanied it.[104] After heated debate and extended congressional hearings,[105] majorities in both houses of Congress extended this ratification deadline for an additional three years and three months. Questions over the legitimacy of this move became moot when the amendment still failed to be ratified.

The other amendment that failed to be ratified contained a ratification deadline of seven years within its text. It would have treated Washington, D.C., as a state for purposes of congressional representation.[106] Since the failure of this amendment to be ratified, some have attempted to accomplish, so far without success, this same object through legislation.[107]

Recent years have witnessed sustained movements for a number of amendments including an amendment to overturn Supreme Court precedents[108] and permit vocal prayer in public schools,[109] an amendment to reverse Supreme Court decisions accepting flag-burning as constitutionally protected expression under the First Amendment,[110] an amendment to mandate a balanced federal budget,[111] an amendment to make English the nation's official language,[112] and others.[113]

Perhaps the most bizarre recent development in regard to the amending process has been the belated ratification of an amendment first proposed back in 1789 along with eleven other amendments, ten of which became the bill of rights. Designed to prevent a sitting Congress from raising its own salary, the amendment received only six ratifications by 1791 and then went into a long hiatus receiving a single ratification in 1873 and another in 1978 before being rediscovered by Gregory Watson, a political science student and later an aide to a Texas legislator, who made its ratification his calling. The necessary number of states finally ratified on May 8, 1992, and the amendment received congressional approval despite the long hiatus between proposal and ratification which called into question the idea of contemporary consensus specified in *Dillon v. Gloss*.[114]

Like earlier controversies over the Fourteenth Amendment, the unsuccessful Child Labor Amendment, the proposed Equal Rights Amendment, and the unused constitutional convention mechanism of Article V, this controversy indicates the need for fresh thinking and renewed attention to the key which is capable of unlocking the Constitution.[115] That is the primary purpose of this book.

NOTES

1. *The Political Writings of James Harrington,* ed. by Charles Blitzer (Indianapolis, IN: Bobbs-Merrill, 1955), p. 41.

2. See Edward S. Corwin, *The "Higher Law" Background of American Constitutional Law* (Ithaca, NY: Cornell University Press, 1965), pp. 84–88.

3. For reflections on the current state of comparative constitutionalism, see Donald L. Robinson, "The Comparative Study of Constitutions: Suggestions for Organizing the Inquiry," *PS: Political Science and Politics* 25 (June 1992), pp. 272–80.

4. Michael Kammen reports that some individuals have held the belief that the Constitution is "divinely inspired." See *A Machine that Would Go of Itself: The Constitution in American Culture* (New York: Alfred A. Knopf, 1987), p. 225. A woman traveling abroad in 1840 is said to have referred to "our own glorious Constitution (whose every article should be held as sacred and unchangeable as were the laws of the Persian and the Mede)." See Kammen's, "The Problem of Constitutionalism in American Culture," Expansion of Bicentennial Lecture on Constitutionalism in America, University of Dallas, Irving, Texas, 1985, p. 1.

5. Mark A. Grabner, "Our (Im)Perfect Constitution," *Review of Politics* 51 (Winter 1989), pp. 86–106.

6. Words taken from the Preamble, U.S. Constitution. There are a large number of good accounts of the deliberations of the U.S. Constitutional Convention. See, among others, Clinton Rossiter, *1787: The Grand Convention* (New York: W. W. Norton, 1966); Carl Van Doren, *The Great Rehearsal* (New York: Viking Press, 1948); William Peters, *A More Perfect Union* (New York: Crown Publishers, 1987); Catherine D. Bowen, *Miracle at Philadelphia* (Boston: Little, Brown, 1966); Max Farrand, *The Framing of the Constitution of the United States* (New Haven, CT: Yale University Press, 1913); and William L. Miller, *The Business of May Next: James Madison & the Founding* (Charlottesville: University Press of Virginia, 1992). For the best primary accounts of the convention, which include James Madison's meticulous notes, see Max Farrand, *The Records of the Federal Convention of 1787,* 5 vols. (New Haven, CT: Yale University Press, 1966).

7. For an elaboration of this theme, see Edmond Cahn, "An American Contribution," *Supreme Court and Supreme Law,* ed. Edmond Cahn (Bloomington: Indiana University Press, 1954).

8. This Article reads as follows:

> The Congress, whenever two thirds of both Houses shall deem it necessary, shall propose Amendments to this Constitution, or, on the Application of the Legislatures of two thirds of the several States, shall call a Convention for proposing Amendments, which, in either Case, shall be valid to all Intents and Purposes, as Part of this Constitution, when ratified by the Legislatures of three fourths of the several States, or by Conventions in three fourths thereof, as the one or the other Mode of Ratification may be proposed by the Congress; Provided that no Amendment which may be made prior to the Year One thousand eight hundred and eight shall in any Manner affect the first and fourth Clauses in the Ninth Section of the first Article; and that no State, without its Consent, shall be deprived of its equal Suffrage in the Senate.

It should further be noted that, by guaranteeing each state "a republican form of government," Article IV, Section 4, of the Constitution left states relatively free to alter their own state constitutions. William M. Wiecek, *The Guarantee Clauses of the U.S. Constitution* (Ithaca, NY: Cornell University Press, 1972), p. 76.

9. Edward C. Beatty, *William Penn as Social Philosopher* (New York: Octagon Books of Farrar, Strauss and Giroux, 1975), p. 61.

10. See *The Federal Convention and the Formation of the Union*, ed. Winton Solberg (Indianapolis, IN: Bobbs-Merrill, 1958), p. 34.

11. One state that did not provide for such amendment was Rhode Island. The result was eventual civil war, the so-called Dorr's Rebellion in the 1840s that led to the Supreme Court's decision in *Luther v. Borden*, 48 U.S. 1 (1849). See John R. Vile, "John C. Calhoun on the Guarantee Clause," *South Carolina Law Review* 40 (Spring 1989), pp. 676–72.

12. See Gordon S. Wood, *The Creation of the American Republic, 1776–1787* (New York: W. W. Norton, 1969), pp. 303–43.

13. For development of these mechanisms, see Roger J. Traynor, "The Amending System of the United States Constitution, An Historical and Legal Analysis," (Ph.D. diss., University of California, 1927), pp. 61–62. For a work specifically examining the council of censors mechanism, see Lewis A. Meador, "The Council of Censors," *Pennsylvania Magazine of History and Biography* 22 (1898), pp. 265–300.

14. Thus, Article II provided that, "Each state retains its sovereignty, freedom, and independence, and every Power, Jurisdiction and right, which is not by this confederation expressly delegated to the United States, in Congress assembled." Solberg, p. 42.

15. The relevant provision of the Articles of Confederation was Article XIII which provided that

> the Articles of this confederation shall be inviolably observed by every state, and the union shall be perpetual; nor shall any alteration at any time hereafter be made in any of them; unless such alteration be agreed to in a congress of the united states, and be afterwards confirmed by the legislatures of every state. Solberg, p. 51.

16. This author agrees with Richard Kay's argument that the Constitution was technically illegal, although he does not believe that this fact in any way detracts from the document's greatness. See Kay, "The Illegality of the Constitution,"

Constitutional Commentary 4 (Winter 1987), pp. 57–80. For the Framers' defense of their extraconstitutional actions, see *Federalist* No. 40.

17. Farrand, *The Records of the Federal Convention,* vol. 1, p. 203.

18. Alexander Hamilton, James Madison, and John Jay, *The Federalist Papers,* ed. Clinton Rossiter (New York: New American Library, 1961), pp. 278–79, from No. 43.

19. For an elaboration of Jefferson's views and their reception by other American Founding Fathers, see John R. Vile, *The Constitutional Amending Process in American Political Thought* (New York: Praeger, 1992), pp. 59–78.

20. For the contrast between the experience at the state and national levels, see "The American Constitutional Tradition: Its Impact and Development," and "The Politics of State Constitutional Revision, 1820–1930," both in *The Constitutional Convention as an Amending Device,* ed. Kermit L. Hall, Harold M. Hyman, and Leon V. Sigal (Washington, DC: American Historical Association and American Political Science Association, 1981). For accounts of one of the early waves of state constitutional reform, see Merrill D. Peterson, ed. *Democracy, Liberty, and Property: The State Constitutional Conventions of the 1820's* (Indianapolis, IN: Bobbs-Merrill, 1966). For comments on constitutional revision in a particular state, see Z. Melissa Lawrence, "Constitutional Revision by Amendment—A Louisiana Tradition," *Louisiana Law Review* 51 (March 1991), pp. 849–60.

21. For records of the debates at the state conventions, see Jonathan Elliot, *The Debates in State Conventions on the Adoption of the Federal Constitution,* 5 vols. (New York: Burt Franklin, 1888). The best selection of Federalist writings is still *The Federalist Papers.* The most complete collection of Anti-Federalist critiques is Herbert J. Storing, ed., *The Complete Anti-Federalist,* 7 vols. (Chicago: University of Chicago Press, 1981). For a state by state account of debates over ratification of the Constitution, see *Ratifying the Constitution,* ed. Michael A. Gillespie and Michael Lienesch (Lawrence: University Press of Kansas, 1989). Also useful is Kurt T. Lash, "Rejecting Conventional Wisdom: Federalist Ambivalence in the Framing and Implementation of Article V," 1992.

22. Thomas Jefferson's role is thought to have been particularly important in influencing James Madison. For correspondence on this subject, see Alpheus T. Mason and Gordon E. Baker, *Free Government in the Making,* 4th ed. (New York: Oxford University Press, 1985), pp. 276–94.

23. For some of this discussion, see Thomas J. Moyer, "The Bill of Rights—Its Origins and Its Keepers," *Judicature* 75 (August–September 1991), pp. 57–61.

24. This was a particular concern of James Madison. See Sanford Levinson, " 'Veneration' and Constitutional Change: James Madison Confronts the Possibility of Constitutional Amendment," *Texas Tech Law Review* 21 (1990), pp. 2443–61 and Paul J. Weber, "Madison's Opposition to a Second Convention," *Polity* 20 (Spring 1988), pp. 498–517. More generally, see Edward P. Smith, "The Movement Towards a Second Constitutional Convention in 1788," *Essays in the Constitutional History of the United States in the Formative Period, 1775–1789,* ed. John F. Jameson (Boston: Houghton Mifflin, 1909), pp. 49–115.

25. In debates on June 8, 1789, in the U.S. House of Representatives, Jackson thus noted:

> Our constitution, sir, is like a vessel just launched, and lying at the wharf, she is untried, you can hardly discover any one of her properties; it is not

known how she will answer her helm, or lay her course; whether she will bear in safety the precious freight to be deposited in her hold. But, in this state, will the prudent merchant attempt alterations? Will he employ two thousand workmen to tear off the planking and take asunder the frame? He certainly will not. Let us gentlemen, fit out our vessel, set up her masts, and expand her sails, and be guided by the experiment in our alterations. If she sails upon an uneven keel, let us right her by adding weight where it is wanting. In this way, we may remedy her defects to the satisfaction of all concerned; but if we proceed now to make alterations, we may deface a beauty, or deform a well proportioned piece of workmanship.

Helen Veit, Kenneth Bowling, and Charlene Bickford, eds., *Creating the Bill of Rights: The Documentary Record from the First Federal Congress* (Baltimore, MD: The Johns Hopkins University Press, 1991), pp. 70–71.

26. There appears to have been little thought given to the possibility of submitting amendments to state conventions. The most likely explanation is that the Framers may have joined the idea of congressional proposal to state legislative ratification, and convention proposal to convention ratification. This, of course, was not specifically dictated by the terms of Article V. See Philip L. Martin, "Madison's Precedent of Legislative Ratification for Constitutional Amendments," *Proceedings of the American Philosophical Society* 109 (February 1965), pp. 47–52.

27. For adoption and history of the Bill of Rights, see Robert A. Rutland, *The Birth of the Bill of Rights, 1776–1791* (Chapel Hill: University of North Carolina Press, 1955); Irving Bryant, *The Bill of Rights: Its Origin and Meaning* (Indianapolis, IN: Bobbs-Merrill, 1965); Bernard Schwartz, *A History of the American Bill of Rights* (New York: Oxford University Press, 1977); and Bernard Schwartz, ed., *The Roots of the Bill of Rights,* 5 vols. (New York: Chelsea House, 1980).

For good contemporary treatments of the Bill of Rights, see Robert S. Peck, *The Bill of Rights & the Politics of Interpretation* (St. Paul, MN: West Publishing Company, 1992); Kermit L. Hall, ed., *By and For the People: Constitutional Rights in American History* (Arlington Heights, IL: Harlan Davidson, 1991); Allen Alderman and Caroline Kennedy, *In Our Defense: The Bill of Rights in Action* (New York: William Morrow, 1991); and Geoffrey R. Stone, Richard A. Epstein, and Cass R. Sanstein, eds., *The Bill of Rights in the Modern State* (Chicago: University of Chicago Press, 1992).

For the argument that the amending process does not pose a threat to the Bill of Rights, see John R. Vile, "Proposals to Amend the Bill of Rights: Are Fundamental Rights in Jeopardy?" *Judicature* 75 (August–September 1991), pp. 62–67. For a survey of key works on the Bill of Rights, see James H. Hutson, "The Birth of the Bill of Rights: The State of Current Scholarship," *Prologue* 20 (Fall 1988), pp. 143–61.

28. Donald S. Lutz, *A Preface to American Political Theory* (Lawrence: University Press of Kansas, 1992), pp. 49–88.

29. Akil R. Amar notes that sometimes the Framers exercised "clever bundling" by tying less popular provisions to more popular ones within the same amendment. See "The Bill of Rights as a Constitution," *Yale Law Journal* 100 (1991), p. 1181. The Framers may, however, have associated guarantees—between "personal liberty" and "property rights"—for example, in ways that would not be as apparent

today. See James W. Ely, Jr., *The Guardian of Every Other Right: A Constitutional History of Property Rights* (New York: Oxford University Press, 1992), p. 54.

30. See, especially, Justice Arthur Goldberg's opinion in *Griswold v. Connecticut,* 381 U.S. 479 (1965).

31. See, for example, Randy Barnette, ed., *The Rights Retained by the People: The History and Meaning of the Ninth Amendment* (Fairfax, VA: George Mason University Press, 1989). Also see, Bennett B. Patterson, *The Forgotten Ninth Amendment* (Indianapolis, IN: Bobbs-Merrill, 1955).

32. Although quite popular early in the twentieth century when the Supreme Court often voided national economic regulations on the basis that they interfered with states' rights, the Tenth Amendment has largely fallen out of favor, once leading Justice Stone to comment that "the Tenth Amendment . . . states but a truism that all is retained which has not been surrendered." See *United States v. Darby,* 312 U.S. 100, 124 (1941).

33. For analysis of these two amendments, see Akil Reed Amar, "The Bill of Rights as a Constitution," *Yale Law Journal* 100 (1991), pp. 1137–46; and George Anastaplo, "Amendments to the Constitution of the United States: A Commentary," *Loyola University Law Journal* 23 (Summer 1992), pp. 679–81. For texts of all amendments proposed by Congress but not ratified by the states, see Appendix L, George Anastaplo, *The Constitution of 1787: A Commentary* (Baltimore, MD: The Johns Hopkins University Press, 1989), pp. 198–99. For analysis of these amendments, see Morton Keller, "Failed Amendments to the Constitution," *The World & I* 2 (September 1987), pp. 87–93.

34. For historical analysis, see John V. Orth, *The Judicial Power of the United States: The Eleventh Amendment in American History* (New York: Oxford University Press, 1987). Also see Clyde E. Jacobs, *The Eleventh Amendment and Sovereign Immunity* (Westport, CT: Greenwood Press, 1972).

35. 2 Dallas 419 (1793).

36. See especially *Marbury v. Madison,* establishing judicial review of national legislation, 5 U.S. 137 (1803). In "An American Contribution," Edmund Cahn notes the main lines of this development and its relationship to the amending process.

37. Alexis de Tocqueville, *Democracy in America,* trans. George Lawrence, ed. J. P. Mayer (Garden City, NY: Anchor Books, 1969), pp. 101–2.

38. 3 U.S. 378 (1798). But see Charles L. Black, Jr., "Correspondence: On Article I, Section 7, Clause 3—and the Amendment of the Constitution," *Yale Law Journal* 87 (1978), pp. 896–900.

39. *Washington's Farewell Address: The View from the 20th Century,* ed. Burton I. Kaufman (Chicago: Quadrangle Books, 1969), p. 21. For further analysis of Washington's views, see Vile, *The Constitutional Amending Process in American Political Thought,* pp. 47–57.

40. John J. Turner, Jr., "The Twelfth Amendment and the First American Party System," *The Historian* 35 (1973), pp. 221–37. Also see Richard B. Bernstein, "Fixing the Electoral College," *Constitution* 5 (Winter 1993), pp. 42–48.

41. Although the practice has been for electors to cast their votes for a president and a vice-president of the same party, this is not required by the Twelfth Amendment. For the suggestion that ticket-splitting might be appropriate in this area, see Akil R. Amar and Vik Amar, "President Quayle?" *Virginia Law Review* 78 (May 1992), 913–47. For a more comprehensive view of the electoral college mechanism,

see Walter Berns, ed. *After the People Vote: A Guide to the Electoral College.* rev. ed. (Washington, DC: American Enterprise Institute, 1992).

42. See, for example, Judith Best, *The Case Against Direct Election of the President: A Defense of the Electoral College* (Ithaca, NY: Cornell University Press, 1975).

43. Keller, "Failed Amendments," p. 88.

44. See Stephen Keogh, "Formal & Informal Constitutional Lawmaking in the United States in the Winter of 1860–1861," *Journal of Legal History* 8 (1987), pp. 275–99. Also see R. Alton Lee, "The Corwin Amendment in the Secession Crisis," *Ohio Historical Quarterly* 70 (January 1961), pp. 1–26; and Harold M. Hyman, "The Narrow Escape from a 'Compromise of 1860': Secession and the Constitution," in *Freedom and Reform: Essays in Honor of Henry Steele Commanger,* ed. Harold M. Hyman and Leonard S. Levy (New York: Harper & Row, 1967), pp. 149–66.

Much earlier than these efforts, John C. Calhoun had attempted to read his theory of concurrent majorities into Article V. See Vile, *The Constitutional Amending Process in American Political Thought,* pp. 79–94.

45. This oft-repeated analogy appears to have been coined by Joseph Story. See his *Commentaries on the Constitution of the United States,* ed. Ronald D. Rotunda and John E. Nowak (Durham, NC: Carolina Academic Press, 1987), p. 680.

46. Sidney George Fisher, *The Trial of the Constitution* (New York: Da Capo Press, 1972. Reprint of J. B. Lippincott, 1862). Noah Webster had taken a similar position in an earlier era. Fisher's views on the amending process are analyzed in Vile, *The Constitutional Amending Process in American Political Thought,* pp. 97–105; for Webster's views, see Philip A. Hamburger, "The Constitution's Accommodation of Social Change," *Michigan Law Review* 88 (November 1989), pp. 280 and 300.

47. See Article V of the Confederate Constitution, *The Federalist,* ed. Paul L. Ford (New York: Henry Holt and Company, 1898), p. 731. More generally, see Charles Robert Lee, Jr., *The Confederate Constitutions* (Chapel Hill: The University of North Carolina Press, 1963) and Marshall L. DeRosa, *The Confederate Constitution of 1861* (Columbia: University of Missouri Press, 1991), pp. 43–44.

48. John A. Jameson, *A Treatise on Constitutional Conventions: Their History, Powers, and Modes of Proceeding,* 4th ed. (New York: Da Capo Press, 1972. Reprint of Callaghan and Company, 1887). See Vile, *The Constitutional Amending Process in American Political Thought,* pp. 102–03, for analysis.

49. Moreover, in 1876, the Senate came but four votes shy of proposing the Blaine Amendment which had been proposed by a 180 to 7 vote in the House. The amendment provided that

> No State shall make any law respecting an establishment of religion, or prohibiting the free exercise thereof; and no money raised by taxation in any State for the support of public schools, or derived from any public fund therefor, nor any public lands devoted thereto, shall ever be under the control of any religious sect; nor shall any money so raised or lands so devoted be divided between religious sects or denominations.

See Steven K. Green, "The Blaine Amendment Reconsidered," *American Journal of Legal History* 36 (January 1992), p. 38.

50. Michael P. Zuchert, "Completing the Constitution, The Thirteenth Amendment," *Constitutional Commentary* 4 (1987), pp. 259–83. For a provocative attempt

to give this and the Fourteenth Amendment new meaning, see Akil Reed Amar, "The Case of the Missing Amendments: *R.A.V. v. City of St. Paul,*" *Harvard Law Review* 106 (November 1992), pp. 124–61.

51. 19 Howard 393 (1857).

52. Abraham Lincoln was arguably responsible for providing the impetus to transfer this idea from the Declaration of Independence to the Constitution. See Garry Wills, *Lincoln at Gettysburg: The Words that Remade America* (New York: Simon & Schuster, 1992).

53. For the mixed motives behind this amendment, see William E. Nelson, *The Fourteenth Amendment: From Political Principle to Judicial Doctrine* (Cambridge, MA: Harvard University Press, 1988).

54. 83 U.S. 36 (1873). For a good explication of this case, see Ronald M. Labbe, "New Light on the Slaughterhouse Monopoly Act of 1869," in *Louisiana's Legal Heritage,* ed. Edward F. Haas (Pensacola, FL: Perdido Bay Press, 1983), pp. 143–62.

55. 109 U.S. 3 (1883)

56. 163 U.S. 537 (1886). These and other contemporary developments are outlined in Chapter 10 of John R. Vile, *A Companion to the United States Constitution and Its Amendments* (Westport, CT: Praeger, 1993).

57. 347 U.S. 483 (1954). In a companion case, *Bolling v. Sharpe,* 347 U.S. 397 (1954), the Court also ruled that segregation in the schools in Washington, D.C., was in violation of the Fifth Amendment, thus effectively reading an equal protection component into this amendment as well.

58. See, for example, *Frontiero v. Richardson,* 411 U.S. 677 (1973) applying equal protection analysis to gender classifications and *Trimble v. Gordon,* 430 U.S. 762 (1977) applying the clause to illegitimacy. In his dissenting opinion in the latter case, Justice (later Chief Justice) William Rehnquist argued that equal protection analysis should be reserved to classifications dealing with race and/or national origin, but his position has not prevailed.

59. This development had begun much earlier in the century but reached a peak during the years of the Warren Court. See Melvin I. Urofsky, *A March of Liberty* (New York: Alfred A. Knopf, 1988), pp. 640–43, and 800–25. For a creative interpretation of the relationship between the due process clause and the Bill of Rights, see Akil R. Amar, "The Bill of Rights and the Fourteenth Amendment," *Yale Law Journal* 101 (April 1992), pp. 1193–1284.

60. See, for example, Justice William Brennan's opinion in *Katzenbach v. Morgan,* 384 U.S. 641 (1966).

61. Joseph B. James, *The Ratification of the Fourteenth Amendment* (Macon, GA: Mercer University Press, 1984), p. 278. If these states were counted, 28 ratifications would be needed; otherwise, 22 states would do.

62. Ibid., p. 283, p. 286.

63. Ibid., p. 297.

64. Ibid., p. 298.

65. The best-argued critique of the congressional promulgation model is Walter Dellinger, "The Legitimacy of Constitutional Change: Rethinking the Amending Process," *Harvard Law Review* 97 (December 1983), pp. 380–432. This critique is examined in the next two chapters of this book.

66. These last two issues and their relation to constitutional change are treated

in a particularly able fashion in Clement Vose, *Constitutional Change: Amendment Politics and Supreme Court Litigation since 1900* (Lexington, MA: Lexington Books, 1972), pp. 21–66 and 287–326.

67. For a particularly vivid example, see Bernard Taper, *Gomillion v. Lightfoot: Apartheid in Alabama* (New York: McGraw-Hill, 1962).

68. In 1898, Goldwin Smith suggested the repeal of the Fifteenth Amendment because it was not being enforced. See "Is the Constitution Outworn?" *North American Review* 166 (March 1898), p. 267.

69. An especially keen observer and advocate of this development was Christopher Tiedeman, a prominent law professor who authored *The Unwritten Constitution of the United States* (New York: G. P. Putnam's Sons, 1890). For analysis of Tiedeman's views, see Vile, *The Constitutional Amending Process in American Political Thought,* pp. 115–136.

For later works with similar emphases on the development of customs and usages, see Herbert Horwill, *The Usages of the American Constitution* (London: Oxford University Press, 1925); Don K. Price, *America's Unwritten Constitution: Science, Religion and Political Responsibility* (Cambridge, MA: Harvard University Press, 1985); and Michael Foley, *The Silence of Constitutions: Gaps, 'Abeyances' and Political Temperament in the Maintenance of Government* (London: Routledge, 1989).

70. Vile, *The Constitutional Amending Process in American Political Thought,* pp. 136–56.

71. Raymond G. Brown, "The Sixteenth Amendment to the United States Constitution," *American Law Review* 54 (1920), pp. 843–54. Also see David E. Kyvig, "Can the Constitution Be Amended? The Battle over the Income Tax, 1895–1913," *Prologue* 20 (Fall 1988), pp. 181–200.

72. *Springer v. United States,* 102 U.S. 586 (1881).

73. *Pollock v. Farmers' Loan & Trust Company,* 158 U.S. 601 (1895).

74. The provision in Article I, Section 9, provides that, "No Capitation, or other direct, Tax shall be laid, unless in Proportion to the Census or Enumeration herein before directed to be taken." The Constitution does not, however, define what is meant by a direct tax.

75. For a modern critique of the effect of this amendment on American federalism, however, see Ronald M. Peters, Jr., "Repeal the Seventeenth!" *Extensions* (Spring 1990), pp. 2, 16–17.

On a related matter, Laura E. Little, "An Excursion into the Uncharted Waters of the Seventeenth Amendment," *Temple Law Review* 64 (Fall 1991), pp. 629–58, critically examines the case of *Trinsey v. Pennsylvania,* 766 F. Supp. 1338, 941 F. 2d 224 (1991), in which the Appeals Court upheld a Pennsylvania law permitting the state party committee to nominate candidates for Senate vacancies without holding a primary open to the public.

76. See Marc Leepson, "Calls for Constitutional Conventions," *Editorial Research Reports* 1 (March 16, 1979), p. 198.

77. See David E. Kyvig, *Repealing National Prohibition* (Chicago: University of Chicago Press, 1979).

78. For details, see David E. Kyvig, ed., *Alcohol and Order: Perspectives on National Prohibition* (Westport, CT: Greenwood Press, 1985).

79. For analysis of the long-running series of arguments contending that the

Eighteenth and other contemporary amendments were substantively invalid, see Vile, *The Constitutional Amending Process in American Political Thought,* pp. 157–82.

80. 253 U.S. 221 (1920).

81. 253 U.S. 350 (1920).

82. 256 U.S. 368 (1921).

83. 258 U.S. 130, 137 (1922).

84. 282 U.S. 716 (1931).

85. Everett S. Brown, "The Ratification of the Twenty-First Amendment," *The American Political Science Review* 29 (December 1935), pp. 1005–17. Also see *Ratification of the Twenty-First Amendment to the Constitution of the United States,* Department of State Publication No. 573 (Washington, DC: U.S. Government Printing Office, 1934); and *Ratification of the Twenty-First Amendment to the Constitution of the United States; State Convention Records and Laws,* compiled by Everett S. Brown (Ann Arbor: University of Michigan Press, 1938).

For contemporary advocates of the convention method of state ratification of amendments, see William H. Pedrick and Richard C. Dahl, "Let the People Vote! Ratification of Constitutional Amendments by Convention," *Arizona Law Review* 30 (1988), 1243–56; and Walter Dellinger, "Another Route to the ERA," *Newsweek* 100 (August 2, 1982), p. 8. For an earlier piece, see George S. Brown, "The People Should be Consulted as to Constitutional Change," *American Bar Association Journal* 16 (1930), 404–6.

86. The Fourteenth Amendment had been particularly disappointing for advocates of woman suffrage since it was the first amendment actually to use the word *male* in describing voters.

87. *Leser v. Garnett,* 258 U.S. 130 (1922).

88. Stephen B. Wood, *Constitutional Politics in the Progressive Era: Child Labor and the Law* (Chicago: University of Chicago Press, 1968).

89. 247 U.S. 251 (1918). This decision overruled an exercise of congressional authority based on the commerce clause.

90. 259 U.S. 20 (1922). This decision overruled an exercise of congressional authority based on congressional taxing powers.

91. 307 U.S. 433 (1939). In a companion case, *Chandler v. Wise,* 307 U.S. 474 (1939), the Supreme Court ruled that a state's ratification of an amendment was conclusive once received by the person designated by Congress, then the administrator of the General Services Administration.

92. *United States v. Darby,* 312 U.S. 100 (1941). For Franklin D. Roosevelt's decision to stack the Court rather than pursue the demanding amending option, see David E. Kyvig, "The Road Not Taken: FDR, the Supreme Court and Constitutional Amendment," *Political Science Quarterly* 104 (Fall 1989), pp. 463–81; and William E. Leuchenburg, "The Origins of Franklin D. Roosevelt's 'Court-Packing' Plan," *Supreme Court Review,* ed. Philip Kurland (Chicago: University of Chicago Press, 1966), pp. 347–400.

For an excellent discussion of why some efforts to reverse judicial decisions are more effective than others, see Mark E. Herrmann, "Looking Down From the Hill: Factors Determining the Success of Congressional Efforts to Reverse Supreme Court Interpretations of the Constitution," *William and Mary Law Review* 33 (Winter 1992), pp. 543–610. Also relevant to this issue is Edward Keynes with Randall K. Miller, *The Court vs. Congress: Prayer, Busing, and Abortion* (Durham, NC: Duke University

Press, 1989) and Rafael Gely and Palbo T. Spiller, "The Political Economy of Supreme Court Constitutional Decisions: The Case of Roosevelt's Court-Packing Plan," *International Review of Law and Economics* 12 (1992), pp. 45–67. For a study of the influence of legal arguments on change in judicial doctrine, see Lee Epstein and Joseph F. Kobylka, *The Supreme Court and Legal Change: Abortion and the Death Penalty* (Durham: University of North Carolina, 1992).

X   93. Stephen W. Stathis, "The Twenty-Second Amendment: A Practical Remedy or Partisan Maneuver?" *Constitutional Commentary* 7 (Winter 1991), pp. 61–68.

X   94. For a critique of this amendment, see Ronald Reagan et al., *Restoring the Presidency: Reconsidering the Twenty-Second Amendment* (Washington, DC: The National Legal Center for the Public Interest, 1990).

95. *Harper v. Virginia Board of Elections*, 383 U.S. 663 (1966).

96. John D. Feerick, *The Twenty-Fifth Amendment: Its Complete History and Earliest Applications*, 2d ed. (New York: Fordham University Press, 1992).

97. Russell L. Caplan, *Constitutional Brinkmanship* (New York: Oxford University Press, 1988), p. 69.

98. Duane Tananbaum, *The Bricker Amendment Controversy: A Test of Eisenhower's Political Leadership* (Ithaca, NY: Cornell University Press, 1988).

99. *Baker v. Carr*, 369 U.S. 186 (1962) had decided that apportionment was a justiciable question rather than a "political question." *Reynolds v. Sims*, 377 U.S. 513 (1964) had applied the "one person, one-vote" formula to both houses of the state legislatures.

100. One called for making the amending process easier, the second would have restricted judicial jurisdiction over legislative apportionment, and the third called for a Court of the Union composed of chief justices of state supreme courts who would have power to void judgments of the U.S. Supreme Court. See John R. Vile, *Rewriting the United States Constitution: An Examination of Proposals from Reconstruction to the Present* (New York: Praeger, 1991), pp. 97–100.

101. See, for example, the "Symposium on the Article V Convention Process," in *Michigan Law Review* 66 (March 1968), pp. 837–1017.

102. *Oregon v. Mitchell*, 400 U.S. 112 (1970).

103. For discussion, see Jane J. Mansbridge, *Why We Lost the ERA* (Chicago: University of Chicago Press, 1986); and Mary F. Berry, *Why ERA Failed* (Bloomington: Indiana University Press, 1986).

104. The best scholarly defense of distinguishing time limits within amendments and those within their authorizing resolutions is found in Dellinger's, "The Legitimacy of Constitutional Change," pp. 406–11, which is discussed at greater length in Chapters 2 and 3.

The situation at the time of the Equal Rights Amendment controversy was further complicated by the fact that five states (Nebraska, Tennessee, Idaho, Kentucky, and South Dakota) attempted to rescind their ratifications prior to the end of the original seven year period. See *Idaho v. Freeman*, 529 F. Supp. 1107, 1112 (1981).

105. For contrasting views on the subject, see Ruth B. Ginsberg, "Ratification of the Equal Rights Amendment: A Question of Time," *Texas Law Review* 57 (1979), pp. 919–45 and Grover Rees III, "Throwing Away the Key: The Unconstitutionality of the Equal Rights Amendment Extension," *Texas Law Review* 58 (May 1980), pp. 875–932.

106. See Jules B. Gerard, *The Proposed Washington D.C. Amendment* (Jefferson

City: Missouri Council for Economic Development, 1979); Clement Vose, "When District of Columbia Representation Collides with the Constitutional Amendment Institution," *Publius: The Journal of Federalism* 9 (Winter 1979), pp. 105–25; and Dottie Horn, "Another Star for the Stripes?" *Endeavors* 8 (Fall 1990), pp. 4–6.

107. Peter Raven-Hansen, "The Constitutionality of D.C. Statehood," *George Washington Law Review* 60 (November 1991), pp. 160–93. Also see Jonathan M. Moses, "Statehood for Washington Faces Hurdle," *The Wall Street Journal*, December 9, 1992, p. B14.

108. See, especially, *Engel v. Vitale*, 370 U.S. 421 (1962) and *Abington School District v. Schempp*, 374 U.S. 203 (1963). Both were based on Supreme Court interpretations of the Establishment Clause in the First Amendment of the Constitution. A recent similar case, *Lee v. Weisman* 112 S. Ct. 2649 (1992) prohibited prayers delivered by members of the clergy at public school graduations.

109. See William M. Beaney, "Prayer and Politics: The Impact of Engel and Schempp on the Political Process," in *The Impact of Supreme Court Decisions*, 2d ed., ed. Theodore L. Becker and Malcolm M. Feeley (New York: Oxford University Press, 1973), pp. 22–36.

110. The cases were *Texas v. Johnson*, 109 S. Ct. 2533 (1989) and *United States v. Eichman*, 110 S. Ct. 2404 (1990). See Robert J. Goldstein, "The Great 1989–1990 Flag Flap: An Historical, Political, and Legal Analysis," *University of Missouri Law Review* 45 (September 1990), pp. 19–106.

111. See *The Constitution and the Budget*, ed. W. S. Moore and Rudolph G. Penner (Washington, DC: American Enterprise Institute for Public Policy Research, 1980). Also see, "The Balanced Budget Amendment: An Inquiry into Appropriateness," *Harvard Law Review* 96 (May 1983), pp. 1600–1620.

112. For discussion of this idea, see Dennis Baron, *The English-Only Question* (New Haven, CT: Yale University Press, 1990).

113. There have been a number of surveys and analyses of amendments proposed during the course of American history. See Herman Ames, *The Proposed Amendments of the Constitution of the United States during the First Century of its History* (New York: Burt Franklin, 1970. Reprint of 1896 edition.); *Proposed Amendments of the Constitution of the United States Introduced in Congress from December 4, 1889, to July 2, 1926*, arranged by Charles C. Tansill (Washington, DC: U.S Government Printing Office, 1926); M. A. Musmanno, *Proposed Amendments to the Constitution* (Washington, DC: U.S. Government Printing Office, 1929); *Proposed Amendments to the Constitution of the United States Introduced in Congress from the 69th Congress, 2d Session through the 84th Congress, 2d Session, December 6, 1926 to January 3, 1957* (Washington, DC: U.S. Government Printing Office, 1957); *Proposed Amendments to the Constitution of the United States of America Introduced in Congress from the 69th Congress, 2d Session through the 87th Congress, 2d Session, December 6, 1926, to January 3, 1963* (Washington, DC: U.S. Government Printing Office, 1963); *Proposed Amendments to the Constitution of the United States of America Introduced in Congress from the 88th Congress, 1st Session through the 90th Congress, 2d Session, January 9, 1963, to January 3, 1969* (Washington, DC: U.S. Government Printing Office, 1969); and Richard Davis, *Proposed Amendments to the Constitution of the United States of America Introduced in Congress from the 91st Congress, 1st Session, through the 98th Congress, 2nd Session, January 1969—December 1984* (Washington, DC: Congressional Research Service Report No. 85–36 GOV, February 1, 1985). Some of the difficulties of doing research in these diverse and

incomplete sources are noted in Thomas E. Heard, "Proposed Constitutional Amendments as a Research Tool: The Example of Prohibition," *Law Library Journal* 84 (Summer 1992), pp. 499–508.

For proposals for more major constitutional changes, see Vile, *Rewriting the Constitution*. Also see William R. Pullen, "Applications of State Legislatures to Congress for the Call of a National Constitutional Convention, 1788–1867." (Master's thesis, University of North Carolina at Chapel Hill, 1948); and Fred P. Graham, "The Role of the States in Proposing Constitutional Amendments," *American Bar Association Journal* 49 (December 1963), pp. 1175–83.

For a discussion of which amendments are favored by the American people, see Austin Ranney, "What Constitutional Changes Do Americans Want?" in *This Constitution: Our Enduring Legacy* (Washington, DC: Congressional Quarterly, 1986), pp. 277–86.

114. See Richard L. Berke, "1789 Amendment Is Ratified But Now the Debate Begins," *New York Times,* May 8, 1992, p. 1; and Bill McAllister, "Congress Backs Madison, But Does It Really Matter?" *Washington Post,* May 21, 1992, p. A23. For a more extended discussion written before state ratification of the amendment, see Robert S. Miller and Donald O. Dewey, "The Congressional Salary Amendment: 200 Years Later," *Glendale Law Review* (1991), pp. 92–109. For a critical view, see John R. Vile, "Just Say No to 'Stealth' Amendment," *National Law Journal* 14 (June 22, 1992), pp. 15–16.

115. The analogy is that of Rees in "Throwing Away the Key."

Chapter 2

The Question of Justiciability— Which Branch of Government Should Have the Ultimate Say Over Issues Involving the Amending Process?

In choosing to be governed by a Constitution, the American Framers eschewed many of the more embracive claims for social and economic rights that were to be advanced in a number of constitutions in the next century, preferring to limit their claims to political rights which could in turn be enforced in courts of law.[1] One can certainly take exception to some of the implications of Justice William Howard Taft's statement that "we are under a Constitution, but the Constitution is what the Court says it is."[2] Nonetheless, in legal terms, at least, it is fair to say that where there is no legal remedy, there is no legal right. Thus, had the United States not developed the institution of judicial review, few constitutional rights would be worth more than the paper on which they are written.

Of course, the Constitution does much more than limit rights through a series of negative prohibitions. Much of the support the Constitution provides to liberty stems rather from the system of separation of powers which attempts to provide checks and balances against abuses of any of the three main branches of government.[3] Thus, for example, both the division of Congress into two houses and the presidential veto are designed to prevent improvident and unwise legislation, while the possibility of impeachment is a protection against executive and judicial excess.

According to Article III of the U.S. Constitution, the judicial power extends to all cases arising under the laws and/or the Constitution of the United States. In recent times, this power has become broad indeed, and today, as in Alexis de Tocqueville's time, there are few political issues that do not eventually become legal issues.[4] Nonetheless, not only have judges and justices often made note of the difference between that which is illegal and that which is unwise but the courts have also designated certain questions as political matters best left for resolution to the elected branches of government. Thus, in *Luther v. Borden,* the Supreme Court declared that the question involving which of two rival state governments was legitimate, or "republican" under the terms of Article IV of the Constitution, was a question for Congress to decide, a doctrine that has subsequently been extended to other matters, especially those involving foreign affairs.[5]

COLEMAN V. MILLER AND THE POLITICAL QUESTIONS DOCTRINE

In *Coleman v. Miller,* the Supreme Court suggested that at least some issues involving the amending process might fall into this political questions category.[6] This case arose as a series of disputes over the child labor amendment proposed in 1924. Initially rejected by the Kansas state legislature in 1925, the legislature subsequently voted again to propose the amendment in 1937. At this time, the state senate equally divided its vote, with the legitimacy of the lieutenant governor's tie-breaking ballot subsequently challenged by some losing members of the legislature. Additionally, the challengers argued that prior rejection of the amendment had been conclusive and that the amendment had not been ratified "within a reasonable time."[7] All these claims were rejected by the Kansas Supreme Court from which an appeal was filed.

Citing cases such as *Hawke v. Smith,*[8] and *Leser v. Garnett,*[9] the Supreme Court, in an opinion by Chief Justice Charles Evans Hughes which was joined by Justices Harlan Fiske Stone and Stanley Reed, agreed that the parties had standing and that the Court had jurisdiction over what was acknowledged to be a federal question.[10] On the matter of whether the lieutenant governor was part of the legislature with the power to cast the deciding vote, however, the Court was "equally divided,"[11] being uncertain as to "whether this contention presents a justiciable controversy, or a question which is political in its nature and hence not justiciable."[12]

The next issue for consideration was the effect of prior state rejection of an amendment. Was such rejection (perhaps on the order of prior ratifications) final, or, was it of no effect, the Constitution addressing only the matter of ratification and not of rejection? The Court attempted to look to the history of the Thirteenth and Fourteenth Amendments indicating that, at least in these instances, "the political departments of the Government dealt with the effect both of previous rejection and of attempted withdrawal and determined that both were ineffectual in the presence of an actual ratification."[13] Rather than establish the precedent that all rescissions were invalid and all ratifications were valid, however, the opinion for the Court (joined by the four concurring justices) concluded that

We think . . . the question of the efficacy of ratifications by state legislatures, in the light of previous rejection or attempted withdrawal, should be regarded as a political question pertaining to the political departments, with the ultimate authority in the Congress in the exercise of its control over the promulgation of the adoption of the amendment.[14]

The Court thus refused to enjoin state officials from certifying to the secretary of state that Kansas had ratified the amendment.

Left was the issue of timeliness. The Court recognized that its earlier decision in *Dillon v. Gloss* permitted Congress to set a time limit as a condition to ratification.[15] Moreover, it cited a host of reasons for such limits:

there was a strong suggestion . . . that proposal and ratification were but succeeding steps in a single endeavor; that as amendments were deemed to be prompted by necessity, they should be considered and disposed of presently; and that there is a fair implication that ratification must be sufficiently contemporaneous in the required number of States to reflect the will of the people in all sections at relatively the same period; and hence that ratification must be within some reasonable time after the proposal.[16]

However, the Court then proceeded to limit the force of the *Dillon* precedent by suggesting that it had not committed itself to making a judgment of timeliness where Congress had not so acted.

It is here that the Court's explanation for its political questions doctrine emerged. Citing the variety of answers that had been given as to what period of time would be appropriate for ratifications, the Court noted that

When a proposed amendment springs from a conception of economic needs, it would be necessary, in determining whether a reasonable time had elapsed since its submission, to consider the economic conditions prevailing in the country, whether these had so far changed since the submission as to make the proposal no longer responsive to the conception which inspired it or whether conditions were such as to intensify the feeling of need and the appropriateness of the proposed remedial action. In short, the question of reasonable time in many cases would involve, as in this case it does involve, an appraisal of a great variety of relevant conditions, political, social and economic, which can hardly be said to be within the appropriate range of evidence receivable in a court of justice.[17]

These questions were as appropriate for the Congress as they were inappropriate for the Court:

The questions they involve are essentially political and not justiciable. They can be decided by the Congress with the full knowledge and appreciation ascribed to the national legislature of the political, social and economic conditions which have prevailed during the period since the submission of the amendment.[18]

If met with ratifications by three-fourths of the states, Congress could decide the issue, and that decision "would not be subject to review by the courts."[19]

Looking more broadly at the political questions doctrine, the Court noted that two considerations prevailed: "the appropriateness under our system of government of attributing finality to the action of the political departments and also the lack of satisfactory criteria for a judicial determination."[20] The precedents it cited, however, had to do with foreign relations and with the guaranty clause.[21]

A concurring opinion by Justice Hugo Black in which Justices Owen Roberts, Felix Frankfurter, and William Douglas joined, went much further than the opinion for the rest of the Court. In the judgment of the concurring justices, "The Constitution grants Congress exclusive power to control submission of constitutional amendments," and "final determination by Congress that ratification has taken place 'is conclusive upon the courts.' "[22]

The four concurring justices thus denied all authority to the courts in regard to amending issues. Part of their objection to judicial interference centered on the need for finality that was mentioned in the opinion for the Court. The concurring justices, thus, for example, said that congressional proclamation "will carry with it a solemn assurance by the Congress that ratification has taken place as the Constitution commands."[23] Similarly, they opposed any judicial actions that would "inevitably embarrass the course of amendment by subjecting to judicial interference matters that we believe were entrusted by the Constitution solely to the political branch of the government."[24] As the latter part of this quotation indicates, however, the main consideration of the concurring justices seems to have centered on their view that Article V vests all amending power in Congress:

No such division between the political and judicial branches of the government is made by Article V which grants power over the amending of the Constitution to Congress alone. Undivided control of that process has been given by the Article exclusively and completely to Congress. The process itself is 'political' in its entirety, from submission until an amendment becomes part of the Constitution, and is not subject to judicial guidance, control or interference at any point.[25]

This emphasis is different from the opinion for the Court which also stressed the lack of satisfactory criteria by which the courts could render judgment.

Yet another concurring opinion authored by Justice Frankfurter and joined by the same justices who took part in the other concurring opinion denied that the parties to the suit had any legitimate judicial standing. They claimed that the legislators in question had no specialized claim apart from that of any other citizens of Kansas, or indeed, of any other U.S. citizen.[26]

Justice Pierce Butler authored an opinion joined by Justice James McReynolds agreeing with the Chief Justice that the parties had standing but dissenting from the Court's characterization of a number of issues as political questions. Butler's strategy was to contrast the Court's posture in *Coleman* with its statements in *Dillon v. Gloss,* from which he quoted a full four paragraphs.[27] Butler further observed that the argument that the issue of timeliness was a political question "was not raised by the parties or by the United States appearing as amicus curiae; it was not suggested by us when ordering reargument."[28] Butler argued for adherence to the precedent in *Dillon v. Gloss.*

In reviewing the Court's opinion in *Coleman v. Miller,* it appears that a total of three arguments were advanced for treating some or all Article V issues as political questions. These were (1) the need for finality; (2) the lack of judicial criteria for making such judgments; and (3) the argument that the Constitution itself vested all amending decisions in Congress.

THREE CONTEMPORARY CASES AND THE POLITICAL QUESTIONS DOCTRINE

The political questions doctrine has, of course, developed considerably since 1939, the most important decision being *Baker v. Carr,*[29] in which the Court reversed its plurality opinion in *Colegrove v. Green,*[30] and declared that it would now consider questions of state legislative apportionment to be justiciable, albeit under authority of the equal protection clause rather than the guarantee clause which had been invoked in previous cases. In his opinion for the Court, Justice William Brennan identified six elements, any one of which could implicate the political questions doctrine:

Prominent on the surface of any case held to involve a political question is found [1] a textually demonstrable constitutional commitment of the issue to a coordinate political department; [2] or a lack of judicially discoverable and manageable standards for resolving it; [3] or the impossibility of deciding without an initial policy determination of a kind clearly for nonjudicial discretion; [4] or the impossibility of a court's undertaking independent resolution without expressing lack of the respect due coordinate branches of government; [5] or an unusual need for unquestioning adherence to a political decision already made; [6] or the potentiality of embarrassment from multifarious pronouncements by various departments on one question.[31]

In a second case, *Powell v. McCormack,* the Supreme Court was called upon to decide on the legitimacy of the exclusion of Congressman Adam Clayton Powell from the House of Representatives.[32] One claim was that Congress had been vested with the exclusive power to decide on the qualifications of its own members. The Court rejected this contention as an obstacle to review, arguing that it first had the responsibility of deciding whether the Constitution granted this power to Congress or not. It ultimately decided that, although Congress could—by a two-thirds majority—expel, it could not exclude anyone who met the formal constitutional qualifications for membership, despite several historical precedents which seemed to suggest otherwise.

In *Goldwater v. Carter,* the Court subsequently faced the question of

whether the president had unconstitutionally invalidated a treaty with Tai-
wan.[33] Six justices (Thurgood Marshall, Lewis Powell, William Rehnquist,
Warren Burger, Potter Stewart, and John Paul Stevens) voted to dismiss
the complaint; Justice Powell filed a concurring opinion; Rehnquist filed a
statement jointed by Burger, Stewart, and Stevens; Byron White and Harry
Blackmun voted for a full hearing; and Justice William Brennan issued a
concurring opinion affirming a lower court judgment validating the president's actions. In rejecting Justice Rehnquist's view that the issue involved
was a political question, Justice Lewis Powell reduced the considerations in
Baker v. Carr to three:

(i) Does the issue involve resolution of questions committed by the text of the
Constitution to a coordinate branch of Government? (ii) Would resolution of the
question demand that a court move beyond areas of judicial expertise? (iii) Do
prudential considerations counsel against judicial intervention?[34]

While ultimately deciding that the issue involved in this case was not ripe
for resolution, Justice Powell did not believe that any of these three concerns
precluded judicial resolution in a properly raised case. In a fascinating footnote, Justice Powell did note that the case for application of the political
questions doctrine in *Coleman v. Miller* had been enhanced by the fact that,
in the unique circumstances of the case, judicial review "would have compelled this Court to oversee the very constitutional process used to reverse
Supreme Court decisions."[35]

Justice Rehnquist's plurality opinion in *Goldwater v. Carter* is of value,
although it was joined by only one other member of the current Court.[36]
Significantly, Rehnquist cited the rationale in *Coleman v. Miller* as the justification for his opinion, arguing that the Court should not intervene in
cases where the Constitution was silent.[37] His was a minority opinion,
however, and was rendered in the course of a decision that did not directly
bear on the amending process.

A review of these three cases does reveal that the three considerations
listed by the justices in *Coleman* remain relevant, if such considerations are
in fact present. Two lower court decisions, as well as a number of contemporary scholars, however, call into question the application of these principles to the amending context.

DYER V. BLAIR

The first of these decisions is potentially a particularly important one
because it was written by John Paul Stevens, then a U.S. district judge but
now a Supreme Court justice.[38] The case arose from the state of Illinois
where ratification of the proposed Equal Rights Amendment was at issue.
The Illinois Constitution specified both that ratification votes required a

three-fifths majority and that no such vote could occur "unless a majority of the members of the General Assembly shall have been elected after the proposed amendment has been submitted for ratification."[39] The senate reported a resolution to the lower house by a majority vote that fell shy of this specified two-thirds.

In subsequently considering resolutions to govern the proposal of amendments, the Illinois house adopted its own rule requiring a three-fifths vote, after being advised by the state attorney general that both the three-fifths requirement and the waiting period within the state constitution were invalid, because they conflicted with Articles V and VI of the U.S. Constitution. The vote in the Illinois house on the Equal Rights Amendment won a majority but failed to get the three-fifths vote that had been specified by the house resolution. Four members of the house subsequently brought suit to require that W. Robert Blair, speaker of the Illinois house, authenticate the state's ratification of the Equal Rights Amendment. This suit underwent a number of permutations before finally being accepted for review by a three-court district court on which Judge Stevens sat.

The court began with the issue as to whether either the question for resolution in this case or amending issues generally were political questions left to Congress to resolve. Here Stevens said it was necessary to examine the four-person concurring opinion in *Coleman v. Miller* in light of more recent decisions. Almost summarily rejecting the argument that the text of the Constitution required Congress rather than the Courts to resolve amending issues (one of the three arguments cited in *Coleman*), the court asked instead if "the issue is one which may produce an unseemly conflict between coordinate branches of government."[40] Relying on *Powell v. McCormack,* the district court found no such conflict.[41] In the court's view, "Decision of the question presented requires no more than an interpretation of the Constitution. Such a decision falls squarely within the traditional role of the federal judiciary to construe that document."[42]

This led the court to consider whether there were adequate "judicially discoverable and manageable standards" for resolving the controversy, an issue squarely raised in *Coleman v. Miller,* albeit in regard to timeliness rather than in respect to the legislative majorities needed.[43] Stevens now denied that the parallel governed:

Although the issue in these cases is somewhat comparable to the lapse of time issue in Coleman in that the criteria for judicial determination are, perhaps, equally hard to find, the answer does not depend on economic, social or political factors that vary from time to time and might well change during the interval between the proposal and the ratification.[44]

To the contrary, Stevens argued that the word " 'ratification'. . . must be interpreted with the kind of consistency that is characteristic of judicial, as opposed to political, decision making."[45] He further indicated that "the Constitution permits many aspects of the ratification procedure to be determined by representatives of the several states."[46]

Stevens identified five possible standards with regard to the appropriate state ratifying majorities. One such standard, drawn from the required number of state concurrences required by Article V, would likewise require a three-fourths majority within each state legislature. A second standard would be patterned on "a lesser extraordinary majority—such as the Illinois three-fifths requirement—of the legislatures elected and eligible to vote."[47] This could, in turn, be reduced to "an extraordinary majority of the legislators present and voting,"[48] to "a vote of 51% of the elected legislators," or, in option five, to "a simple majority, a majority of a quorum—or more precisely of the legislators present when a quorum is present."[49]

Stevens cited the 21 to 20 vote of the Kansas legislature that was sanctioned in *Coleman v. Miller* as proving that, "an extraordinary majority is not *required* by federal law" while indicating in a footnote that this did not necessarily preclude the possibility of permitting such a majority.[50] Citing some historical evidence that the Framers of Article V probably assumed that states would act by majority vote, Stevens sided with the equally consistent view "that the framers did not intend to impose either of those alternatives upon the state legislators, but, instead, intended to leave that choice to the ratifying assemblies."[51] Acceptance of this position accorded with the Framers' view of federalism and would prevent the court from having to choose among the five alternatives Stevens had outlined.[52] Stevens accordingly concluded that

Article V identifies the body—either a legislature or a convention—which must ratify a proposed amendment. The act of ratification is an expression of consent to the amendment by that body. By what means that body shall decide to consent or not to consent is a matter for that body to determine for itself.[53]

Stevens's analysis now took a turn. State legislatures or conventions may decide by what majority to ratify amendments, but since a state could not require a popular referendum as a condition to ratification,[54] then the requirements for intervening elections or for super majorities that were contained within the Illinois Constitution were invalid.[55] Stevens distinguished the "states" from the "designated ratifying bodies."[56] Thus, any language within the state constitution was "precatory" (recommendatory) only, and state legislatures could be governed by their own rules of procedure in such instances.[57] While thereby denying that Illinois had ratified the Equal Rights Amendment, Judge Stevens indicated that he believed this was an appropriate area for judicial supervision, albeit oversight that was deferential to a wide range of state choices.

IDAHO V. FREEMAN AND THE POLITICAL QUESTIONS DOCTRINE

Judge Marion Callister of the U.S. district court in Idaho rendered a second decision on the Equal Rights Amendment that casts light on the current state of the political questions doctrine and its relation to the amending process.[58] Two main issues dominated—a state's right to rescind ratification of a pending amendment and Congress's right to extend the deadline for ratification of such an amendment.[59] The Court set both questions against the general background of the Equal Rights Amendment that was reviewed in the first chapter.

The court began with an extended analysis designed to show that the parties to the case (legislators and other leaders of three states that had attempted to rescind the Equal Rights Amendment) had properly invoked standing and that the issues they raised were ripe ones. Perhaps most important in this regard was the court's rejection of the argument that it should not intervene unless and until three-fourths of the states ratified an amendment:

The Court is not aware of nor has it been referred to any case under article V that has been dismissed on the grounds that the case is not ripe because all the steps have not been taken. Rather, it appears that numerous Supreme Court and lower court cases have resolved specific substantive and procedural questions relating to article V prior to ratification by three-fourths of the states.[60]

In turning to the political questions issue, the Idaho Court invoked each of the six criteria set forth in *Baker v. Carr*. In ascertaining whether there was a "textually demonstrable constitutional commitment to a Coordinate Political Department," Judge Callister further noted the defendants' claim that Congress "is granted exclusive and plenary control over all phases of and questions arising out of the amendatory procedure."[61] Pointing out that Judge Stevens had rejected this view in *Dyer v. Blair,* the court further observed that, "the judiciary, while only dealing with article V in a handful of cases, has nevertheless dealt with virtually all the significant portions of that article."[62] Moreover, Judge Callister argued that vesting Congress with plenary power ran counter to the intentions of the Framers who blended state and national powers in a unique federal concoction in creating the Article V mechanism.[63] In Callister's view, the states determine whether to ratify an amendment; in turn, Congress decides whether such ratifications are sufficiently contemporaneous: "Therefore, when the states act on an amendment and certify that determination to Congress, that certification binds Congress leaving it only with the determination of the question of contemporaneousness."[64]

Callister did not, however, decide that congressional decision making, even in the area of ratification, is plenary; rather, he viewed this too as an appropriate arena for judicial review. Arguing that the division of authority between Congress and the states in the area of constitutional amendment indicated the need for a neutral third party like the courts to intervene, Callister argued that

The question of whether or not a rescission of a prior ratification is a proper exercise of a state's power under article V is one that is not committed to Congress, and should not be, but is appropriate for judicial interpretation under the Court's authority to "say what the law is." Furthermore, while the question of the reasonableness of the ratification period is one committed to Congress, such is not the question presented here. Rather, the question presented to the Court is one of procedure under article V and these procedural questions have been held to be ones which the Court must decide.[65]

Moreover, in a footnote, Judge Callister indicated that the political questions doctrine was not even an absolute bar to review of congressional judgments of contemporaneousness.[66]

Given Callister's understanding that the Constitution made no textual commitment precluding judicial review, he turned next to the issue raised in *Baker v. Carr* as to whether the judiciary had a set of "manageable standards" that it could apply to this area.[67] Judge Callister drew heavily from Judge Stevens's opinion in *Dyer v. Blair* as well as from Justice Rehnquist's decision in *Goldwater v. Carter*[68] from which he derived a two-part test. Rehnquist had said that judicial intervention was inappropriate where: (1) no constitution provision governed, and where (2) "different answers might be appropriate in different situations."[69] Although Judge Callister agreed that the Constitution was silent as to the precise issue under consideration, he ruled that, "it is equally evident that the question of the state's ability to rescind and the propriety of changing an established time limitation are ones which should not be answered 'in different ways for different amendments.' "[70] Differing standards would lead to inconsistency and uncertainty, resulting in disorder. Thus, Callister concluded that judicial standards were not lacking.

Following Justice Powell's lead in *Goldwater v. Carter,* Callister combined the last four issues in *Baker v. Carr* (the presence of an initial policy decision for nonjudicial discretion, lack of respect for coordinate branches, the need for adherence to a preexisting decision, and the possibility of embarrassment from multifarious pronouncements) under the heading of "prudential considerations."[71] The most important consideration was whether there was a need for "unquestioning adherence to a political decision already made."[72] Here Callister sought to distinguish the *Coleman* decision from the present case, noting both that the earlier case did not specifically deal with the same issue and that Congress has itself never made a final decision on the matter.[73]

Coleman had suggested that congressional action in regard to the Civil War amendments might be conclusive, but Callister argued otherwise, pointing out that while Congress chose to count rescinding states when promulgating the amendment, it was not clear that these states were actually needed for ratification.[74] Moreover, in subsequently deciding on ratification of the Fifteenth Amendment, Congress did not refer to the Fourteenth Amendment precedent:

> From the foregoing it is plain that Congress has not come to any conclusion regarding the question of rescission. The fact that congressional action could be viewed at best as equivocal would indicate that even if the Court felt compelled to defer to a decision made by Congress, it would be impossible to do so.[75]

Callister followed this analysis with the view that prior rejection and rescission were different issues; thus, the Coleman precedent need not apply to both. In Callister's judgment, if Congress could ignore state rescissions, this would "destroy the balance created in article V and remove the state's power to create a barrier to encroachment by the national government."[76] Like Judge Stevens, then, Judge Callister called into question the scope, if not the existence of, the political questions doctrine as applied to the amending process. Ultimately, Judge Callister questioned both the extension of the Equal Rights Amendment and the majority by which this action was taken, while sanctioning a state's decision to rescind its ratification. The wisdom of these specific judgments is assessed in the next chapter.

WALTER DELLINGER AND THE POLITICAL QUESTIONS DOCTRINE

Of all the essays on the amending process that have been published in the last two decades, probably few have been more widely read than the piece published by Professor Walter Dellinger of the Duke University Law School in a 1983 issue of *The Harvard Law Review*.[77] This piece is forcefully and elegantly written and came at a time when there was still great dispute about the congressional decision extending the ratification time for the Equal Rights Amendment. Part of the attractiveness of Dellinger's argument may well have stemmed from the fact that his argument justified the action Congress had taken in extending ratification in this case while otherwise subjecting congressional discretion to judicial limitations and providing a set of clear answers as to what position the courts should take on the outstanding issues surrounding the amending process. Dellinger made two main points in his article: first, that the judiciary should accept jurisdiction over constitutional amending issues; and second, that in doing so, it should apply a formalistic analysis. This chapter addresses only the first matter, leaving the second for the chapter which follows.

After summarizing the Court's decision in *Coleman v. Miller,* Dellinger argued that the model of congressional promulgation which completely left judgments of timeliness and the effects of prior rejection to Congress had a number of fatal weaknesses. First, "because the decisions of one Congress cannot bind a subsequent Congress,"[78] Dellinger argued that a decision in regard to one amendment would not set useful precedents in regard to others. Thus, this model would lead to uncertainty, even to the extent of allowing one Congress to reverse the judgment of a previous one. Second, Dellinger argued that there was no foundation for the application of the political questions doctrine to this area in the constitution text or in prior "congressional practice" or "judicial precedent."[79] Textually, the Constitution adds no requirement of congressional promulgation to congressional proposal and state ratification. Moreover, the addition of such a step is particularly problematic when applied to the alternative convention mechanism for amendment which was included largely as a way of bypassing a recalcitrant Congress.[80] As to congressional practice, only the Fourteenth Amendment had been promulgated, and this action "was taken without any floor discussion of the basis for the assumed congressional power to determine whether an amendment had been properly ratified."[81] Moreover, *Dillon v. Gloss* later established that amendments become effective when ratified by the last state and not when promulgated by Congress or someone acting in a ministerial capacity on behalf of that body. As to judicial precedents in general, cases from *Hollingsworth v. Virginia* through *United States v. Sprague* had demonstrated that the Court could play an important function in the amending area.[82] Such review did not preclude a role for Congress; here Dellinger advanced the view that Congress could set unalterable time limits by including them within the text of amendments (where they would be self-enforcing) rather than attaching them to accompanying authorizing resolutions.[83]

Dellinger argued that judicial oversight of the amending process was justified on the same basis as other exercises of judicial review and was sometimes essential to vindicate the rights of litigants in real cases and controversies. Furthermore, "the requirement of written opinions justifying results reached, the doctrine of stare decisis, and the judiciary's relative disinterestedness in the ebb and flow of momentary public opinion all tend to give the courts an institutional advantage in establishing and applying fundamental norms."[84] Moreover, written opinions would provide precedents to guide future decisions.

In considering the most common objections to judicial review of the amending process, Dellinger looked at the foundation upon which Laurence Tribe, in answering Dellinger's article, built most of his critique—the fear that "such review would provide the Court with the opportunity to invalidate amendments designed to overturn decisions of the Court."[85] Dellinger responded by observing that only four of twenty-six amendments adopted to the date of his article had modified judicial decisions, and one of these (the Twenty-Sixth Amendment) was not a true reversal.[86] Moreover, he argued that past decisions—one involving the constitutionality of an amendment reversing the Supreme Court—had established the Court's ability to act fairly in such circumstances.[87] He concluded that the Court was unlikely to jeopardize its general powers by making an unprincipled decision about a single amendment to which it objected. Moreover, some amendments, like the proposed Balanced Budget Amendment, are aimed at *congressional* practices rather than judicial decisions and thus would be vulnerable to congressional attack. While the timing of judicial decisions may be unfortunate, since Congress would first have to act so that a real case would exist, Dellinger contended that this is a short-term rather than a long-term problem. In sum, Dellinger believed that judicial review could have an important role to play in resolving controversial amending issues.

GROVER REES III AND THE POLITICAL QUESTIONS DOCTRINE

One of the most explicit answers to Dellinger's article was written by Grover Rees III, a former law professor at the University of Texas who was then Chief Justice of the High Court of American Samoa.[88] Like Dellinger, Rees was particularly concerned about the debates over extension of the ratification of the Equal Rights Amendment. Whereas Dellinger was able to justify this extension, Rees thought that it was unwarranted.[89] Much of Rees' response accordingly deals with the standards that Dellinger proposes for judicial review and with constitutional convention issues not directly relevant in this chapter. What is interesting about Rees's critique, which can be taken as an indication of thinking on the more conservative end of the political spectrum, however, is that Rees was equally emphatic about rejecting Dellinger's formalistic model of judicial review and the model of plenary congressional power which he identified with *Coleman v. Miller*. This latter critique is relevant for our current discussion.

As Rees viewed the situation, the preferred model for amending issues is what he called the "Classical Model" or that of "Contemporaneous Consensus," which he found articulated in *Dillon v. Gloss* but implicit in a number of other decisions in which the Courts reviewed amending issues.[90] This model regards the Constitution as a contract to be interpreted according to "the manifest intentions of the parties—the States, either in their own capacity or as agents for the people—should not be defeated by construction."[91]

Rees opposed the decision in *Coleman v. Miller* for calling this model into question. Not only did this decision break with precedents but it also unwisely made Congress "the judge in its own case,"[92] and set the framework for those who would encourage Congress to do whatever it chose regardless of "the intentions of other participants in the amending process."[93] Like Dellinger, Rees objected to the seeming imposition of a third step in the amending process, that of a "final 'acceptance' by Congress."[94] Rees argued that this new model was particularly unwarranted when judging issues involving a convention called at the request of the states.

Rees extended his analysis of the political questions doctrine later in his article. Rees was particularly critical of Justice Black's concurring opinion in *Coleman v. Miller,* arguing that it stemmed not from an actual statement within the Constitution delegating amending issues to the political branches (Black made this assertion but pointed to no such provision) but was rather motivated by fears that if the Court intervened, especially in an amendment designed to overturn its child labor rulings, the Court would be considered to be a "super legislature."[95]

Rees argued that the solution to judicial abuse is not judicial abstinence but the exercise of sound judicial judgment.[96] Moreover, Rees argued that the courts are much more likely to be able to adjudicate amending issues fairly than is the Congress; the judiciary is the branch "*most likely* to find and apply the law without injecting its own interests and passions."[97] Also, the judiciary would be able to adjudicate more consistently than the Congress.[98]

Rees further argued that the decisions in *Baker v. Carr* and *Powell v. McCormack* had undercut *Coleman v. Miller.* Rees argued that decisions about constitutional amendments were no more complicated than were decisions that the courts routinely make in reapportionment cases.[99] *Powell v. McCormack* had further narrowed application of the political questions doctrine and indicated that past congressional practice was not conclusive of current constitutionality.[100] Rees therefore concluded that the political questions doctrine should not apply in the amending area, a judgment heightened in his view by what he considered to be the unseemly way that Congress had accepted extension of the ratification deadline for the Equal Rights Amendment.

LAURENCE TRIBE AND THE POLITICAL QUESTIONS DOCTRINE

One of the nation's leading constitutional theorists, Harvard law professor Laurence Tribe, like Rees, responded to Dellinger's views of judicial review of the amending process.[101] Initially, it appears that Tribe's objections to Dellinger's arguments for judicial review were less to the idea of review itself and more to the extent of this review and to the formalistic criteria Dellinger had suggested for such review. Tribe thus characterized Dellinger's arguments against plenary congressional control as "a straw man"[102] and indicated the need "to recognize a role for the federal judiciary in policing the outer boundaries of the amendment process."[103] Tribe accordingly advocated "substantial, albeit less than total, deference when courts are faced with challenges to ratification procedures approved by Congress."[104]

Drawing from Justice Powell's opinion in *Goldwater v. Carter*, Tribe did point to the danger "of having the Supreme Court closely oversee the very constitutional process used to reverse [its] decisions."[105] Granting that most amendments are not directly aimed at overturning judicial decisions, Tribe nonetheless observed that

when *Congress* proposes an amendment to the states (as it has proposed all the amendments thus far adopted), the suggestion of a change in the Constitution's text almost inevitably reflects a deep national dissatisfaction with the way constitutional law—elaborated in our system principally by the courts—has theretofore resolved a matter. The resort to amendment—to constitutional *politics* as opposed to constitutional *law*—should be taken as a sign that the legal system has come to a point of discontinuity, a point at which something less radical than revolution but distinctively more radical than ordinary legal evolution is called for.[106]

In elaborating on an idea to which this author returns in Chapter 7, Tribe further suggested that questions involving "the merit," or substance, of a proposed amendment might be "a true 'political question'—a matter that the Constitution addresses, but that it nevertheless commits to judicially unreviewable resolution by the political branches of government."[107]

Tribe's position at the hearings over extension of the Equal Rights Amendment indicates that his view may be less supportive of judicial review and more along the lines of the plenary congressional power model that his exchange with Dellinger indicated. Indeed, there was considerable justification for Dellinger to use Tribe's and similar views as foils in formulating and defending his own formalistic model.[108] Of all the testimony given, Tribe's testimony, particularly at the first set of hearings, might have led to the greatest possibility for confusion. He advocated the right not only of Congress to extend a ratification deadline but also to shorten it. In his words, "I don't think it is consistent with constitutional history or theory to say that the snowball keeps rolling downhill."[109] Moreover, by Tribe's analysis, one Congress is not bound by the decision of a former one. As to rescission, this too became a matter for ad hoc congressional decision. Thus, when asked whether extension of the period for ratification also would permit states to rescind, Tribe responded:

Not automatically. That is, the power to rescind is the power on the part of a State to advise the Congress that, in determining whether an amendment has been validly ratified, the State is no longer in favor of the amendment; how Congress treats that action by the most recent legislature is a matter of delicate congressional judgment, depending on a wide variety of facts and circumstances in each case.[110]

Indeed, Tribe even suggested that, in the middle of the ratification process, Congress would have power to change state ratification from that given by the legislatures to that given by convention.[111]

The problem with such analysis, of course, is that it leaves Congress in complete control of the amending process even after its duty is done and amendments have been sent to the states. Moreover, absent any fixed guidelines, it is unlikely that such a highly political body would be able to establish the kinds of stable precedents that one would want to set as a guide for the future. Tribe's testimony, like Dellinger's and Rees's analyses, seems ultimately to point to the need for some kind of judicial review.

CONCLUSION

Obviously, there are many others who have spoken on the application of the political questions doctrine to the constitutional amending process. The cases and opinions surveyed in this chapter should, however, be sufficient to draw at least a tentative answer to the question addressed in the title of this chapter, namely, which branch of government should have the ultimate say over issues involving the amending process?

This writer believes the precedents and arguments advanced in this chapter are sufficient to show, in the very least, that the amending area is not an area for complete judicial abnegation. After being barraged by a host of cases asking the courts to void amendments because their substance was invalid, it is understandable that the Court might have wished to wash its hands of the whole area, especially when confronted with an amendment—the child labor amendment—that was aimed at overturning the effects of two of its own decisions.[112]

The arguments advanced in *Coleman v. Miller* for declaring almost all matters of procedure to be political questions, however, have not held up very well. Although Article V does divide responsibilities for proposing and ratifying amendments between Congress and the states (which would itself seem to call for occasional judgment calls about whether one institution was exercising powers committed to the other), there simply is no blanket textually demonstrable commitment of amending issues to the political branches of government. Standards for resolving amending issues would not appear on their face to be any more difficult than those required in a host of other areas where the courts have intervened. There is no reason to argue that judicial review of amending issues will show any more disrespect, or lead to any greater governmental embarrassment, than is evidenced by review of other issues.

There is some danger, which Justice Powell and Laurence Tribe have emphasized, in having the courts serve as judges in cases of amendments designed to modify or overturn their decisions, but the alternative is to leave Congress (at whom amendments are also aimed) as judge in its own case, and the structure and experience of the judicial branch make it less likely to enter partisan judgments in this area than the legislative branch. Moreover, especially over time, consistent judicial opinions would likely lead to greater stability in this area than a series of ad hoc congressional decisions each tailored to specific, and at times, highly partisan, circumstances. It thus appears that judicial judgments are appropriate in the amending area. The next chapter focuses on what these standards should be.

NOTES

1. For a defense of this approach, see Maurice Cranston, *What Are Human Rights?* (New York: Taplinger, 1973), pp. 51–72. Also see William Van Alstyne, "Notes on a Bicentennial Constitution: Part I, Processes of Change," *University of Illinois Law Review,* 1984, pp. 935–37.

2. This quotation is cited and critiqued in Ralph A. Rossum and G. Alan Tarr, *American Constitutional Law, Cases and Interpretation,* 3d ed. (New York: St. Martin's Press, 1991), pp. 1–3.

3. M. J. C. Vile, *Constitutionalism and the Separation of Powers* (Oxford: Clarendon Press, 1969). Also see *Separation of Powers—Does It Still Work?*, ed. Robert A. Goldwin and Art Kaufman (Washington, DC: American Enterprise Institute for Public Policy Research, 1986).

4. De Tocqueville thus noted that, "There is hardly a political question in the United States which does not sooner or later turn into a judicial one." *Democracy in America,* ed. J. P. Mayer (Garden City, NY: Anchor Books, 1969), p. 270.

5. 48 U.S. 1 (1849).

6. 307 U.S. 433 (1939). In a companion case, *Chandler v. Wise,* 307 U.S. 474, the Court denied standing to those who challenged the governor's certification of the child labor amendment to the U.S. secretary of state.

7. *Coleman v. Miller,* p. 436.

8. 253 U.S. 221 (1920).

9. 258 U.S. 130 (1922).

10. On this point, it took the votes of the two dissenting justices to make a majority. See "Sawing a Justice in Half," *Yale Law Journal* 48 (1939), p. 1457.

11. *Coleman v. Miller,* p. 447. Apparently, Justice McReynolds had been absent from the last conference. See Lester B. Orfield, *The Amending of the Federal Constitution* (Ann Arbor: University of Michigan Press, 1942), p. 19. This division shows, however, that the modern court is not the only one to be guilty of delivering precedents extremely difficult to interpret. For a recent critique of the Court in this vein, see Joseph Goldstein, *The Intelligible Constitution* (New York: Oxford University Press, 1992).

12. *Coleman v. Miller,* p. 447.

13. Ibid., p. 449.

14. Ibid., p. 450.

15. 256 U.S. 368 (1921).

16. *Coleman v. Miller,* p. 452.

17. Ibid., p. 453.

18. Ibid., p. 454.

19. Ibid.
20. Ibid., pp. 454–55.
21. See *Ware v. Hylton,* 3 Dall. 199 (1796), and *Luther v. Borden,* 7 How. 1 (1849).
22. *Coleman v. Miller,* p. 457 citing *Leser v. Garnett,* 258 U.S. 130, 137.
23. *Coleman v. Miller,* p. 457.
24. Ibid., p. 458.
25. Ibid., p. 459.
26. Ibid., pp. 464–65.
27. Ibid., pp. 471–72.
28. Ibid., p. 474.
29. 369 U.S. 186 (1962).
30. 328 U.S. 549 (1946).
31. 369 U.S. 186, 217.
32. 395 U.S. 486 (1969).
33. 444 U.S. 996 (1979).
34. Ibid., p. 998.
35. Ibid., p. 1001, note 2. Powell cites Fritz W. Scharpf, "Judicial Review and the Political Question: A Functional Analysis," *Yale Law Journal* 75 (1966), p. 589. A problem with this analysis would be the difficulty the Court might have in consistently accepting review of cases where its power was not at issue and rejecting those cases where it was.
36. Aligned with Rehnquist were Burger, Stewart, and Stevens. Only the latter is currently on the Court, and as the following analysis demonstrates, he is on record elsewhere as arguing that at least some amending issues are not political questions.
37. Rehnquist cited the dictum in *Dyer v. Blair,* 390 F. Supp. 1291, 1302, that "A question that might be answered in different ways for different amendments must surely be controlled by political standards easily characterized as judicially manageable."
38. *Dyer v. Blair,* 390 F. Supp. 1291 (1975).
39. Ibid., p. 1295.
40. Ibid., p. 1300.
41. 395 U.S. 486 (1969).
42. *Dyer v. Blair,* p. 1301.
43. Ibid.
44. Ibid., p. 1302.
45. Ibid., p. 1303.
46. Ibid., p. 1304.
47. Ibid., p. 1305.
48. Ibid.
49. Ibid.
50. Ibid.
51. Ibid., p. 1306.
52. Ibid., p. 1307.
53. Ibid.
54. *Hawke v. Smith* (No. 1), 253 U.S. 221; *National Prohibition* cases, 253 U.S. 350.
55. *Dyer v. Blair,* p. 1308.
56. Ibid.

57. Ibid.

58. *Idaho v. Freeman,* 529 F. Supp. 1107 (1981). Callister was a regional representative of the Mormon Church which opposed the Equal Rights Amendment, leading the author of one note who was quite critical of the opinion to suggest that he should have recused himself from the case. See John Carroll, "Constitutional Law: Constitutional Amendment. Rescission of Ratification. Extension of Ratification Period. State of Idaho v. Freeman," *Akron Law Review* 16 (Summer 1982), p. 154, note 24.

59. For a sampling of law reviews which address this issue, see Norman Vieira, "The Equal Rights Amendment: Rescission, Extension and Justiciability," *Southern Illinois University Law Journal* (1981), pp. 1–20; "Comments, The Equal Rights Amendment and Article V: A Framework for Analysis of the Extension and Rescission Issues," *University of Pennsylvania Law Review* 127 (1978), pp. 494–532; Yyonne B. Burke, "Validity of Attempts to Rescind Ratification of the Equal Rights Amendment," *University of Los Angeles Law Review* 8 (1976), pp. 1–22; Leo Kanowitz and Marilyn Klinger, "Can a State Rescind Its Equal Rights Amendment Ratification: Who Decides and How?" *Hastings Law Journal* 28 (March 1978), pp. 979–1009; A. Diane Baker, "Comments, ERA: The Effect of Extending the Time for Ratification on Attempts to Rescind Prior Ratifications," *Emory Law Journal* 28 (1979), pp. 71–110; and Raymond M. Plannel, "The Equal Rights Amendment: Will States Be Allowed to Change Their Minds?" *Notre Dame Lawyer* 49 (February 1974), pp. 657–70.

60. *Idaho v. Freeman*, p. 1122.

61. Ibid., p. 1125.

62. Ibid., p. 1126.

63. Judge Callister here refers for support to Lester Orfield's, *The Amending of the Federal Constitution.*

64. *Idaho v. Freeman,* p. 1135.

65. Ibid., pp. 1135–36.

66. Ibid., p. 1136. Callister cites a colloquy at oral argument which leads him to conclude, "Therefore, at some point the courts could review a determination by Congress and theoretically overrule its finding of what constitutes a reasonable time period."

67. Ibid.

68. 444 U.S. 996 (1979).

69. Cited in *Idaho v. Freeman,* p. 1138.

70. Ibid., p. 1139.

71. Ibid.

72. Ibid., p. 1140.

73. Ibid., p. 1141.

74. Ibid., p. 1144.

75. Ibid., pp. 1144–45.

76. Ibid., p. 1146.

77. Walter Dellinger, "The Legitimacy of Constitutional Change: Rethinking the Amending Process," *Harvard Law Review* 97 (December 1983), pp. 380–432.

78. Ibid., p. 392.

79. Ibid., p. 398.

80. Ibid., p. 399.

81. Ibid., p. 400.

82. Ibid., pp. 404–05.

83. Ibid., pp. 406–11.

84. Ibid., p. 413. In a similar vein, Bruce A. Ackerman has argued that "*Coleman v. Miller* has given us a half-century of increasingly partisan congressional 'interpretation' on the one hand, scholarly and judicial silence, on the other." Ackerman, "The Storrs Lectures: Discovering the Constitution," *Yale Law Journal* 93 (1984), p. 1065.

85. Dellinger, "The Legitimacy of Constitutional Change," p. 414.

86. Ibid., pp. 414–15. Dellinger notes that, while the Twenty-Sixth Amendment overturned the effect of the Supreme Court's decision in *Oregon v. Mitchell*, 400 U.S. 112 (1970), "nothing in the twenty-sixth amendment in any way repudiated that interpretation of the fourteenth amendment." (415).

87. Ibid., p. 415. Dellinger's reference is to *Hollingsworth v. Virginia*, 3 U.S. (3 Dall.) 378 (1798), where the Court decided that presidential signature was not necessary for ratification of the Eleventh Amendment. This amendment overturned the Court's decision in *Chisholm v. Georgia*, 2 U.S. (2 Dall.) 419 (1793).

88. Grover Rees III, "The Amendment Process and Limited Constitutional Conventions," *Benchmark* 2 (1986), pp. 67–108.

89. Grover Rees III, "Throwing Away the Key: The Unconstitutionality of the Equal Rights Amendment Extension," *Texas Law Review* 58 (May 1980), pp. 875–932.

90. Rees, "The Amendment Process," p. 70.

91. Ibid.

92. Ibid., p. 71.

93. Ibid. In this regard, it is worth noting that in the debate on the penultimate draft of an amending process at the Constitutional Convention (the one that omitted a convention mechanism altogether), the Convention rejected a proposal by Roger Sherman to strike the requirement for ratification by three-fourths of the states, "leaving future Conventions to act in this matter, like the present Conventions according to circumstances." See Max Farrand, *The Records of the Federal Convention of 1787* (New Haven, CT: Yale University Press, 1966), vol. II, pp. 629–30. To the extent that this vote represented a sentiment to withhold issues of ratification from the bodies that proposed amendments, such sentiment would also mitigate against the plenary congressional power model.

94. Rees, "The Amendment Process," p. 72.

95. Ibid., p. 101.

96. Ibid., p. 102.

97. Ibid.

98. Ibid., p. 103.

99. Ibid., p. 104.

100. Ibid., p. 106.

101. Laurence Tribe, "A *Constitution* We Are Amending: In Defense of a Restrained Judicial Role," *Harvard Law Review* 97 (December 1983), pp. 433–45.

102. Ibid., p. 433.

103. Ibid., p. 434.

104. Ibid., p. 444.

105. Ibid., p. 435.

106. Ibid., p. 436.

107. Ibid., p. 443. Apparently, Walter Dellinger agrees. See his "Constitutional Politics: A Rejoinder," *Harvard Law Review* 97 (December 1983), pp. 447–48.

108. Dellinger, "The Legitimacy of Constitutional Change," pp. 393–96.

109. Testimony of Laurence Tribe as found in *Equal Rights Amendment Extension,* Hearings before the Subcommittee on Civil and Constitutional Rights of the Committee on the Judiciary, House of Representatives, 95th Congress, 1st and 2nd Session on H.J. Res. 638. Nov. 1, 4, and 8, 1977; May 17, 18, 19, 1978, p. 42.

110. Ibid., p. 45.

111. Ibid., p. 57. In the second set of hearings, Tribe asserted that Congress could extend the time limit for amendment ratifications by a simple majority without the need for presidential approval. He believed Congress can prohibit rescissions and that congressional silence does not necessarily allow rescission, but he was unsure whether Congress could allow rescissions, in part because he is unsure what the Court would do in such circumstances. See *Equal Rights Amendment Extension,* Hearings before the Subcommittee on the Constitution of the Committee on the Judiciary, United States Senate, 95th Congress, 2d Session on S.J. Res. 134, August 2, 3, and 4, 1978, pp. 238–51.

112. I have previously made this point in "The Amending Process: Alternative to Revolution," *Southeastern Political Review* 99 (Fall 1983), p. 74.

Chapter 3

The Question of Standards—What Rules Are Most Appropriately Applied to Procedural Issues Surrounding the Amending Process?

In the chapter which preceded, the question centered on which institution of government should oversee amending controversies; in this chapter, the focus is on the desirable standards themselves. There are a number of ways to proceed. One temptation is simply to identify and address important issues—should states be permitted to rescind ratifications of pending amendments, does Congress have power to extend the time limits for amendments and the like—individually. While this writer thinks it is important to provide plausible answers to these questions and does so later in this chapter, he thinks it is more profitable to begin the process by putting individual issues within a larger context by ascertaining if there is some overarching principle, or set of standards, under which specific issues can be addressed.

REES'S THREE MODELS OF THE AMENDING PROCESS

One of the participants in amendment debates, Grover Rees III, has delineated three models of the amending process which can serve as a useful starting point.[1] These models are the classical model emphasizing contemporaneous consensus; the political questions and plenary congressional power model; and what Rees calls the formalist model.[2]

The second model should be familiar to readers of the previous chapter; this model makes Congress the sole judge of amending issues or gives almost complete deference to all such decisions. The argument in the previous chapter should have demonstrated that this view has the potential for undermining the legitimacy of the Constitution by leaving questions concerning its amendment to be decided in a partisan fashion. This leads to a look at the other two models.

Rees advocated the contemporary consensus model.[3] He believed this model is consistent with the view of amendments held by the Framers (hence his designation of this as the classical model) and subsequently articulated by the Supreme Court in *Dillon v. Gloss*[4] and in other opinions prior to *Coleman v. Miller*.[5] Rees combined this model with an argument from intent. Thus, this model views the Constitution as "a kind of contract," with gaps and ambiguities to be "resolved according to the principle that the manifest intentions of the parties—the States, either in their own capacity or as agents for the people—should not be defeated by construction."[6]

If Rees's contemporary consensus model is to be accepted, it could probably best be modified, as Rees himself might be quite willing to do, to indicate that Article V does not call for a contemporary consensus of the people per se, but for a contemporary consensus as expressed through the states.[7] This writer accordingly dubs this revised model as the federal contemporary consensus model. Critics of the amending process can point to the possibility that amendment desired by popular majorities will not always be adopted; there are even remote theoretical cases where a minority of the population concentrated in the smallest 38 states might ratify amendments that are opposed by the majority.[8] These possibilities exist because the Framers did not aim for a contemporary consensus per se but for a contemporary consensus of the states. That is, they aimed for "*nationally distributed* majorities."[9] Their goal in so doing, partly a concession to the Anti-Federalists who feared domination by the large states, was "to insure that no amendments could be passed simply with the support of a few populous states or sections."[10] It would be impossible for any amendment to be adopted in the present system that drew support, however strong, from only one state or region in the country.

DELLINGER'S FORMALISTIC MODEL AND ITS APPLICATION

It should be apparent that one of Rees's main targets is the view proposed by Walter Dellinger. It is, therefore, time to return to this view which Dellinger advanced in the same article that was the focus in the last chapter.[11] Dellinger's concern in that article was that the current amending process is too uncertain, leaving basic issues such as the legitimacy of extension of ratifications and of rescissions in doubt. Opposing the view that the amending process was intended to reflect "the goal of consensus," Dellinger argued that "Article V is more properly viewed as a provision establishing a fixed mechanism for recording assent to an amendment than as a directive mandating a quest for elusive policy goals."[12] Subsequently criticizing both the model of contemporary consensus and that of congressional promulgation of amendments, Dellinger advocated the application of " 'fixed' rules" rather than "principles."[13] His goal was to create "certainty" and "the restraint of official arbitrariness," which in turn enhances "legitimacy."[14] Viewing Article V as "a series of formalities," Dellinger argued that such formalities were "more likely to provide clear answers" than is the search for contemporary consensus.[15] Dellinger's approach to consensus was more nuanced than it might first appear. He argued not so much that such consensus was undesirable per se as that such consensus was already sufficiently obtained by the series of steps outlined in Article V.[16]

In outlining his formalistic approach to Article V, Dellinger examined three main issues, namely, the effect of prior rejections, subsequent rescissions, and untimely ratifications. In addressing prior rejections, Dellinger argued that they should have no effect whatsoever. He sagely pointed out that it would be difficult to ascertain precisely what actions would constitute definitive state rejection. Moreover, contrary to the argument advanced against the actions of the Kansas state legislature in *Coleman v. Miller,* it is possible for a state convention to convene and ratify a constitution, or amendment, after a previous convention had rejected one or the other, and so there should logically be no problem with a legislature doing the same.[17]

Dellinger's argument here is sound. Interestingly, however, it is doubtful that Dellinger's approach to prior rejections would be any different than that advocated by proponents of the contemporary consensus model who, almost by definition, would be bound by the last official state action, at least up to the time that the necessary number of ratifications were received.

This led Dellinger to consider the issue of rescissions. It is important to recognize that a formalistic model would be consistent either with choosing to accept or choosing to reject all rescissions. Dellinger chose the latter course. He recognized that, in outlining amending procedures, the Constitution is silent about the matter. He also believed the historical record is ambiguous.[18] Ultimately, Dellinger came down on the side of rejecting all subsequent rescissions believing that this would lead to greater certainty and would promote greater deliberation, each state recognizing that any ratification it gave was final.

The first part of Dellinger's argument is circular. He advocates certainty. Certainty will be enhanced either by accepting or rejecting all rescissions.[19] As to the argument that deliberation would be enhanced if a legislature knows its ratification is final, it seems difficult to make the argument for finality here and reject it for state rejections of amendments.[20] Moreover, if states fear that they are entering into agreements they can never void no matter how great the potential dangers, some might become overly cautious, thus delaying or forestalling the adoption of needed constitutional changes.[21]

Dellinger did make a convincing case that, especially over the course of time, formal rules here are more desirable than ad hoc determinations.[22]

Those who argue for the contemporaneous consensus model, however, get the same certainty while furthering the idea of contemporary consensus. Their approach would further empower the states that are the very ones deciding whether or not to approve ratifications. Clearly, the contemporary consensus model is superior here.

Perhaps the most difficult issue Dellinger faced is the issue of the timeliness of state ratifications. Consistent with his earlier analysis,[23] Dellinger argued that the only legitimate limits on the timeliness of ratifications are those imposed within the texts of amendments themselves. This enabled him to support extension of the ratification deadline for the Equal Rights Amendment.

It is not clear, however, that this conclusion is necessarily any more formalistic than a standard that would enforce Congress's initial deadline, whether incorporated within the text or in an accompanying authorizing resolution. Moreover, Dellinger arguably undercut his argument against paying attention to contemporary consensus by suggesting that a Court worried about amendments proposed more than a hundred years ago could "invoke a doctrine of desuetude and declare the amendments dead."[24] The time frame either matters or it does not; Dellinger sought to have it both ways.

In any case, Dellinger argued that in *Coleman v. Miller* the Court would have been fully justified in declaring that the ratifications of the child labor amendments were still timely. Although Congress was familiar with such limits from the Eighteenth Amendment, it had refused to set a limit here, and at no point had debate over the amendment been fully dormant.

This author believes that Dellinger is correct with regard to ratifications of the child labor amendment. As a practical matter, however, Dellinger's case for allowing states to continue ratifying amendments where Congress had set no deadlines would be strengthened if he also allowed states to rescind their ratifications of pending amendments. Moreover, while the only self-enforcing limit on constitutional limits may indeed be those within the text, once the legitimacy of judicial review is acknowledged in this area, there is no reason that the courts should not themselves enforce limits on amendments when Congress has specifically agreed to limits (a consideration which does not appear to have been the case prior to the Eighteenth Amendment where this innovation was introduced) and included them within the authorizing resolutions sent to the states.

A number of fairly compelling reasons suggest that in the case of the Equal Rights Amendment such time limits were not a mere incidental matter left to alteration by later congresses, but a vital concomitant of the package of compromises under which the amendment was considered by the states. First, the seven-year limit was consciously introduced by opponents of the amendment and adopted over expressions of concern by its supporters.[25] Second, the initial decision—first made at the time of the Twenty-Third

Amendment—to include seven-year limits in the authorizing resolution instead of the amendment's text apparently stemmed from a desire not to clutter the constitutional text rather than from an intention to open such limits to further changes.[26] Third, since the resolution containing the time limit was sent to the states along with the formal text of the amendment, there is a good chance that some such states reasonably relied on this limitation when deciding whether or not to ratify, especially since no such prior time limits had ever been altered.[27] Such limits would not, of course, doom amendments whose time limits had expired but for which a contemporary consensus existed. Rather, these limits would require that the existing consensus be demonstrated by mustering another two-thirds vote of both houses of Congress and the subsequent ratification of three-fourths of the states.

In comparing and contrasting the federal contemporary consensus and formalistic models, it appears that the former model is sounder. This model would permit states both to ratify amendments previously rejected and to rescind ratifications given. This model would further allow courts to enforce congressionally established time limits, whether within the text of amendments themselves or within the text of the authorizing resolutions. In cases where Congress failed to set limits, the courts could still insist that ratifications would not be good forever. If the amendment receives a timely challenge in the courts, there is simply no good reason, for example, for them to accept the legitimacy of the ratification of the Twenty-Seventh Amendment, no matter how definitively Congress has spoken.[28] If the amendment really represents the considered judgment of the people, their representatives in Congress and the states can discuss it openly and vote for it within a reasonable time period. If not, it has no business being in the Constitution.[29]

DYER V. BLAIR AND *IDAHO V. FREEMAN* REVISITED

In the previous chapter, this writer examined two district court decisions on the political questions doctrine. *Dyer v. Blair* raised essentially one key question, namely, the legitimacy of rules providing that states ratify amendments by more than a majority vote.[30] Consistent with the federalism emphasis of Article V, Judge John Paul Stevens left the determination of such a majority to the ratifying bodies, specifying, however, that these bodies and only these bodies had the right to set extraordinary majorities. This seems to be a reasonable solution which takes into account federal concerns. The conclusion would not, however, necessarily be compelled by either the contemporary consensus or formalistic models.

Idaho v. Freeman dealt with a broader range of issues.[31] The court's view of rescissions in that case is consistent with the view of contemporary consensus advocated in this chapter. Indeed, Judge Marion Callister may actually have strengthened the case for contemporary consensus by tying the acts of a state legislature acting in regard to a proposed amendment to the expression of "the consent of the people:"

All of the cases which have considered article V have reaffirmed the vision of the founding fathers that the essential democratic value of the will of the people be inextricably linked with the state's action in considering ratification.[32]

Permitting states to rescind ratification of pending amendments, just as permitting them to ratify amendments previously rejected, "would promote the democratic ideal by giving a truer picture of the people's will as of the time three-fourths of the states have acted in affirming the amendment."[33] As Callister argued:

To make a state's ratification binding with no right to rescind would give ratification a technical significance which would be clearly inappropriate considering that the Constitution through article V gives technical significance to a state's ratification at only one time—when three-fourths of the states have acted to ratify.[34]

An equally important question in *Idaho v. Freeman* was the issue of whether Congress had authority to extend the ratification time for the Equal Rights Amendment. Here Callister cited *Dillon v. Gloss* to show that Congress could set a time limit for ratification but was not obligated to do so.[35] Judge Callister concluded from *Dillon,* however, that, because deadlines were adopted to enhance certainty, once such a deadline was set, it was binding. Seeing proposal of an amendment as integrally tied to its ratification, Callister concluded that

Once the proposal has been formulated and sent to the states, the time period could not be changed any more than the entity designated to ratify could be changed from the state legislature to a state convention or vice versa. Once the proposal is made, Congress is not at liberty to change it.[36]

Judge Callister did not fully draw upon the contemporary consensus model, but his opinion is certainly consistent with such a model—as it is with a formalistic model which accepts all initial congressional time limit conditions as final. States ratify amendments in the presence of certain understandings. If these understandings are changed, the ratifications, and the consensus of opinion they are designed to represent, are questionable.

Judge Callister sought to reinforce his argument here by contending that, even if Congress were recognized as having the right to extend ratification of an amendment, it would have to do so by a two-thirds vote.[37] Although this position received some support (from Charles Black, Jr., among others) at the Equal Rights Amendment extension hearings,[38] this author is not convinced that his argument, which rests on reading "two-thirds of both houses of Congress" as synonymous with Congress throughout Article V, here is sound.[39] The argument is not, in any case, relevant once the unconstitutionality of the vote for extension is itself established.

COLEMAN V. MILLER REVISITED

Having examined the consequences of applying the contemporary consensus model to lower court decisions, it is now also timely to see how the Court might have addressed the issues in *Coleman v. Miller* using the contemporary consensus and formalistic models.

The decision in *Dyer v. Blair* and more general considerations of federalism suggest that the issue of the tie-breaking vote cast by the lieutenant governor was a matter for the state to decide and that certification of the amendment to the General Services administrator should have been conclusive on this point. This finding would be consistent both with a formalistic model and with a federal contemporary consensus model.

The issue of prior rejection of an amendment was similarly irrelevant under either set of standards. Advocates of both the formalistic model and the federal contemporary consensus model would counsel that the later action of ratification should be accepted. There is no reason that such issues should have been treated as a political issue to be left to the discretion of each Congress.

As to timeliness, the Court again properly decided that it should not void Kansas' late ratification. Noting that Congress had not itself set a deadline and that debates over the amendment had never ended, the Court erred only in suggesting that ratifications would, in such circumstances, be left completely to congressional discretion. While such a position is consistent with one version of the formalistic model, it is inconsistent with any view of federal contemporary consensus and tempts Congress to exercise partisan judgments about constitutional issues. Such a view also promotes instability by allowing one Congress to overturn actions of a preceding one.

OTHER ISSUES: THE WISDOM OF ADHERING TO JUDICIAL PRECEDENTS

From time to time throughout the nation's history, other legal issues have surfaced in regard to the constitutional amending process. Such issues could not and have not always been answered simply by plugging in the formalistic and/or contemporary consensus models. Still, there is no need to question clear existing legal precedents in this area once it is recognized that one of the greatest virtues of judicial review of amending issues (advocated in chapter 2) is that over time such review can provide reasonably clear and consistent answers to questions which might otherwise be resolved by Congress in a partisan fashion from one amendment to another.[40] Moreover, it would be particularly foolish to overturn precedents on which most existing amendments were clearly predicated.

Thus, the accepted understanding that a governor's signature is not required for state petitions for ratifications of amendments should be perpetuated.[41] Similarly, there is no reason at this time in history to begin requiring presidential signatures on amendments,[42] or to overturn the Supreme Court's earlier judgment that the two-thirds majority of both houses of Congress required by Article V is, as Congress has itself previously determined, two-thirds of those present (assuming the presence of a quorum) rather than two-thirds of the entire membership.[43] The effects of all of the last three decisions, if indeed they can be measured, would be to facilitate constitutional changes, and, given the paucity of amendments ratified over the last 200-year period, it can hardly be argued that the result has been to make the process too easy.[44] This practical consideration thus confirms the argument above for adhering to precedent.

NOTES

1. Grover Rees III, "The Amendment Process and Limited Constitutional Conventions," *Benchmark* 2 (1986), pp. 67–108.
2. Ibid., pp. 70–72.
3. There is further, albeit indirect, support for this model in Charles L. Black, Jr., "The Proposed Amendment of Article V: A Threatened Disaster," *Yale Law Journal* 72 (1963), pp. 959 and 961.
4. 256 U.S. 368 (1921).
5. 307 U.S. 433 (1939).
6. Rees, "The Amendment Process," p. 70.
7. Akil Reed Amar arguably undermines this emphasis in his proposal for ratifying amendments by referendum. See his "Philadelphia Revisited: Amending the Constitution Outside Article V," *University of Chicago Law Review* 55 (Fall 1988), pp. 1043–1104. This work is discussed at greater length in Chapter 6.
8. For note of such arguments, see Martin Diamond, Winston M. Fisk, and Herbert Garfinkel, *The Democratic Republic* (Chicago: Rand McNally, 1966), p. 98.
9. Ibid., p. 99.
10. Ibid.
11. Walter Dellinger, "The Legitimacy of Constitutional Change: Rethinking the Amending Process," *Harvard Law Review* 97 (December 1983), pp. 380–432. This author has previously analyzed Dellinger's views in "Judicial Review of the Amending Process: The Dellinger-Tribe Debate," *The Journal of Law & Politics* 3 (Winter 1986), pp. 21–50, but his views in this chapter are much more complete than in the earlier article.
12. Dellinger, "The Legitimacy of Constitutional Change," pp. 388–89.
13. Ibid., p. 417.
14. Ibid., p. 417–18.
15. Ibid., p. 418.

16. Ibid., pp. 418–19.

17. Ibid., p. 421.

18. Both these points are made in John R. Vile, "Permitting States to Rescind Ratifications of Pending Amendments to the U.S. Constitution," *Publius: The Journal of Federalism* 20 (Spring 1990), pp. 110–13.

19. Ibid., p. 116.

20. Ibid., p. 117.

21. Ibid., p. 119. I thus noted that, "a legislature would be freer to commit itself to an amendment because it would be freer to retract it."

22. This author has previously suggested that courts should look with deference on a law whereby Congress specifically detailed beforehand when it would accept or reject rescissions. One compromise solution would be to reject all rescissions within the first three or four years while permitting rescissions thereafter. See Vile, "Permitting States to Rescind Ratifications," p. 122.

23. Dellinger, "The Legitimacy of Constitutional Change." This position was discussed in the previous chapter.

24. Ibid., p. 425. Dellinger further noted that, "No such need . . . is likely to arise." The recent acceptance of the Twenty-Seventh Amendment by the necessary number of states some 203 years after it was proposed suggests that Dellinger, along with practically every other observer of this process, was mistaken.

The dispute over extension of the ratification deadline for the Equal Rights Amendment, as well as the experience with the Twenty-Seventh Amendment surely make it politically unlikely that Congress will ever report another amendment to the states without a self-enforcing time limit within its text. This is one issue that may well be resolved without further judicial intervention.

25. Grover Rees III, "Throwing Away the Key: The Unconstitutionality of the Equal Rights Amendment Extension," *Texas Law Review* 58 (May 1980), p. 916.

It is interesting that the first seven-year limit ever proposed—for what became the Eighteenth Amendment—was apparently offered by then-Senator Warren G. Harding with similar motivations. See David E. Kyvig, "Alternative to Revolution: Two Hundred Years of Constitutional Amending," *The Embattled Constitution: Vital Framework or Convenient Symbol,* ed. Adoph H. Grundman (Malabar, FL: Robert E. Krieger Publishing, 1986), pp. 141–42.

26. Rees, "Throwing Away the Key," pp. 917–19. In thus arguing, like Walter Dellinger, for such a distinction, Ruth Bader Ginsberg, whose own conclusions are phrased tentatively, (the change "may reflect an underlying recognition that setting a time for ratification entails a determination qualitatively different from agreement on the substantive content of an amendment") points to no evidence for such an understanding prior to debates over extension of the Equal Rights Amendment in 1978, a rather late date to discover such an important distinction. See "Ratification of the Equal Rights Amendment: A Question of Time," *Texas Law Review* 57 (1979), p. 932.

27. Rees, "Throwing Away the Key," pp. 919–24.

28. The vote to promulgate the amendment was 414 to 3 in the House and 99 to 0 in the Senate. See Bill McAllister, "Congress Backs Madison: But Does It Really Matter?" *Washington Post* (May 21, 1992), p. A21.

There are at least two respects in which the congressional pay raise amendment is on firmer ground than a belatedly ratified Equal Rights Amendment would have been. First, no deadline of any type was set for the first amendment. Second, no states apparently attempted to rescind ratification of the former as they did the latter.

29. By the same token, it is probably reasonable to say that the amendment must be accepted as part of the Constitution if it does not receive a timely legal challenge. There simply will come a point in such circumstances where judicial intervention would cross the line from concern over procedure to one of substance. Russell L. Caplan thus notes, in regard to amendments that are outside the scope of a proposing convention, "if an irregularly adopted amendment is not contested over a period of years, probably decades, the amendment can attain a secure place in the Constitution by virtue of public acquiescence." See *Constitutional Brinkmanship: Amending the Constitution by National Convention* (New York: Oxford University Press, 1988), p. x.

30. 390 F. Supp. 1291 (1975).

31. 529 F. Supp. 1107 (1981).

32. Ibid., p. 1148.

33. Ibid., pp. 1148–49.

34. Ibid., p. 1150.

35. Ibid., p. 1152.

36. Ibid., p. 1153.

37. Ibid.

38. Testimony of Charles Black, *Hearings before the Subcommittee on Civil and Constitutional Rights of the Committee on the Judiciary,* House of Representatives, 95th Cong., 1st and 2d Session, on H.J. Res. 638, November 1977 and May 1978 (Washington, DC: U.S. Government Printing Office, 1978), pp. 69–108.

39. This reading is problematic among other reasons because it would suggest that when faced with demands for a convention from two-thirds of the states, Congress could not call a convention until it mustered a two-thirds vote. As the discussion in the next chapter indicates, this would seem to be an unnecessary and undesirable obstacle in the path of getting Congress to do its constitutional duty.

40. For a particularly good discussion of the role of precedents, see Michael J. Gerhardt, "The Role of Precedent in Constitutional Decisionmaking and Theory," *George Washington Law Review* 60 (November 1991), pp. 68–159.

41. William Edel, *A Constitutional Convention: Threat or Challenge?* (New York: Praeger, 1981), pp. 107–8. It is not altogether clear that there is a direct legal precedent on this subject.

42. Ibid. The relevant legal precedent is *Hollingsworth v. Virginia,* 3 Dall., 378 (1798).

43. *Rhode Island v. Palmer,* 253 U.S. 386 (1920).

44. Mary F. Berry, "How Hard It Is to Change," *New York Times Magazine* (September 13, 1987), pp. 93–98.

Chapter 4

The Question of Safety: Are There Adequate Rules and Enforceable Limits on Article V Conventions?

One of the most discussed contemporary aspects of the constitutional amending process is the still untried provision for an Article V convention. Stimulated by earlier calls for a convention to overturn the Supreme Court's reapportionment decisions, the American Bar Association (ABA) issued an influential report on this subject in the 1970s,[1] and there have subsequently been numerous articles and several books on the issue,[2] as well as a number of unsuccessful attempts to pass legislation to deal with this contingency.[3]

ISSUES AND FRAMEWORKS

Although questions involving the convention are legion, a number of basic issues appear responsible for most of the controversy. These include the length of time that petitions for a convention should remain valid, how similar these petitions must be for them to be aggregated together as a single call for a convention, and whether states may call a limited convention or whether a convention would necessarily be at liberty to consider and propose anything. This last question is linked, in turn, to the key question as to whether a convention would be a safe option or not. Specifically, could a convention be limited by one or another institution of government, or would it be sovereign?[4]

The temptation in this area, as in amending matters generally, is to treat each issue separately; ultimately, no matter what framework is adopted, some questions simply require a prudent choice among alternatives, none of which is compelled by any single principle or set of principles. On some of the major issues, however, it is both possible and desirable to address such questions within a larger context. Here the earlier analysis in this book about general criteria for assessing amending issues may prove to be of considerable service.

To review briefly, previous chapters identified three basic approaches to the amending process: The first is an ad hoc approach that leaves resolution of individual amending issues for Congress to decide in accord with its judgments as to contemporaneous and the like. This is the approach that was effectively sanctioned in *Coleman v. Miller,*[5] and that Congress accepted in extending ratification of the Equal Rights Amendment. For reasons which should become clear in reviewing the history of the convention mechanism at the Constitutional Convention, this model is especially inappropriate when applied to the convention mechanism which was largely designed to empower the states and bypass an unresponsive Congress. A second approach is the formalistic approach that was described and defended by Walter Dellinger as a means of promoting certainty.[6] A third approach is to apply the contemporary consensus standard outlined by Grover Rees III.[7] This model, it may be recalled, can best be modified so as to be called the federal contemporary consensus model in recognition that the amending process does not provide for contemporary consensus per se but for contemporary consensus as expressed by the states. One advantage of continuing to use these models is that the two most prominent advocates of the second and third models have also addressed the Article V convention issue, albeit in light of the text and history of the Article V convention mechanism.

THE CONSTITUTIONAL TEXT AND HISTORY

As the first chapter indicated, the U.S. Constitution says little about the convention mechanism, simply providing that

on the Application of the Legislatures of two thirds of the several States, [the Congress] shall call a Convention for proposing Amendments, which . . . shall be valid to all Intents and Purposes, as Part of this Constitution, when ratified by the Legislatures of three fourths of the several States, or by Conventions in three fourths thereof.[8]

Textually, this provision might seem to require that a convention propose more than one amendment, but this is clearly a case where historical practice has firmly established that the grammatical plural is designed to include singular amendments as well—otherwise Congress would also have to propose more than one amendment at a time, which it clearly has not always done. As to historical construction, since no such Article V convention has been called since 1787, there are simply no clear precedents as to calling and operating such a convention.[9]

Limited but important light, however, is cast on the convention mechanism by the record of deliberations at the Constitutional Convention.

Indeed, the first real attempt to formulate an amending mechanism at the convention (reported by the Committee of Detail on August 6, 1787) provided that "on the Application of the Legislatures of two thirds of the States in the Union, the Legislature of the United States shall call a Convention for that purpose."[10] This proposal was criticized on September 10, first by Elbridge Gerry, who feared that a convention majority could subvert the states, and by Alexander Hamilton, who thought that Congress was more likely to perceive constitutional dangers than the states.[11] James Madison, who was especially concerned about the ambiguity of the convention mechanism, subsequently introduced a resolution that eliminated the convention proposal mechanism and left Congress to propose amendments by a two-thirds vote or after receiving petitions from two-thirds of the states.[12] In history that is examined in somewhat greater detail later in this chapter, the convention option was reintroduced on September 15, after a number of objections including George Mason's expressed fears that the Madison proposal would denigrate the states.[13] After several minor changes, Article V was formulated into the mechanism it is today.

Madison, it may be remembered, commended Article V for equally enabling "the general and the State governments to originate the amendment of errors, as they may be pointed out by the experience on one side, or on the other."[14] Specifically commenting on the convention mechanism in *Federalist* No. 85, undoubtedly with a view toward alleviating any remaining state fears, Hamilton asserted that Congress would have no power to thwart state desires for a convention but would be obliged to call a convention requested by the states.[15]

In the first hundred years or so of the nation's history, states that applied for conventions, while undoubtedly stimulated by specific concerns, called for a *general* convention.[16] One commentator has, however, noted that this term "primarily referred not to deliberative scope but to breadth of attendance."[17] Moreover, there is at least one nineteenth-century legal precedent, *Smith v. Directors of Union Bank of Georgetown*,[18] which can be interpreted as sanctioning a limited convention. In any case, from the late nineteenth century forward, most state petitions calling for conventions have listed a specific subject that they want the convention to treat.

Both because of the precedent of the Confederate states as well as because of some overblown assertions of state sovereignty in a number of state conventions, Judge John Jameson authored a massive book after the Civil War in which he argued that conventions were subordinate to state constitutions, or where such constitutions were silent, to the legislatures that called them.[19] Jameson's most important contribution may have been his designation of four types of conventions: the spontaneous convention or public meeting; the legislative convention or general assembly; the revolutionary convention; and the constitutional convention.[20] This classification, and particularly the distinction between the revolutionary and constitutional conventions, enabled Jameson to domesticate the latter mechanism, claiming that it was not a sovereign, but a constitutional, body subordinate to the people. All scholars, however, have not shared Jameson's view,[21] and a number of twentieth-century commentators, many writing for popular audiences, have paraded a host of horribles that might arise in connection with such conventions.[22] Some of these scenarios are predicated on the view that once in session, a convention cannot be limited.

DELLINGER'S FORMALISTIC MODEL AND UNLIMITED CONSTITUTIONAL CONVENTIONS

This view of an unlimitable convention is most closely associated with three scholars, namely Walter Dellinger of Duke and Charles Black, Jr., and Bruce Ackerman of Yale.[23] The first two have made especially powerful constitutional arguments that are examined later along with responses by William Van Alstyne, Grover Rees III, and Paul Weber and Barbara Perry. Before looking at the specific arguments, however, it is interesting to note a parallel between the views that advocates of an unlimitable convention have expressed and the formalistic model that Walter Dellinger has proposed in another context.[24]

Under Dellinger's understanding, most troubling issues connected with the convention mechanism are less likely to arise because the mechanism is not as likely to be used if its use automatically entails the possibility of a complete rewriting of the Constitution than if a convention can be confined to a single topic. Just as important, Congress would have the clearest possible guidelines for carrying out its Article V responsibility to call a constitutional convention when it received petitions from two-thirds of the states. Simply stated, under Dellinger's plan, the Congress would be free to ignore all calls except those recognizing or predicated upon a wide open convention. Moreover, once a convention was called, most if not all attempts to limit it from the outside would be ipso facto invalid. One of the critics of Dellinger's view that conventions cannot be limited, colleague William Van Alstyne, nonetheless acknowledged the advantage of this feature of Dellinger's view:

it eliminates the plain and arbitrary difficulty of expecting a reasonable Congress to decide whether, given different forms in which these state resolutions are submitted . . . a sufficient "consensus" has in fact been expressed for a given kind of limited convention. It avoids, too, the plain and related problem of what Congress is expected to do in describing the agenda for a convention thus called.[25]

No scheme will, of course, eliminate all questions. Thus, Dellinger and other advocates of an open convention have to decide such issues as whether to aggregate all calls for general conventions together or whether to accept time limits, whether to permit states to withdraw memorializing petitions, and the like.[26] Still, if any model of the convention process would provide clear guidelines for Congress to follow, it is undoubtedly the view that would accept only calls for a general convention.

CHARLES BLACK'S ARGUMENTS FOR AN UNLIMITABLE ARTICLE V CONVENTION

One of the best-known proponents of the argument that Article V requires a general convention or none at all is Charles Black, Jr. of Yale University, who advanced this view in writing in opposition to the Ervin Bill which would have established rules to govern a constitutional convention.[27] Like more recent advocates of legislation, Senator Sam Ervin and other sponsors of this bill made provision for limited constitutional conventions which Black argued were a constitutional nullity. Because applications for a limited convention were invalid, thirty-four would be similarly invalid. As Black put it, "Thirty-four times zero is zero."[28]

It is difficult to separate Black's constitutional argument against a limited convention from his view of the undesirability of such proceedings. This opinion is, in turn, linked to belief in the adequacy of the more regularized Article V procedures and the lack of opposition between the national government and the states.[29] Moreover, in apparent contrast to the beliefs of those who included the alternate amending mechanism within the Constitution, Black argued that

there is not a shred of support for the notion that it ever was or now is more "desirable and practical" to use this alternative machinery for the piecemeal amendment of the Constitution. On the contrary, the hitherto used and time-proven method is quite desirable and practical, responsive enough when one is dealing with so successful a Constitution, and just as obedient to the will of the people, fully represented as they are, State by State, in Congress and in the ratifying legislatures, as any system can be without destroying stability.[30]

Black made two main arguments against the limited convention option. His first argument was historical. Black pointed out that of all the applications for conventions in the first century, only one (Alabama's petition in 1833 for a convention to deal with the tariff) appears to have called for a convention limited to a specific topic, and he concluded that the theory of limited conventions is therefore a twentieth-century invention.[31] Black's second argument was textual:

It seems to me that the most natural meaning of the words "a Convention for proposing Amendments" is "a convention for proposing such amendments it decides to propose"—that is, a general convention—and that the importation of a limitation not in the text is quite unwarranted.[32]

Black went on to suggest that the convention mechanism should be reserved to deal with "extraordinary occasions" that might not be adequately addressed by the more tried and true path of amendments.[33] In short, Black saw no real need for a convention mechanism except for those contingencies where wholesale constitutional changes are desired or needed. He believed the regular Article V processes were adequate to all other contingencies.

Black elaborated on his arguments at greater length in another article,[34] specifically directed against the influential report of the American Bar Association which had supported the idea of a limited convention.[35] Black's central argument was one drawn from what he described as "plain meaning." Attempting to "track" the words of Article V, he says it is clear that states can apply for "a [general] convention for proposing amendments."[36] The question as he viewed it was whether the states could also apply for another type, "a different power, not at all obviously meant by Article V," that is for a limited convention.[37] Indeed, Black argued that the two kinds of convention are "as different in kind as (1) the freedom to marry; and (2) the freedom to marry one of two or three people designated by somebody else."[38]

Grover Rees has noted that while Black is persuasive, his argument from the text ignores the fact that the section of Article V which Black examined is essentially a grant of power to the states. Accordingly, Rees argued that "the phrase 'convention for proposing Amendments' admits easily of the construction 'such amendments as the States wish the convention to consider.' "[39] Countering Black's analogy, Rees says that forcing the states to call an unlimited convention they do not want is equivalent to forcing someone to commit beforehand to marry someone selected by someone else.[40] He therefore concludes that Article V did not intend to force states to call an unlimited convention to remedy a limited problem or set of problems.

This leads into Black's argument, however, from the debates in the Convention of 1787. Reviewing the ABA Report, Black denied that the Article V convention method was a state method or that such a conclusion could be drawn from the sketchy convention debates. Black cited the portion of the Convention record quoted by the ABA as the origin of the Article V convention mechanism. The Convention was debating a provision with no convention clause that provided that Congress would propose amendments when two-thirds of its members decided to or when two-thirds of the state legislatures petitioned for them.[41] During debates over these provisions, a number of points were made. Roger Sherman feared that states' rights were in jeopardy, and he accordingly proposed an amendment to "provide that no State should be affected in its internal police, or deprived of its equality in the Senate."[42] George Mason feared that the process was too dependent on Congress and not enough on "the people."[43] Robert Morris and Elbridge Gerry subsequently moved to require a convention at the request of two-thirds of the states.[44] While foreseeing potential problems with this mechanism, James Madison did not oppose the measure outright, and it was subsequently adopted.[45] Reviewing these proceedings, Black argued that the birth of the convention mechanism at the Constitutional Convention could just as well be traced to Sherman's fears that amendment was too easy as to Mason's fears that it was too difficult.[46] The convention, "another, nationally-oriented body," might thus "more plausibly be seen as a response to Sherman's fears of 'the States'."[47]

What this analysis ignores is the fact that Sherman's fears that the amending process might go too far clearly were not remedied by the convention mechanism. Rather, as will become clearer in Chapter 7, Sherman's objections became the basis for debate over whether states should be affected in their internal affairs, whether slave importation should be guaranteed, and whether states should be guaranteed equal suffrage in the Senate.[48] These discussions became the basis for Article V's two entrenchment clauses. Moreover, Sherman renewed this debate after adoption of the convention mechanism.[49]

Black says, however, that Mason's fears that the convention mechanism was too difficult might also have been addressed by a general convention mechanism, which was then thought to be representative of popular sovereignty.[50] Undoubtedly, the Framers had high regard for the convention mechanism. Moreover, Mason specifically identified Congress as a potential problem.[51] Neither side of the debate over conventions, however, is denying the possibility of a general convention. The question is simply whether Mason and others intended to require the state to open the entire Pandora's box of constitutional reform simply to bypass a recalcitrant or unresponsive Congress. On this matter, Rees has correctly noted,

there is absolutely *no* evidence that *anybody* intended the change to deprive the State legislatures of a power that they were clearly to have under the penultimate draft [that is, the draft the convention was debating]: the power to initiate the proposal of particular amendments.[52]

In the end, Black admits that his arguments from convention notes, like those of the ABA, prove "next to nothing."[53] He is left with his arguments from "plain meaning" and his arguments from history. Here Black's citations of early calls for a "general convention"[54] may be undercut by the fact that such a general convention could have referred to the source of the delegates rather than the scope of its deliberations.[55] Moreover, it is possible that states that initially requested a convention thought a complete reconsideration of the Constitution was a necessity and that the errors they perceived simply could not be met by a single amendment or set of amendments.

WALTER DELLINGER'S ARGUMENTS FOR AN UNLIMITABLE CONSTITUTIONAL CONVENTION

While Charles Black responded to arguments about the deliberations of the Constitutional Convention but believed they ultimately proved nothing, Walter Dellinger introduced his arguments against a limited constitutional convention largely on the basis of a comprehensive view of the deliberations of the Constitutional Convention of 1787, including the passages just cited. From this survey, Dellinger identified two themes, namely, that

Congress should not have exclusive power to propose amendments; and state legislatures should not be able to propose and ratify amendments that enhance their power at the expense of the national government.[56]

Dellinger used this second theme to argue against limiting the agenda of a convention. Arguing that the Founders did not want "a process of state proposal followed by state ratification without the substantive involvement of a national forum," Dellinger further contended that "permitting the states to limit the subject matter of a constitutional convention would be inconsistent with this aim."[57]

Citing a case where a state called a convention specifically to vote up or down on the text of a single amendment, Dellinger argued that such an assembly would effectively bypass the requirement for an intervening national body, and that, had the Framers aimed at giving states the power both to propose and ratify amendments, conventions would have been unnecessary.[58] In such a case, it is unlikely that the Framers would have sanctioned such a serious mechanism for such a frivolous purpose.

Dellinger believed this same logic was compelling when applied to a convention limited not to a single amendment but to a single subject area. Practically, limiting such a convention might prove detrimental by preventing accommodation and compromise.[59] Moreover, this would vest Congress with undue control over the convention, a control that "should be left to the convention itself."[60] Such a view would, of course, require that Congress reject all applications premised on a limited convention. Consistent with his emphasis on formalism elsewhere, however, Dellinger argued that an initial precedent establishing that

applications are valid if and only if applying states understand that the convention will be free to set its own limits, [would ultimately] be significantly less intrusive than if Congress were to undertake with each set of applications to infer and enforce limits on the subject matter authority of the convention.[61]

Dellinger concluded that all state calls for a convention limited to a single amendment or subject area are invalid unless "it is clear that the suggested limit is only a recommendation."[62] Looking specifically at the state requests for a convention to deal with a balanced budget, Dellinger argued that most such calls were invalid because they call for something that is not possible under Article V.[63]

Dellinger did proceed to distinguish his views somewhat from those of Ackerman and Black by arguing that, while states cannot authoritatively limit an Article V convention, such a convention would not be affirmatively obligated to consider wholesale constitutional revision. Such a convention would be as free as Congress to consider whatever amendments it chose, but "it is reasonable to expect that a convention would choose to confine itself to considering amendments addressing the problem that led states to apply for the convention," and delegates might even run on a platform thus to confine their deliberations.[64] Such a limit would, however, be self-imposed rather than required by the states beforehand or by Congress itself.

WILLIAM VAN ALSTYNE'S ARGUMENTS FOR A LIMITED ARTICLE V CONVENTION

William Van Alstyne, a law professor at Duke University, has written at least two articles in which he responded to those who believed that the states had no authority to call a limited Article V convention. The first was directed to Ackerman and Black and the second to Walter Dellinger.

In the first piece, Van Alstyne acknowledged the "expediency" but doubted the "rightness" of Black's and Ackerman's interpretation.[65] Pointing to the uncertainty at the Constitutional Convention of how or whether the new Constitution would work, Van Alstyne thought it very important that the delegates provide a "state mode" of amendment in the event that Congress proved to be unresponsive in adopting needed changes; he further argued that this mode "was not to be contingent upon any significant cooperation or discretion in Congress."[66] Congress "was supposed to be mere clerk of the process," with no role "as a hostile censor, a body entitled to impose such stringent requirements upon the states as effectively to render the state mode of securing particular amendments nearly impossible."[67] Therefore, in tracking the wishes of the Framers, Van Alstyne concluded that

a generous construction of what suffices to present a valid application by a state, for consideration of a particular subject or of a particular amendment in convention, is far more responsive to the anticipated uses of article V than a demanding construction that all but eliminates its use in response to specific, limited state dissatisfactions.[68]

Van Alstyne further pointed out that there are some cases where it might be necessary to call a convention to address specific congressional shortcomings. In such a case, it would not be appropriate for Congress to place "a wholly unexpected price tag (a 'Catch 22' as it were) on that right," that is the requirement that the states open the Constitution up for the prospect of wholesale constitutional reform, nor did Van Alstyne think that this was the Framers' intention.[69] Indeed, Van Alstyne argued that, while permitted by Article V, "such a [general] convention is the least likely to be the foreseeable object of states expected to make use of their collective authority in article V."[70] Van Alstyne thus concluded that

if two-thirds of the state legislatures might perchance agree on the exact wording of an amendment they would wish to be reviewed in a called convention for discussion and vote, this would seem to me to state the paradigm case in which Congress should proceed with the call—and limit the agenda exactly in accordance with the unequivocal expressions of those solely responsible for the event.[71]

Van Alstyne undertook a similar theme in responding to his colleague Walter Dellinger. In reexamining Convention proceedings, Van Alstyne emphasized the concern of some of the delegates about giving Congress any role in the amending process.[72] In analyzing the intent of the Convention, Van Alstyne came to two conclusions:

The first point is that securing a way to propose and to submit for ratification amendments other than those that might originate in or be congenial to extraordinary majorities in Congress was a steadfast determination in the Philadelphia Convention. The second point is that the most expected use of that authority would be in response to alleged usurpations, whether of states' rights or of personal liberties, by the national government itself.[73]

Using the language of Article V to reject the view that the text of the Constitution therefore requires a limited convention,[74] Van Alstyne nonetheless again argued against a Catch 22 approach that forced states to call a convention they did not want.

Agreeing with Dellinger that the Framers intended to put an obstacle between direct state proposal and state ratification of an amendment, he found that a limited convention did still provide for such a check in a variety of ways. First, he believed that the final convention mechanism left Congress with some power "to compose that convention as it believes best serves national interests."[75] Second, such a convention would encompass broader viewpoints by including all the states and not just those that joined in the call. Third, the convention would debate the proposal and might conclude that it was "not as simple or as free from disabling criticism as it may first have appeared to the states."[76] The time the convention itself took would serve as a fourth buffer and would be followed by a fifth, namely the congressional discretion as to how the convention proposals would be ratified. In short, Van Alstyne believed that the Framers had proposed a perfectly safe mechanism for constitutional change and that the states should not be forced to call an unlimited convention to achieve more limited goals.

GROVER REES'S ARGUMENTS FOR A LIMITED CONVENTION OPTION

Van Alstyne's critique of Ackerman's, Black's, and Dellinger's views rests on a view of original intent that stresses the Framers' desire to give states protection within the new system of government and equally to enable the states to introduce amendments. Grover Rees III tried further to tie this view of state power back to his view of contemporary consensus and to the view of participants engaged around a bargaining table.

Rees argued that the central flaw in the arguments of those who believe that states can only call a general convention is that their view rests on the mistaken notion that the convention was "a direct grant of power to the convention itself."[77] To the contrary, Rees emphasized the way that this was designed to empower the states. Since Congress can propose amendments "without thereby creating an organism . . . that Congress opposes," so, too, can the states.[78] As to Dellinger's argument that the Framers intended that states should not be able to enhance their power at the expense of the federal government, Rees found no solid foundation for this contention.[79] To the contrary, he argued that the formulation of the convention method was "almost certainly intended to *secure* (not eliminate) the power of State legislatures to initiate amendments."[80] In Rees's view, the alternate amending mechanism is thus well worth preserving.

On the related issue of who would control a convention, as earlier, Rees accepted a limited legislative role while rejecting the view of plenary congressional control. Returning to the notion of contemporary consensus, Rees argued that Congress had power "to facilitate, but not to obstruct, the expression of a consensus among the participants in each stage of the convention process."[81] Accordingly dividing congressional responsibilities into three parts, Rees would tabulate state convention petitions with a view to determining whether such states desired a convention and what kind they wanted; he favored convention rules designed to express the will of the convention within the parameters of its call; and he advocated rules for ratification designed "to detect rather than to obstruct the expression of a consensus among three-fourths of the State ratifying bodies."[82]

This author believes that the arguments of Van Alstyne, Rees, and other advocates of the states' right to call a limited constitutional convention are persuasive and consistent with the intention of the Framers and ratifiers of Article V.[83] The model which allows, but does not require a limited convention, is best designed to facilitate the adoption of needed amendments and to balance congressional powers under the more regularized Article V process.[84] The language of Article V does not require a general convention and should not be tortured into doing so.

PAUL WEBER AND BARBARA PERRY ASSESS THE POLITICAL SAFETY OF CONSTITUTIONAL CONVENTIONS

While there is therefore much to be gained from an examination of constitutional arguments, these arguments may not be completely dispositive, leaving at least residual doubts as to the safety and efficacy of the Article V convention mechanism. Addressing this very issue, Paul Weber and Barbara Perry have made a valuable contribution to the debates by directing attention from purely legalistic arguments to what they call "political 'safety latches' " as well.[85] Acknowledging that no preordained scenario could with absolute certainty predict what a convention could do, they believe that focus on certain political factors can lead to reasonable inferences about what a convention would in fact do.[86] Their survey of such factors led them to argue that "a constitutional convention would be an extraordinarily safe political procedure."[87]

Weber and Perry have identified a number of political protections. They cited the requirement that two-thirds of the states first must agree on a call. While some such calls may be adopted in a cavalier fashion, Weber and Perry identified a "fourth-quarter cautiousness" that usually develops as the number of states begins to approach this limit.[88] Consistent with the conclusion in Chapter 2, they further argued that Congress and the courts have the power to resolve disputes about such issues as what constitutes a valid application, whether a convention can be limited, and the like. Delegate selection processes would almost surely give an advantage to established political figures with the backing of politically responsive groups. Such delegates might even run on a platform designed to assure that they rein in discussion to that issue or issues which prompted a convention call. The character of such delegates as well as intense media attention during the convention itself would be likely to prevent a runaway convention. Moreover, Congress would be able to examine the amendments before proposing them to the states for ratification. In assessing the safety of such a convention, Weber and Perry concluded that:

It requires a consensus of at least 75 percent of the state legislatures or assemblies in addition to the active cooperation of Congress and the courts, and at least some established political elites and interest groups to pass an amendment by this means. It is a procedure that requires so much time that short-term passions or temporary coalitions could not prevail.[89]

THE DESIRABILITY OF LEGISLATION

In arguing against the Ervin Bill on constitutional conventions, Charles Black made two arguments that deserve particular attention. First, he contended that the legislation was flawed because one Congress had no power to bind successors "on questions of constitutional law and policy."[90] Second, he argued that

Even if (as is not the case) the 92d Congress could bind its successors, it would be foolish to settle great constitutional and prudential questions at a time when public and professional attention are not focused on them, and when (with respect to the prudential questions) the conditions of the future are unknowable.[91]

It is difficult to imagine two contentions that are more mistaken.

As to the first, there is great wisdom in the view suggesting that because they are so important, constitutional issues can never be decided solely by precedent. This fact should, however, no more keep Congress from making reasoned constitutional judgments than it should preclude the Supreme Court from doing so. Some of the most important laws that Congress has adopted—the Judiciary Act of 1789, the War Powers Resolution, and the Impoundment Act, to name only a few—deal with important constitutional matters. Some of these laws have and can be changed, but certainty and the perception of fairness are both enhanced when such procedures are outlined beforehand.

As to Black's second argument, this too seems to state things exactly in reverse. The great problem in constitutional matters is to formulate rules and standards that can be applied generally without an eye to specific ad hoc issues of policy about which one is self-interested. Such general rules are most likely to be formulated at a time when such specific policies are not under current consideration. One of the problems with the debates over the extension of the ratification time for the Equal Rights Amendment was the perception by opponents of this extension that the decision to extend was not made on the basis of neutral legal principles but rather with a view to its effect on the specific amendment in question. This is more generally the problem with the ad hoc model of congressional decision making critiqued in Chapter 2. Naturally, Congress would have power to change legislation in the middle of a crisis if such changes proved to be necessary, but surely it would be better if preestablished standards had been set that would be presumptively valid, unless and until a clear need for change demonstrated itself. Surely, for example, it would be better for states to know beforehand whether they could or could not rescind memorializing resolutions for amendments, how many years their petitions would be considered valid, whether calls for a limited convention were considered legitimate, and how states would be represented at such a convention.

THE DIVISION OF STATE AND CONGRESSIONAL RESPONSIBILITY

The most obvious difficulty with a law governing constitutional conventions is to divide state and congressional responsibilities properly. To this writer, at least, it seems clear that there are some functions the states—that form no separate governing body—and the convention (which is not permanent) cannot perform on their own. These questions include, but are not necessarily limited to, issues involving whether calls for a convention are sufficiently contemporaneous and similar as to warrant calling a convention (where there may, however, be an advisory role for the states), when and where the convention would convene, and how states would be represented. Rees correctly argued that such decisions should be made with the intention of facilitating, rather than obstructing, state desires and expressing their contemporary consensus. This is one of the strongest reasons for arguing that Congress has the power to limit a convention if this is the desire of the states. Such limits could be imposed both when the convention is called and when Congress subsequently decides whether to pass its proposals on to the states for ratification. At this time, of course, Congress would also have to decide whether the amendment or amendments proposed by the convention would be ratified by state legislatures or by special conventions within the states.

The states, by contrast, should have full power to decide how their delegates will be selected and how much they will pay them (with Congress perhaps picking up other convention expenses). Moreover, once the convention meets, it should be able to set its own rules, deciding, for example, who it will select as officers, by what majority it will vote on amendments (any legislation by Congress on this issue would be advisory only), what if any committee or subcommittee structures it will establish to facilitate its work, how long it will convene, and how long it will permit debate on individual amendments. Like the initial congressional judgments, these matters should, by the logic of Chapter 2, be subject to judicial review, albeit review which is deferential to the nature of the convention and the state interests it is designed to represent.

The Constitutional Convention Implementation Act of 1991 is a reasonably good law that fits most of the criteria just specified. It allows but does not require a limited convention. It permits states to decide on the rules they will follow in memorializing Congress for a convention. It encourages states to indicate which if any other state applications deal with the same subject, further specifying that petitions are valid for a seven-year period and allowing for state rescission. The bill authorizes Congress to set the time and place for the convention. States would be represented according to the same scheme used in the electoral college, with states deciding how to choose their own delegates. Delegates would take an oath to comply with the Constitution, but would be free to draw up their own rules (with, however, a provision—probably unnecessary and possibly unwise—against unit-rule voting). In submitting amendments to the states, Congress would in turn be authorized to determine if the amendments fit the general subject matter of the convention and how they will be ratified. States would be allowed to reconsider rejections and rescind ratifications prior to approval by three-fourths of the states. All such matters would be subject to judicial review.[92]

CONCLUSION

As with any untried mechanism, numerous questions may never be resolved about an Article V convention unless and until such a gathering is actually called. However, in this author's judgment there is no reason that states should be faced with a Catch 22 in which they must accept the possibility of a completely wide open convention to remedy a distinct problem or set of problems. If the states desire a limited convention, the power to limit it is implicit in Congress's ministerial duty to call a convention as well as in the courts' authority, established in Chapter 2, to say what the law is. Moreover, numerous constitutional and political restraints should serve to distinguish, as Jameson tried in the nineteenth century to do, between a "constitutional convention" and a "revolutionary convention." The former is not a mechanism to be feared. If the latter comes, it is less likely to be the result of a system that allows representative institutions at the state and national levels to initiate changes than to result from a system in which such changes are stymied in the name of some overly restrictive view of what the Constitution does or should mean.

NOTES

1. American Bar Association, Special Constitutional Convention Study Committee, *Amendment of the Constitution by the Convention Method under Article V* (Chicago: American Bar Association, Public Service Activities Division, 1979).

2. See especially, Russell L. Caplan, *Constitutional Brinkmanship: Amending the Constitution by National Convention* (New York: Oxford University Press, 1988); Wilbur Edel, *A Constitutional Convention: Threat or Challenge?* (New York: Praeger, 1981); and Paul J. Weber and Barbara A. Perry, *Unfounded Fears: Myths and Realities of a Constitutional Convention* (New York: Praeger, 1989). Other books and articles are mentioned in the course of discussions in this chapter.

3. In the 1970s, the fight for legislation was led by Senator Sam Ervin of North Carolina. For analysis of his bill see Sam Ervin, Jr., "Proposed Legislation to Implement the Convention Mechanism of Amending the Constitution," *Michigan Law Review* 66 (March 1968), pp. 875–902. Also see "Proposed Legislation on the Convention Method of Amending the United States Constitution," *Harvard Law Review* 85 (June 1972), pp. 1612–48. More recent legislation has been sponsored by Senator

Orrin Hatch of Utah. For his bill, see his speech in *Congressional Record,* Senate, January 15, 1991, S559–S563.

4. Laurence Tribe has attempted to capitalize on this and other ambiguities in opposing a convention to propose a balanced budget amendment. See "Issues Raised by Requesting Congress to Call a Constitutional Convention to Propose a Balanced Budget Amendment," *Pacific Law Journal* 10 (1979), pp. 627–39. On pp. 634–35, Tribe described "three distinct confrontations of nightmarish dimension—confrontation between Congress and the Convention, between Congress and the Supreme Court, and between the Supreme Court and the states."

5. 307 U.S. 433 (1939).

6. Walter Dellinger, "The Legitimacy of Constitutional Change: Rethinking the Amending Process," *Harvard Law Review* 97 (December 1983), pp. 386–432.

7. Grover Rees III, "The Amendment Process and Limited Constitutional Conventions," *Benchmark* 2 (1986), pp. 67–108.

8. U.S. Constitution, Article V.

9. There have, of course, been numerous state conventions, but parallels between these institutions and the Article V mechanism must necessarily be tentative. See Francis H. Heller, "Limiting a Constitutional Convention: The State Precedents," *Cardozo Law Review* 3 (1982), pp. 563–79.

10. Max Farrand, *The Records of the Federal Convention of 1787*, vol. 2 (New Haven, CT: Yale University Press, 1966), p. 159.

11. These views are outlined in John R. Vile, *The Constitutional Amending Process in American Political Thought* (New York: Praeger, 1992), p. 29.

12. Farrand, *Records*, p. 559.

13. Ibid., p. 629.

14. Alexander Hamilton, James Madison, and John Jay, *The Federalist Papers,* ed. Clinton Rossiter (New York: New American Library, 1961), p. 279.

15. Ibid., p. 526.

16. William R. Pullen, "Application of State Legislatures to Congress for the Call of a National Constitutional Convention, 1788–1967" (Master's thesis, University of North Carolina, Chapel Hill, 1948).

17. Caplan, *Constitutional Brinkmanship,* p. xx.

18. 30 U.S. (5 Pet) 518, 528 (1831).

19. John A. Jameson, *A Treatise on Constitutional Conventions: Their History, Powers, and Modes of Proceeding* (New York: Da Capo Press, 1972. Reprint of fourth edition, Chicago, 1887).

20. Ibid., pp. 1–16.

21. See, for example, Roger S. Hoar, *Constitutional Conventions: Their Nature, Powers, and Limitations* (Boston: Little, Brown, 1919).

22. See, for example, Thomas H. Kean, "A Constitutional Convention Would Threaten Rights We Have Cherished for 200 Years," *Detroit College Law Review* 4 (Winter 1986), pp. 1087–91; Theodore Sorenson, "The Quiet Campaign to Rewrite the Constitution," *Saturday Review* (July 15, 1967), pp. 17–20; and Arthur J. Goldberg, "The Proposed Constitutional Convention," *Hastings Constitutional Law Quarterly* 11 (Fall 1983), pp. 1–4. Also see Tribe's, "Issues Raised by Requesting Congress."

23. Ackerman's views, which are not treated in this chapter, are found in "Unconstitutional Convention," *New Republic* 180 (March 3, 1979), pp. 8–9.

24. Dellinger, "The Legitimacy of Constitutional Change." This article is discussed at length in the previous chapter.

25. William W. Van Alstyne, "Does Article V Restrict the States to Calling Unlimited Conventions Only?—A Letter to a Colleague," *Duke Law Journal* (January 1978), p. 1299. For another article that notes the simplicity of the Black and Dellinger positions that all calls for anything other than a general convention are invalid, but which, like Van Alstyne, ultimately rejects this argument as unpersuasive, see Neal S. Manne, "Good Intentions, New Inventions, and Article V Constitutional Conventions," *Texas Law Review* 58 (December 1979), pp. 168–69.

26. Here, if Dellinger were to follow a purely formalistic model under which all petitions (except those that fall prey to desuetude) are valid and all rescissions are invalid, he might have to conclude that Congress already is duty bound to call an Article V convention. For just such a conclusion, see Bruce M. Van Sickle and Lynn M. Boughey, "Lawful and Peaceful Revolution: Article V and Congress' Present Duty to Call a Convention for Proposing Amendments," *Hamline Law Review* 14 (Fall 1990), pp. 1–115.

27. Black had made a similar, but less detailed, argument in "The Proposed Amendment of Article V: A Threatened Disaster," *Yale Law Journal* 72 (1963), pp. 957–66. That article was primarily addressed to the undesirability of three proposals to amend the Constitution proposed by the Council of State Governments and mentioned in the first chapter.

28. Charles L. Black, Jr., "Amending the Constitution: A Letter to a Congressman," *Yale Law Journal* 82 (December 1972), p. 198.

29. Ibid., p. 200.

30. Ibid., p. 201. William F. Swindler, "The Current Challenge to Federalism: The Confederating Proposals," *The Georgetown Law Review* 52 (Fall 1963), pp. 1–41 at p. 16 took the position that the Article V convention mechanism had a limited historical purpose and that it is now obsolete. He wrote:

> The thrust of all the writing [in *The Federalist*] concerning the convention proviso would seem to be that once the constitutional system was demonstrably operative, the proviso itself would become inoperative since its only function was to provide a means of correcting the system if it failed to become self-sustaining.

31. Black, "Amending the Constitution," pp. 202–3.

32. Ibid., p. 203.

33. Ibid.

34. Charles L. Black, Jr., "Amendment by National Constitutional Convention: A Letter to a Senator," *Oklahoma Law Review* 32 (1979), pp. 626–44.

35. American Bar Association, *Amendment of the Constitution.*

36. Black, "Amendment by National Constitutional Convention," p. 629.

37. Ibid.

38. Ibid., p. 630.

39. Rees, "The Amendment Process," p. 76. A similar view of state powers is advanced by Bill Gaugush, "Principles Governing the Interpretation and Exercise of Article V Powers," *The Western Political Quarterly* 35 (June 1982), pp. 217–18.

40. Rees, "The Amendment Process," p. 77.

41. Farrand, *Records,* vol. 2, p. 629.

42. Ibid.

43. Ibid.

44. Ibid.

45. Ibid., p. 630.

46. Black, "Amendment by National Constitutional Convention," p. 635.

47. Ibid.

48. Farrand, *Records,* vol. 2, pp. 630–31.

49. Rees, "The Amendment Process," p. 78.

50. Black, "Amendment by National Constitutional Convention," p. 637.

51. Farrand, *Records,* vol. 2, p. 629.

52. Rees, "The Amendment Process," p. 78. Underlining Rees's. Similarly, Robert M. Rhodes notes the convention debates reveal that "Madison and Hamilton viewed the two modes of initiating amendments as equivalent alternatives and that they envisioned a process whereby both the state and National Legislatures would be able to apply to Congress for specific constitutional amendments." See "A Limited Constitutional Convention," *University of Florida Law Review* 26 (Fall 1983), p. 7.

53. Black, "Amendment by National Constitutional Convention," p. 637.

54. Ibid., pp. 638–43.

55. See Caplan, p. xx.

56. Walter Dellinger, "The Recurring Question of the 'Limited' Constitutional Convention," *Yale Law Review* 88 (1979), 1623–40.

57. Ibid.

58. Ibid., p. 1632.

59. Ibid., p. 1633.

60. Ibid., p. 1634.

61. Ibid., p. 1635.

62. Ibid., p. 1636.

63. For a very similar view, see William T. Barker, "A Status Report on the 'Balanced Budget' Constitutional Convention," *John Marshall Law Review* 20 (1986), pp. 29–96. This position is almost directly the opposite of that of Van Sickle and Boughey in "Lawful and Peaceful Revolution," who believe Congress is already obligated to call a constitutional convention. A related argument is made by James E. Bond and David E. Engdahl, "The Duties and Powers of Congress Regarding Conventions for Proposing Amendments," in *The Constitutional Convention: How Is It Formed? How Is It Run? What Are the Guidelines? What Happens Now?* Washington, DC: (National Legal Center for the Public Interest, 1987), who believe that Congress had independent authority to call a convention on its own.

64. Dellinger, "The Recurring Question," p. 1639.

65. Van Alstyne, "Does Article V Restrict the States," p. 1302.

66. Ibid., p. 1303.

67. Ibid.

68. Ibid.

69. Ibid., p. 1304.

70. Ibid., p. 1305.

71. Ibid., pp. 1305–06. In this regard, it might be useful to recall that a number of scholars unsuccessfully objected to the conventions that ratified the Twenty-First

Amendment repealing Prohibition on the basis that Article V called only for deliberative conventions and not for conventions that simply cast an up or down vote.

72. William Van Alstyne, "The Limited Constitutional Convention—The Recurring Answer," *Duke Law Journal* (September 1979), p. 988.

73. Ibid., p. 990.

74. Such a view has been advocated by Ann S. Diamond in "A Convention for Proposing Amendments: The Constitution's Other Method," *Publius: The Journal of Federalism* 11 (Summer 1981), pp. 113–46. For a critique of this view, see John R. Vile, "Ann Diamond on an Unlimited Constitutional Convention," *Publius: The Journal of Federalism* 19 (Winter 1989), pp. 177–83.

75. Van Alstyne, "The Recurring Answer," p. 993.

76. Ibid., p. 994.

77. Rees, "The Amendment Process," p. 75. Rees's views are also presented in his "Constitutional Conventions and Constitutional Arguments: Some Thoughts About Limits," *Harvard Journal of Law and Public Policy* 6 (1982), pp. 79–91.

78. Rees, "The Amendment Process," p. 79.

79. Ibid., p. 80.

80. Ibid., p. 82.

81. Ibid., p. 85.

82. Ibid.

83. I have not treated Russell Caplan's generally helpful *Constitutional Brinkmanship* here, both because I have treated it elsewhere and because, while arguing for a limited convention, Caplan does not directly answer critics who argue that such conventions are not constitutional. I also think there is some problem with Caplan's reliance on precedents that occurred prior to the writing of Article V. For more detailed reflections, see John R. Vile, "Book Review, Filling a Void in Scholarship: Russell L. Caplan on Constitutional Conventions," *Journal of Law & Politics* 6 (Fall 1989), pp. 125–34.

84. There may well be merit in the idea that a convention called simply to debate the text of a single amendment would be unwise and unproductive. The expense alone would appear to mitigate against such a narrow single-issue convention. This writer is not of the opinion, however, that such a convention would therefore be unconstitutional. In this, at least, he differs from the author of the 1991 Convention Bill discussed later.

85. Weber and Perry, *Unfounded Fears,* p. 105. These arguments were previously presented in Paul J. Weber, "The Constitutional Convention: A Safe Political Option," *Journal of Law & Politics* 3 (Winter 1986), pp. 51–70.

86. Weber and Perry, *Unfounded Fears,* p. 106.

87. Ibid., p. 109.

88. Ibid.

89. Ibid., p. 119.

90. Black, "Amending the Constitution," p. 191. Italics omitted.

91. Ibid., p. 194. Italics omitted.

92. This law is effectively summarized and defended by Senator Orrin Hatch in a speech in the *Proceedings and Debates of the 102d Congress,* First Session, 137 (January 15, 1991), pp. S559–S563. The text of the bill follows on pp. S563–S565.

Chapter 5

The Question of Exclusivity—Can Any Constitutional Changes Be Adopted Without Using Article V?

JUDICIAL REVIEW AND THE AMENDING PROCESS

As the narrative in the first chapter should indicate, at least since *Marbury v. Madison* affirmed the power of judicial review of national legislation,[1] the formal constitutional amending process has been somewhat in tension with changes effected by judicial interpretations and congressional and presidential practices.[2] While the formal amending process can be used to modify the Constitution and even to reverse judicial decisions and evolving practices, the judiciary interprets not only the Constitution itself but also amendments added to it.

Moreover, justices, particularly those who put special emphasis on the original intent and/or the plain words of the Founders, have frequently accused their more non-interpretivist or activist brethren of improperly "amending" the Constitution.[3] Thus dissenting from an innovative interpretation of the contracts clause in *Home Building & Loan Association v. Blaisdell,* Justice George Sutherland (one of the four conservative justices then on the Supreme Court) noted that

What a court is to do, therefore, is to declare the law as written, leaving it to the people themselves to make such changes as new circumstances may require. The meaning of the constitution is fixed when it is adopted, and it is not different at any subsequent time when a court has occasion to pass upon it.[4]

Similarly objecting to the Court's discovery of a right of privacy in *Griswold v. Connecticut* (the Connecticut birth control case), Justice Hugo Black also rejected such judicial innovation:

For myself, I must with all deference reject that philosophy. The Constitution makers knew the need for change and provided for it. Amendments suggested by the people's elected representatives can be submitted to the people or their selected agents for ratification. That method of change was good enough for our Fathers, and being somewhat old-fashioned I must add that it is good enough for me.[5]

In a more nuanced position, Justice Lewis Powell rejected the plurality's attempt in *Frontiero v. Richardson* to include gender classifications within the category of "suspect categories":

The Equal Rights Amendment, which if adopted will resolve the substance of this precise question, has been approved by the Congress and submitted for ratification by the States. If this Amendment is duly adopted, it will represent the will of the people accomplished in the manner prescribed by the Constitution. By acting prematurely and unnecessarily, as I view it, the Court has assumed a decisional responsibility at the very time when state legislatures, functioning within the traditional democratic process, are debating the proposed amendment. It seems to me that this reaching out to pre-empt by judicial action a major political decision which is currently in process of resolution does not reflect appropriate respect for duly prescribed legislative processes.[6]

It is difficult to imagine a constitutional history of the United States that focused alone either on the Constitution and its amendments or on judicial interpretations—omitting, for example, either the Civil War Amendments or cases such as *Plessy v. Ferguson* and *Brown v. Board of Education*.[7] This is enough to persuade this author that it is too late in the day to argue that the amending process is the exclusive means of effecting any constitutional changes.

STEPHEN MARKMAN'S ARGUMENTS FOR JUDICIAL RESTRAINT

Stephen Markman, one-time assistant attorney general for legal policy and now a U.S. attorney for the eastern district of Michigan, has written at least two articles in which he has argued that the relation between judicial review and constitutional amendment has undergone a fundamental shift which is at odds with the Constitution.[8] In looking at the large number of single issue amendments which have been proposed in the last few decades, Markman concluded that these amendments are not, like most previous amendments, designed "to correct defects in the document's [the Constitution's] text or structure, but to overturn specific conclusions of the Supreme Court."[9] Moreover, these attempts—and Markman picked out abortion, school prayer, and the issue of busing for special attention—have been generated by a Court which has increasingly looked beyond the constitutional text to adopt the Constitution to modern times rather than waiting for the people to exercise their exclusive power under Article V. In Markman's view, attempts at amendment have thus been attempts at constitution restoration rather than constitutional reformation.[10] They have been necessitated because the Supreme Court has failed to recognize Article V as "the sole mode of amendment permitted by the Constitution."[11] By contrast, Article V of the Constitution serves as definitive testimony to the fact

that the Constitution is not "written on water," that its meaning is not to evolve and "mature" over time, and that it matters what the Constitution's words meant to the society that drafted and ratified it. Article V is the ultimate expression that the Constitution is not a mere "parchment barrier" but that its guarantees and principles are permanent and unchanging in the absence of resort to its procedures.[12]

Markman proceeded to argue that judicial usurpations of the amending process and adaptations of the Constitution to changing times are in conflict with three constitutional principles—federalism, separation of powers, and popular rule—each of which is better accommodated by the formal constitutional amending process.[13]

Certainly, despite the difficulty of adopting amendments, there are some powerful arguments to be made for the advantage of inaugurating constitutional changes through the constitutional amending process rather than through judicial innovation[14] as well as some arguments to be made for judicial restraint.[15] Philip Hamburger has also demonstrated that the exercise of the amending process also appears more closely to follow the Framers' intention than do vague notions of adapting the Constitution through judicial or other means.[16] It is difficult, however, to draw as clear a line as Markman advocates between judicial interpretation and judicial usurpation. Debates over whether the courts were interpreting or amending the Constitution date at least as far back as the Marshall Court.[17] Moreover, as current discussions over the value of adhering to judicial precedents indicate, the Court might at times inaugurate greater changes by enforcing its view of original intent than by sticking with earlier understandings. Furthermore, while the pace of judicial opinions, like the pace of most other governmental institutions, has undoubtedly increased (partly aided, as court scrutiny of the school prayer controversy would indicate, by the incorporation doctrine whose implications now seem to have been fairly well worked out), it is not altogether clear that the phenomenon Markman identifies is unique to the last few decades rather than inherent within the political system itself.[18]

As the narrative in the first chapter indicates, for example, those who pushed for the Eleventh Amendment certainly thought they were restoring the Constitution to its original meaning as did those who worked for adoption of the Fourteenth Amendment and later the Sixteenth Amendment. For that matter, those who pressed for adoption of the Bill of Rights thought they were restoring the role of individual rights which they perceived to have been in place under the Articles of Confederation against usurpations by the national government. Moreover, while the modern court has been more activist than many, it has arguably not been uniquely so. Markman's analysis thus is a reason for some caution about judicial usurpation generally but hardly provides answers as to whether judicial intervention is warranted in individual cases involving real litigants.

SANFORD LEVINSON AND CONSTITUTIONAL CHANGE

Texas Law School Professor Sanford Levinson, who has written a number of other pieces on the constitutional amending process, has provided some thoughtful reflections that help put Markman's and similar critiques in historical context.[19] In seeking to "unpack some of the various meanings packed within the term 'amendment,' "[20] Levinson spends considerable time attempting to draw the line between constitutional interpretations and constitutional amendments. Initially, in a distinction with which Markman might well agree, Levinson notes that the difference is a difference "between organic development and the *invention* of entirely new solutions to old problems."[21] As his discussion proceeds, however, Levinson makes it clear that the line between these two categories has been indistinct at least as far back as Marshall's opinion in *McCulloch v. Maryland*.[22] Moreover, Levinson shows that a number of amendments which have been adopted do not really fit the category of invention but may be viewed as having been implicit in the Constitution already.[23]

Ultimately, Levinson develops a "spectrum" of possibilities[24] "in regard to describing any given legal development," which, while not necessarily the last word on the subject, is enough to establish the great difficulty of drawing any absolute line between changes effected by amendments and those effected through other means:

(1) It is, especially if the result of a judicial decision, simply a recognition, called "interpretation," of what was already immanent within the existing body of legal materials; (2) It is, especially if a statute passed by a legislature, a change not disallowed by the constraints established by the Constitution and thus what might be termed an allowable "interpretation" of the powers allowed legislatures by the Constitution; (3) It represents a genuine change not immanent within the pre-existing materials or allowable simply by the use of the powers granted (or tolerated) by the Constitution, although the change, being fairly marginal, allows one to speak of it unproblematically as an "amendment"; (4) It represents a genuine change of such a dimension as to be described as a "revision"—i.e., a special kind of amendment—but that change, nonetheless, is congruent with the immanent values of the constitutional order. . . . (5) It represents a change of such fundamental dimension

as to be called truly revolutionary and thus taken out of the language of amendment at all.[25]

Levinson argues that it is impossible to understand American constitutional history without recognizing that as many or more changes have been effected by constitutional interpretations as by constitutional amendments,[26] and he applauds attempts, such as those of Bruce Ackerman, to extend analysis of this subject.

BRUCE ACKERMAN'S BOOK, FIRST HALF

Ackerman, who is a professor of law and political science at Yale University, has begun the task of providing a firmer basis for extra-Article V changes in the Constitution with the publication of the first volume of a projected three-volume series on the Constitution.[27] Elaborating on hints he had developed in a number of earlier articles,[28] Ackerman's sketch of governmental change in *We the People: Foundations* is still incomplete, but the work is so well-written as well as so provocative and controversial that it is likely to be the focus of scholarly attention for years to come.[29] Drawing insights from law, political science, and history, Ackerman's thought has the potential of cross-fertilizing all three disciplines. Whether, as he seems to hope, the book will be taken as seriously by the general populace,[30] would appear rather more problematical, but, judging from the large number of legal scholars who are already familiar with his articles, his book is likely to have a profound effect in this area.[31]

Like Louis Hartz[32] whom he admires, Ackerman believes that the American historical experience is unique. Indeed, in Ackerman's view, it is so unique that it cannot be adequately understood through use of imported categories, whether these be notions of Lockean liberalism of which Hartz was so fond or whether these be ideas of republicanism that have come to dominate some accounts of the founding since Hartz's day.[33] Ackerman argues that what he describes as dualist democracy is a superior paradigm both to what he calls monistic democracy and to the view he attributes to "rights foundationalists."[34] The monistic democrat, epitomized by Woodrow Wilson, is so struck by the beauty of the British parliamentary system, that this democrat stresses direct political accountability to the electorate and is troubled when the entire platform of the bearer of the latest electoral mandate is not enacted into law. The rights foundationalist, with eyes on Locke, Kant, and other European models, allows certain fundamental rights to trump legislative judgments.[35] Ackerman argues that neither view is complete; America has instituted a dualist democracy that incorporates the insights of both into a larger whole. This system allows representatives to legislate within constitutional parameters but limits wider exercises of power contrary to restraints, or unsanctioned by grants of power, in the higher law of the Constitution.[36] Incidentally, here as elsewhere in his book, Ackerman seems to oversell the importance of his views on the subject by suggesting that he is the first to come to such an insight. In fact, he later argues that his view is consistent with that of Publius in *The Federalist*. Moreover, Ackerman omits others who have articulated similar views— for example, Alpheus Mason who resurrected the term *free government* to express a very similar if not identical balance between majority rule and minority rights.[37]

In assessing what he describes as the professional narrative of American history, Ackerman believes that the story has been distorted by undue emphasis, as evident in the bicentennial celebrations, on the continuity of this experience, albeit with some nod to the achievements and the disjunction of the Civil War era. In Ackerman's view, however, the nation's history can best be understood by dividing it, like Gaul, into three parts: the Founding; the period that culminated in Reconstruction; and, finally, the period that succeeded the New Deal. Each was an extraordinary time of constitutional creativity. Moreover, each was, in purely procedural terms, illegal. The delegates at the Constitutional Convention of 1787 ditched the Articles of Confederation without adhering to its own specifications for constitutional emendation;[38] the Reconstruction Congress forced Southern states to ratify the far-reaching Fourteenth Amendment as a condition to readmission to the Union from which, under Northern theory, they had never technically seceded; and the New Deal democrats brought about major changes in constitutional understanding altogether outside of the exercise of Article V. Reconstruction relied on a congressional model of leadership inconsistent with the federal requirements of Article V while the New Deal showed the potential of presidential leadership and was finalized by a series of transformative judicial decisions and appointments. In each of the three periods, normal politics gave way to a process of higher lawmaking that has forever changed the American political and constitutional landscape. Lesser moments, such as Jeffersonian and Jacksonian democracy and progressivism have also altered constitutional history albeit not, in Ackerman's judgment, to the same extent.[39]

While it is possible that Ackerman has once again overstated the uniqueness of his own story line,[40] the dynamic of his scheme leads to renewed possibilities for understanding constitutional interpretation. Each of these times the nation has changed "regimes," judges have in turn been responsible for interpreting the new regime's relationship to the old. Since each new regime has modified, rather than simply replaced the one(s) that preceded, the task of constitutional interpretation is necessarily difficult, involving the need for "multigenerational synthesis."[41] Reductionists try to solve the problem of interpretation either by focusing on one time or the other. Thus, someone such as Justice Hugo Black exaggerates the clarity and breadth of the Reconstruction amendments while someone like Raoul

Berger makes the opposite error, interpreting these amendments as though they were mere superstatutes.[42] The Reconstruction amendments, like the changes inaugurated by the New Deal outside the classical amending process are, for Ackerman, however, justly viewed as "transformative amendments" and a serious interpreter elaborates "doctrinal principles which harmonize the conflict in a way that does justice to the deepest aspirations of each."[43] The Supreme Court exercises a unique role in the "preservationist function," recognizing that there will be some "failed constitutional moments" as well as successful ones.[44]

Perhaps the most problematical part of Ackerman's theory is the notion that the New Deal represented a constitutional moment equal to the previous two. The main obstacle to such recognition is what Ackerman diagnoses as the myth of constitutional recovery, namely the belief that, in ultimately legitimizing the New Deal, the Court was not sanctioning recent amendments in constitutional understanding but that it was simply returning to an earlier jurisprudence of John Marshall and the early Federalist Court. This view has, according to Ackerman, resulted in too negative a view of the contribution to jurisprudence that the Court made from Reconstruction to the New Deal. Only by recognizing the viability of interpretations rendered during this period can one truly understand how revolutionary the New Deal alterations were.[45]

By focusing on the change initiated by the New Deal Court in footnote four of the *Carolene Products* case[46] and elsewhere, Ackerman hopes to cast further light on contemporary cases, especially *Brown v. Board of Education* (1954)[47] and *Griswold v. Connecticut* (1965).[48] After first suggesting that both cases might be examples of judicial prophesy which initiated new transformational movements, Ackerman ultimately concludes that both interpretations are consistent with, and indeed, representative of "a more comprehensive understanding of the problem of synthesis"[49] than heretofore understood.

Brown v. Board of Education emerges in Ackerman's interpretation not simply as a better understanding of the meaning of the Reconstruction amendments than was *Plessy v. Ferguson,* but as a recognition of the implications of these amendments in light of the more activist state instituted by the New Deal.[50] Ackerman takes his cue from Warren's emphasis in *Brown* on changing times. Given the increased governmental role in education and the importance of education in modern life, it was no longer plausible to suggest that the *Plessy* distinction between social and political equality was still viable (this writer, for one, would question whether it ever was) or that schooling was somehow merely a matter of individual choice rather than a governmental mandate. *Griswold,* in turn, carried this recognition to a still higher level of generality by indicating that however much the New Deal intended to legitimate a more activist role for government, it was not intended to eliminate the personal spheres protected in the first and second regimes by property rights and now reconceptualized under the rubric of privacy. For Ackerman, "*Griswold's* reinterpretation of the Founding texts in terms of a right to privacy, rather than a right to property and contract, is nothing less than a brilliant *interpretive* proposal."[51] Thus judicial interpretation followed upon earlier constitutional transformations.

BRUCE ACKERMAN'S BOOK, SECOND HALF

From this discovery of the Constitution, Ackerman proceeds in the second half of his book to a discussion of Neo-Federalism, where with help from Hannah Arendt and others, he tries in convincing fashion to redeem the revolutionary notion of the American Revolution as against those moderns who see anything less than total continuing revolution as suspect.[52] Ackerman enlists Publius to demonstrate that the Framers rejected permanent revolution while still valuing "public-regarding political activity involving citizen sacrifice of private interests to pursue the common good in transient and informal political assemblies."[53] Like Publius, Ackerman hopes to distinguish times of extraordinary constitution making from more pervasive times of normal politics. In so doing, the Framers recognized that no representative institutions, elected though they may be, are substitutes for the people themselves. In times of normal politics, separation of powers, the multiplicity of factions, and other constitutional mechanisms requiring minimal citizen virtue and participation would work to safeguard the last constitutional synthesis, allowing, however, for more "solemn and authoritative" acts which alter the form of government itself.[54] While one might conclude that the Framers were thus justifying their own extralegal activities and pointing to the need for following Article V channels in the future, Ackerman's interpretation is broader:

He [Publius] leaves open the relationship between these new rules and the kinds of "solemn and authoritative" action that should convince the judges. This failure to insist on strict legality makes sense, of course, given Publius's own frank confessions that the Philadelphia Convention's own actions are illegal.[55]

Thus, the way is opened for full acceptance of Reconstruction actions which dispensed with normal Article V procedures and of the New Deal which ignored them completely.

In elaborating on the Framers' conception of revolution, Ackerman dismissed the Marxian notion that revolution must be a social phenomenon; Ackerman identified revolution rather with "the political consciousness of the engaged participants."[56] Likewise rejecting the views of Charles Beard and other progressive spokesmen, Ackerman saw the Constitution as the fulfillment of the dream articulated in the Declaration of Independence, finely distinguishing his own view from a host of other historians and theorists in the process. Ackerman further argued that it is possible to distinguish "the *revolutionary process* through which the Federalists mobilized popular support for their constitutional reforms, and the *property-oriented substance* of their particular social vision."[57]

Two particularly creative chapters on democratic citizenship follow, with the focus on private citizenship. Most people cannot in most times be "public citizens," nor should they become complete privatists. Forcing people to be free contradicts freedom. The constitutional system can be maintained, however, as long as sufficient numbers of citizens devote enough attention to everyday politics to vote and otherwise contribute to its legitimacy. More will be brought into the process during times of constitutional transformation, but mere systemic maintenance does not require such a high degree of activity nor the need for extraordinary citizen virtue. Here Ackerman offered a cogent critique of parliamentary democracy which has been frequently proposed as an alternative to the American scheme of checks and balances.[58] By his understanding, a parliamentary system exaggerates the extent to which the representative assembly actually speaks for a largely dormant people, thus in fact potentially sanctioning the kind of majority tyranny the American Founders feared. Ackerman's justification of judicial review is tied to Publius's.[59] The Court speaks for the people's will as embodied in the written Constitution (translated more generously, undoubtedly too generously, in Ackerman's scheme to the last constitutional moment) as against any temporary majorities whose representatives might now dominate the elected branches of government.

Times of normal politics are from time to time punctuated by attempts at higher lawmaking which Ackerman divided into four parts. In the "signaling phase" a movement "earns the constitutional authority to claim that, in contrast to the countless ideological factions competing in normal politics, its reform agenda should be placed at the center of sustained public scrutiny."[60] This is followed by a "proposal" phase, by "mobilized popular deliberation," and, if accepted, by a period of "legal codification" during which the Supreme Court translates "constitutional politics into constitutional law."[61] Whereas the "classical system" follows the Article V amending process, the "modern system" relies on presidential leadership, on congressional passage of "transformative statutes," a period of judicial invalidation signaling the change about to be effected, and then either the defeat of the new movement or its eventual triumph recognized in a judicial "switch in time."[62] While this description seems literally tailored to account for a category of one, namely the New Deal, Ackerman believes that it was foreshadowed by other periods in American history, most notably the Jeffersonian and Jacksonian periods and Reconstruction. Ackerman's analysis also allowed him to argue that President Ronald Reagan's failure to get Judge Robert Bork confirmed to the Supreme Court represented a failed constitutional moment—rather heavy weight to assign to a single event which may well have been as influenced by Bork's appearance and personality as his political beliefs.[63]

How is the Court to know when higher lawmaking other than through Article V processes has occurred? Accepting some imprecision, Ackerman focuses on the "depth, breadth, and decisiveness" of popular opinion in such moments,[64] recognizing that there may be occasional "false positives" and "false negatives." Perhaps with a view toward the possibility of "stealth" appointments to the Supreme Court which could have transformative effects short of popular sanction, Ackerman referred back to a proposal which he makes for a change in Article V by which such future signals are more likely to be interpreted correctly. This proposal specifies that a president in his second term could propose amendments to Congress which, if approved by two-thirds of both houses, would be listed on the next two presidential ballots. If approved in both elections by three-fifths of the participating voters, such amendments would be "ratified in the name of the People of the United States."[65]

In his final chapter, in which Ackerman again defends his dualistic vision of democracy, he further suggests the need for a new Bill of Rights that would add economic to political liberties by securing all citizens "against the vagaries of unemployment, disability, sickness, and old age."[66] Believing that current constitutional protections can legally be repealed by subsequent amendments,[67] Ackerman also proposes that "*inalienable* rights" be entrenched in the American, as in the German, Constitution,[68] thus permanently committing the nation "to the *unconditioned* protection of fundamental rights."[69] Ironically, then, Ackerman appeals to the very classical mechanism for constitutional amendment that, by his own analysis, has been superseded in each of the last two major constitutional moments.

EVALUATION

Any full critique of Ackerman's work necessarily awaits the publication of his next two volumes, to be titled *Transformations* and *Interpretations*, respectively. The appearance of *Foundations* is, however, an appropriate occasion to assess Ackerman's project as it has developed so far and to raise questions which might give added focus to his next two volumes.

Perhaps a good starting point is the observation from the first chapter of this book that, over the past 204 years, some twenty-seven formal amendments have been added to the Constitution. From one perspective, even this number may exaggerate the role of constitutional amendment, since the first ten were adopted in a cluster (Amendments 13 through 15 and 16 through 19 were also ratified within relatively short time periods), and one amendment repealed another. From another vantage point, advanced in the beginning of this chapter, the number 27 seriously underrepresents the number of times the Constitution has been changed, since the judicial branch fine-tunes the Constitution on a regular basis, with its more important decisions often being practically indistinguishable from amendments themselves.

Although Article V of the Constitution specifies two ways of proposing amendments, it does not require that minor changes be initiated through one mechanism and major changes be effected by the other. There is thus no a priori way to determine which amendments have been mere adjustments to the document and which were intended to bring about significant transformations. Certainly, the Bill of Rights is generally recognized as quite significant, but it may be viewed as an extension of, rather than as a repudiation of, the Founding philosophy. The Reconstruction Amendments marked and, to some extent, initiated another major transformation in American life, as did the Progressive Era amendments. As Ackerman notes, no amendments mark the New Deal, unless one includes the somewhat belated slap at presidential power implicit in the two-term limit of the Twenty-Second Amendment. The preceding New Deal legal transformation has certainly left its mark, however, in case law, both in the so-called switch in time[70] and in *Carolene Products* and other cases where the Court articulated a new agenda for itself.[71]

In choosing his focus, Ackerman effectively reduced major constitutional changes to three, each of which he portrays as legally suspect. The Founders thus disregarded the provisions for constitutional amendment under the Articles of Confederation in formulating a new Constitution.[72] Authors of the Civil War amendments effectively forced Southern states to consent to the new polity which had been baptized in blood. New Dealers substituted presidential and congressional initiatives for amendments and eventually stacked a Court that affirmed their work. Other more numerous, if less transformative, amendments practically cease to exist in Ackerman's narrative. Thus, despite the success of the Progressive Era and other individual amendments, Ackerman's analysis effectively reduces the role of the classical process to a nullity from the Civil War period forward.

What is strange about this account is that the exceptions have so swallowed the rule that an otherwise uninformed or inattentive reader might never guess that most amendments have been adopted in a procedurally unambiguous way that has engendered little controversy. Moreover, Article V of the Constitution has never been repealed and is frequently invoked by those seeking one or another constitutional change. Indeed, having justified the work of all three constitutional transformations that he describes, Ackerman himself comes to recommend that two new changes be adopted neither by following the Civil War precedent and forcing recalcitrant states to ratify nor by use of the New Deal precedent of presidential leadership and transformative judicial appointments but rather through classical Article V mechanisms!

All this suggests that the Article V process is not as dead or as dormant as Ackerman seems to suggest and that his own narrative is deficient. If he, as a premier student of the process, recommends the classical model, or at least a variant of it, exactly what has he described? Perhaps Ackerman should give less attention to the illegality of the Constitution than to the decision of its authors to provide for a more viable amending mechanism which they praised as a viable alternative to revolution,[73] and as a safety-valve that would make further illegal actions unnecessary.[74] Certainly it is significant that Reconstruction proponents, however much they may have strayed from procedural niceties, saw an advantage in working through the amending process and actually incorporating desired legal changes within the constitutional text. Perhaps, to draw from Stephen Markman's critique, the critical problems with decisions such as *Griswold v. Connecticut* is that they are not so much constitutional interpretations as they are judicial innovations, or judicial amendments in the guise of interpretations.

Had Ackerman adopted the more traditional view that identifies the "switch in time that saved nine" not so much as a repudiation of the Constitution as a rejection of judicial excrescences on the Constitution which had developed from 1890 to 1937, he might have concluded that constitutional transformations that take place outside the Article V arena are rarely likely to have the same force and staying power as those actually incorporated into the Constitution. Arguably, there is some difficulty in proclaiming that all New Deal judicial innovations were simply recognitions of the wisdom of John Marshall's earlier positions. By the same token, there are continuing good reasons to question whether the massive judicial edifice involving "liberty of contract," substantive due process, and such distinctions as those involving the "heart of a contract" versus mere "incidents of employment" could have been so easily and quickly dismantled without amendments in 1937 had such distinctions actually been enshrined in the constitutional text.[75]

While Ackerman's account illumines the metaconstitutional features of the New Deal in a unique way that highlights certain truths otherwise obscured by the more dominant professional narrative, it obscures others. There is surely reason to think twice before discarding this more traditional explanation which so well accounts for the fragility and relatively quick demise of judicial patterns of decision making over the prior four decades. Readers should ask whether Ackerman would seriously suggest that the Court could have made its quick and relatively complete turnaround if there had been amendments to the Constitution specifically prohibiting minimum wage, maximum hour, and child labor legislation and guaranteeing absolute freedom of contract. Similarly, it might be worth asking whether the post New Deal judicial interpretations have the same force and are as legally entrenched as if they had been specifically written into the Constitution.[76]

Proponents of *Griswold v. Connecticut* and *Roe v. Wade* might like to think so, but their concern over recent Supreme Court nominees would indicate otherwise.

As Ackerman recognizes, his proposal for a more liberalized amending provision is hardly new, but it is no less odd, and potentially no less dangerous, on that account.[77] A president whose election truly marked a realigning period in American history might first of all wonder why he must wait until his second term to introduce an amendment and until the first term of a new president (recall the Twenty-Second Amendment's limit on presidential terms) to enact it. Why, moreover, should a president, especially a lucky one, bother at all with an amending process if he could simply stack the Court in the manner of the last constitutional transformation? Would failure to approve such an amendment prove ipso facto that no constitutional moment had occurred or would it simply signal that it has been initiated, like the last such transformation Ackerman recognizes, without the benefit of such an amendment? Is federalism now so moribund that there should be no consideration given to how votes are weighted? If voters in the five or ten largest states are unanimous in desiring an amendment, should it be adopted even though it is opposed by overwhelming majorities in all the others?[78] What if one amendment were adopted in this fashion while another were adopted through the classical amending process? Which would trump the other?

On a more practical note, it is not altogether clear that Ackerman's proposal would do anything to change Article V's most formidable obstacle. Currently, presidents are free, as, for example, both Ronald Reagan and George Bush have done, to propose whatever amendments they choose.[79] The obstacle to such amendments has not been the fact that a president cannot exert personal influence on the process but rather the difficulty of getting two-thirds of both houses of Congress to concur. Of thirty-three such proposals, twenty-seven have been adopted.[80] While the ratification requirement is, to be sure, an obstacle, it is not the central one. Moreover, it is not at all clear that it will be easier to get three-fifths of the people to approve an amendment in two successive presidential elections than it would to get three-fourths of the states to do the same.[81] If this process is not easier, what real incentive will there be to use it?

As to Ackerman's suggestion that a new Bill of Rights embodying social and economic rights needs to be enacted, there are again problems. Traditionally, those nations that have adopted such bills have often viewed them simply as high sounding ideals that could be ignored.[82] Moreover, there are a host of practical questions as to how such amendments should be enforced, particularly in cases of economic depression or catastrophe. Further to entrench such provisions,[83] especially before they have had a chance to be tested in practice, might assure that they will be ignored rather than taken seriously and that they might breed cynicism about the power of constitutional change in general.[84] Clearly, Ackerman has a lot more explaining to do before such a step is taken.

ROBERT LIPKIN AND THE IDEA OF CONSTITUTIONAL REVOLUTIONS

Yet another view of constitutional change—albeit one not yet presented in book form—has been offered by Robert Lipkin of the Widener University School of Law.[85] Lipkin's central model for constitutional change is the model applied to scientific revolutions by Thomas Kuhn.[86] Accordingly, Lipkin divides the processes of constitutional change and judicial decision making into two main classes—periods of revolutionary adjudication in which a new revolutionary paradigm is established and periods of more routine adjudication which follow.[87]

From the perspective of this book, the most notable aspect and the most critical weakness of Lipkin's lengthy account is its complete silence about the processes of establishing and amending constitutions. Indeed, by contrast to Ackerman's more nuanced account, Lipkin also almost completely ignores the role of the people or the role of Congress and/or the president in establishing new constitutional understandings or revising existing ones.

Markman's analysis earlier in this chapter would certainly indicate that there are occasions where judicial interpretations appear to be at odds with the constitutional text, but Lipkin seems to interpret almost every important judicial decision as revolutionary, not simply if it was contrary to the text but if it was not absolutely dictated by it. Lipkin thus identifies *Marbury v. Madison*,[88] *Martin v. Hunter's Lessee*,[89] *McCulloch v. Maryland*,[90] *Gibbons v. Ogden*,[91] *Barron v. Baltimore*,[92] *Brown v. Board of Education*,[93] and *Griswold v. Connecticut*[94] all as revolutionary decisions even though he acknowledges that many of these decisions are consistent with good readings of the constitutional text. Levinson's earlier four-fold classification, however, proves useful in indicating that not every constitutional interpretation is thereby a constitutional revolution.[95] Lipkin's analysis apparently proceeds from the assumption that the political elements are the most important aspect of constitutional adjudication.[96] Undoubtedly, such elements are present, but this does not mean that all constitutional claims are equally valid,[97] or that one should completely obliterate the distinction, which Markman emphasized and Levinson ultimately preserved,[98] between constitutional interpretation and constitutional amendment, whether initiated by the judiciary or through formal Article V mechanisms. Ultimately, then, Lipkin's explanation of constitutional change is even less satisfactory than Ackerman's.

NOTES

1. 5 U.S. 137 (1803).
2. One of the theorists who has devoted the greatest attention to, and indeed

celebrated, this phenomenon was Christopher Tiedeman, *The Unwritten Constitution of the United States* (New York: G. P. Putnam's Sons, 1890).

3. Such charges are documented in John R. Vile, "The Supreme Court and the Amending Process," *Georgia Political Science Association Journal* 8 (Fall 1980), pp. 33–66. Also see John R. Vile, "Constitutional Interpretation and Constitutional Amendment: Alternative Means of Constitutional Change," *Research in Law and Policy Studies,* Vol. 3, ed. Stuart Nagel (Greenwich, CT: JAI Press, 1992).

4. 290 U.S. 398, 452–53 (1934).

5. 383 U.S. 479, 522 (1965).

6. 411 U.S. 677, 692 (1973).

7. Apparently, the same is true of other nations. For focus on this issue in Canadian law, see Andree Lajoie and Henry Quillian, "Emerging Constitutional Norms: Continuous Judicial Amendment of the Constitution—The Proportionality Test as a Moving Target," *Law and Contemporary Problems* 55 (Winter 1992), pp. 285–302.

8. Stephen Markman, "The Amendment Process of Article V: A Microcosm of the Constitution," *Harvard Journal of Law & Public Policy* 12 (1989), pp. 113–21; and Stephen Markman, "The Jurisprudence of Constitutional Amendments," *Still the Law of the Land?* ed. Joseph S. McNamara and Lissa Roche (Hillsdale, MI: Hillsdale College Press, 1987), pp. 79–96. Also see Markman's, "A Poor Choice of Words: Careless Rhetoric About the Constitution," *Detroit College of Law Review* 1991 (Fall), pp. 1325–47.

9. Markman, "The Jurisprudence of Constitutional Amendments," p. 80.

10. Ibid., p. 81.

11. Ibid., p. 87.

12. Markman, "The Amendment Process of Article V," p. 119.

13. Ibid., pp. 117–18.

14. See Vile, "Constitutional Interpretation and Constitutional Amendment."

15. Probably these have been as effectively made by Christopher Wolfe as by anyone. See his *Judicial Activism: Bulwark of Freedom or Precarious Security?* (Pacific Grove, CA: Brooks/Cole, 1991). Also see Stephen C. Halpern and Charles M. Lamb, *Supreme Court Activism and Restraint* (Lexington, MA: Lexington Books, 1982).

16. Philip A. Hamburger, "The Constitution's Accommodation of Social Change," *Michigan Law Review* 88 (November 1989), pp. 325–27.

17. See Sanford Levinson's discussion of *McCulloch v. Maryland,* 17 U.S. 316 (1819), in "Accounting for Constitutional Change (Or, How Many Times Has the United States Constitution Been Amended? (A) <26; (B) 26; (C) >26; (D) All of the Above," *Constitutional Commentary* 8 (1991), pp. 418–20.

18. It is, of course, possible to argue that one should not proceed from a constitutional ought to a constitution is, but, on this point, at least, this author has to agree with Robert J. Lipkin that

> if it is conceded that the theory of constitutional revolutions captures constitutional practices, then it is difficult to see how the critic can insist that it has no prescriptive force. It will only be plausible to argue that actual practice has no prescriptive force if there is a conclusive argument against actual practice.

See "The Anatomy of Constitutional Revolutions," *Nebraska Law Review* 68 (1989), p. 783.

19. See, for example, Sanford Levinson, " 'Veneration' and Constitutional Change: James Madison Confronts the Possibility of Constitutional Amendment," *Texas Tech Law Review* 21 (1990), pp. 2443–60; and Levinson's "On the Notion of Amendment, Reflections on David Daube's 'Jehovah the Good,' " *S'Vara: A Journal of Philosophy and Judaism* 1 (Winter 1990), pp. 25–31. Also relevant is Levinson's, *Constitutional Faith* (Princeton, NJ: Princeton University Press, 1988).

20. Levinson, "Accounting for Constitutional Change," p. 411.

21. Ibid.

22. Ibid., pp. 418–21. Similarly, in an extremely useful paper, Lutz notes that "some constitutions by design, and others by accident, leave so much room for interpretation that what some call amendment-through-interpretation is actually specification in the face of ambiguity." Donald S. Lutz, "Toward a Theory of Constitutional Amendment" (Paper presented at the American Political Science Convention, Chicago, IL, September 1992), p. 7.

23. This writer believes that Levinson needs to give more attention to the role of formal amendments as means of *establishing* existing rights as in *adding* new ones. The greater clarity of a concisely worded amendment incorporated into the constitutional text and changeable only by another formal amendment is indeed one of its greatest advantages over reliance on a series of judicial decisions that may be altered by shifting judicial majorities.

24. In a similar vein, Walter F. Murphy notes that, "One might look on usage, interpretation, and formal amendment as forming a hierarchy of legitimate constitutional change." "The Right to Privacy and Legitimate Constitutional Change," in *The Constitutional Bases of Political and Social Change in the United States* ed. Shlomo Slonim, (New York: Praeger, 1990), p. 219.

25. Levinson, "Accounting for Constitutional Change," p. 417. The last category points ahead to the discussion in a later chapter about the possibility that there are substantive limits on the constitutional amending process.

26. Ibid., p. 428. Levinson thus concludes that while it is necessary to maintain a distinction similar to that involving interpretation and amendment, he "cannot provide the formal criteria by which to distinguish the two." For a critique which argues that Levinson ultimately recognizes too much indeterminacy in the law, see Leslie F. Goldstein, *In Defense of the Text: Democracy and Constitutional Theory* (Savage, MD: Rowman & Littlefield, 1991), pp. 176–81.

27. Bruce Ackerman, *We the People: Foundations* (Cambridge, MA: Belknap Press, 1992). Ackerman refers to this book at p. ix as his "principal preoccupation during the 1980's."

28. Bruce Ackerman, "The Storrs Lectures: Discovering the Constitution," *Yale Law Journal* 93 (May 1984), pp. 1013–72; Ackerman, "Constitutional Politics/Constitutional Law," *Yale Law Journal* 99 (December 1989), pp. 453–547; and Ackerman, "Transformative Appointments," *Harvard Law Review* 101 (1988), pp. 1164–84.

29. On the flyleaf of Ackerman's new book, Sanford Levinson follows up his earlier praise by describing Ackerman's work as, "The most important project now underway in the entire field of constitutional theory," and says that Ackerman's contribution "will easily be not only the most significant work in constitution theory to be published in this decade, but, indeed, perhaps in the past half-century."

Professor Cass R. Sunstein (Chicago) calls it, "one of the most distinguished works on the American Constitution since World War II."

30. This writer draws this conclusion from appeals which Ackerman makes directly to the reader in the second person as well as hints that he does not expect his readers to be familiar with *The Federalist* or with Gordon Wood's *The Creation of the American Republic, 1776–1787* (New York: W. W. Norton, 1969). See Ackerman, *We The People,* pp. 218 and 322.

31. For critiques of Ackerman's articles, see James G. Pope, "Republican Moments: The Role of Direct Popular Power in the American Constitutional Order," *University of Pennsylvania Law Review* 139 (December 1990), pp. 304–5; and Lawrence G. Sager, "The Incorrigible Constitution," *New York University Law Review* 65 (October 1990), pp. 924–35.

32. Hartz's best-known book on the subject is *The Liberal Tradition in America* (New York: Harcourt, Brace & World, 1955).

33. Ackerman particularly cites Wood, *The Creation of the American Republic* and J. G. A. Pocock, *The Machiavellian Moment* (Princeton, NJ: Princeton University Press, 1975).

34. Ackerman, *We the People,* pp. 3–10.

35. The term is borrowed from Ronald Dworkin, *Law's Empire* (Cambridge, MA: Belknap Press, 1986), pp. 70–72.

36. Ackerman, *We the People,* p. 33.

37. Alpheus T. Mason and Gordon Baker, *Free Government in the Making: Readings in American Political Thought,* 4th ed. (New York: Oxford University Press, 1985), pp. 8–16. This author also questions whether Ackerman's descriptions of the democratic monist and the rights foundationalist are not overdrawn, almost to make of each a straw man. Thus, Alexander Bickel [*The Least Dangerous Branch* (Indianapolis, IN: Bobbs-Merrill, 1962)], who is frequently cited by Ackerman as a monistic democrat, seems to this author at least, ultimately to praise judicial review rather than to bury it. Similarly, Woodrow Wilson, however much he admired the British system, ultimately entitled a book, *Constitutional Government in the United States* (New York: Columbia University Press, 1961. Reprint of 1908 edition). In turn, there are few if any "rights foundationalists" cited by Ackerman who would not recognize appropriate areas for actions by popular majorities.

38. Here Ackerman wisely chooses the interpretation of Richard S. Kay, "The Illegality of the Constitution," *Constitutional Commentary* 4 (Winter 1987), pp. 57–80 to that of his colleague, Akil R. Amar, "Philadelphia Revisited: Amending the Constitution Outside Article V," *University of Chicago Law Review* 55 (Fall 1988), pp. 1043–1104.

39. Ackerman's theory seems to borrow much from the theory of critical or realigning elections formulated by V.O. Key and elaborated in works like Walter Burnham's, *Critical Elections and the Mainsprings of American Politics* (New York: W. W. Norton, 1970).

40. Morton J. Frisch and Richard G. Stevens, eds., *The Political Thought of American Statesmen* (Dubuque, IA: Kendall/Hunt, 1973), pp. 2–3, for example, focus on the same three periods that Ackerman does.

41. Ackerman, *We the People,* p. 88.

42. Ibid., p. 91.

43. Ibid., pp. 92 and 94. One wonders what interpretative assumptions might

lie behind this appeal to deeper aspirations. For two modern, albeit divergent, accounts focusing on such aspirations, see Gary J. Jacobsohn, *The Supreme Court and the Decline of Constitutional Aspiration* (Totowa, NJ: Rowman & Littlefield, 1986); and Sotirios Barber, *On What the Constitution Means* (Baltimore, MD: Johns Hopkins University Press, 1984).

44. Ackerman, *We the People*, pp. 101 and 108.

45. Ibid., pp. 62–67.

46. *United States v. Carolene Products*, 304 U.S. 149 (1938).

47. 347 U.S. 483 (1954).

48. 381 U.S. 479.

49. Ackerman, *We the People*, p. 141.

50. 163 U.S. 537.

51. Ackerman, *We the People*, p. 159.

52. Hannah Arendt, *On Revolution* (New York: Viking Press, 1963).

53. Ackerman, *We the People*, p. 171.

54. Ibid., pp. 193 and 195 citing the language of *Federalist* No. 78.

55. Ibid., p. 195.

56. Ibid., p. 203.

57. Ibid., p. 228.

58. For a comprehensive discussion of this and other alternatives to the American Constitution which have been proposed in the last century, see John R. Vile, *Rewriting the United States Constitution* (New York: Praeger, 1991).

59. Ackerman, *We the People*, p. 192, thus cited *Federalist* No. 78 at pp. 467–68:

> Nor does this conclusion by any means suppose a superiority of the judicial to the legislative power. It only supposes that the power of the people is superior to both, and that where the will of the legislature, declared in its statutes, stands in opposition to that of the people declared in the Constitution, the judges ought to be governed by the latter rather than the former.

60. Ackerman, *We the People*, p. 266. Although much of his analysis is otherwise similar to Ackerman's, James G. Pope faults Ackerman for suggesting that the Court's initial role might be to squelch popular legislative initiatives. See Pope's, "Republican Moments: The Role of Direct Popular Power in the American Constitutional Order," *University of Pennsylvania Law Review* 139 (December 1990), p. 357. Pope proceeds to suggest, p. 360, that "Statutes that result from higher track lawmaking—call them 'republican' statutes—should receive a broad construction; products of interest group bargaining should . . . be narrowly constructed."

61. Ackerman, *We the People*, p. 267.

62. Ibid., pp. 267–68.

63. Michael Klarman, "Constitutional Fact/Constitutional Fiction: A Critique of Bruce Ackerman's Theory of Constitutional Moments," *Stanford Law Review* 44 (February 1992), p. 769, notes that, "The Reagan/Bork episode does not even remotely satisfy the criteria Ackerman has enumerated to define successful efforts at higher lawmaking." This reader, for one, also cannot help but wonder if Ackerman would have accepted the confirmation of Judge Bork as a new constitutional moment repudiating the New Deal. This, too, seems, a bit too much weight to assign to such an event. Moreover, if the Bork nomination is classified as a failed constitutional moment, why should not the confirmation of Clarence Thomas (which

probably received even more publicity, including public hearings) be considered a successful one? For similar thoughts, see Suzanna Sherry, "Book Review, The Ghost of Liberalism Past," *Harvard Law Review* 105 (February 1992) pp. 931–32. For additional reflections on the notion of constitutional moments which suggests that such moments are most likely to occur during periods of divided government, see Mark Tushnet, "The Flag-Burning Episode: An Essay on the Constitution," *University of Colorado Law Review* 61 (1990), pp. 50–52.

64. Ackerman, *We the People,* p. 272.

65. Ibid., p. 55. Ackerman apparently rejects the views of a colleague that popular majorities can already amend the Constitution by referenda. See Amar, "Philadelphia Revisited." This view is discussed in the next chapter of this book.

This author is unsure why Ackerman refers to ratification "in the name of the People of the United States." On its face, such language would appear to be superfluous, but there is always the possibility that Ackerman means to suggest that amendments ratified by referendum would be superior to others.

66. Ackerman, *We the People,* p. 319.

67. This writer shares this view which is developed in Chapter 7.

68. Ackerman might need to consider that a number of rights in the German Constitution, for example, the rights to free expression and association, are qualified in ways that they are not in the United States. See S. E. Finer, *Five Constitutions* (Middlesex, England: Penguin Books, 1979), pp. 198–200. Even some political parties have been declared illegal. See Alex N. Dragnich and Jorgen S. Rasmussen, *Major European Governments,* 7th ed. (Pacific Grove, CA: Brooks-Cole, 1986), p. 371.

69. Ackerman, *We the People,* pp. 320–21. This suggestion might call Ackerman's ultimate commitment to dualistic democracy into question, seemingly aligning him more with the "rights foundationalists" whom he has criticized.

70. *N.L.R.B. v. Jones & Laughlin Steel Corporation,* 301 U.S. 1 (1937).

71. 304 U.S. 144 (1938).

72. Suzanna Sherry has correctly noted that, "The illegality of the Founders' own act and their recognition that illegal constitutional change is necessary in some times and places, however, do not mean that the Founders thought that future illegal change would be necessary in America." See "The Ghost of Liberalism Past," p. 925.

73. See George Mason's statement at the U.S. Constitutional Convention in the first chapter.

74. As noted in Chapter 1, this frequently invoked analogy was probably conceived by Justice Story.

75. Alpheus T. Mason, *The Supreme Court from Taft to Warren* (Baton Rouge: Louisiana University Press, 1968), p. 62.

76. A contemporary writer thus points out that

> recent advocates of limited government downplay or deny federal responsibility for social welfare. In the absence of a constitutional directive to follow a different course, a public with a short, selective historical memory finds no reason to demand otherwise. Proponents of a more expansive view can point to a half century of federal practice and judicial approval but no specific constitutional sanction. Without explicit constitutional defense, the New Deal's legislative heritage rests on sand. Fifty years after FDR's attempt to

enlarge the Court, much of the country has apparently returned to a pre-New Deal view of federal duty. It is worth contemplating how the situation might differ had the New Deal felt it possible and important to write its views of federal obligation into the Constitution.

See David E. Kyvig, "The Road Not Taken: FDR, the Supreme Court, and Constitutional Amendment," *Political Science Quarterly* 104 (Fall 1989), p. 481.

77. For a discussion of the multiple proposals from American progressives, see John R. Vile, *The Constitutional Amending Process in American Political Thought* (New York: Praeger, 1992), pp. 137–56.

78. Many progressives thus proposed that amendments would have to be ratified by a majority of voters in a majority of states. See, for example, M. A. Musmanno, *Proposed Amendments to the Constitution* (Washington, DC: U.S. Government Printing Office, 1929), p. 194, for a discussion of Senator La Follette's proposal.

79. One or both of these presidents is thus on record as favoring amendments regarding abortion, prayer in schools, balanced budgets, flag-burning, a line-item veto and repeal of the Twenty-Second Amendment. Similarly, Jimmy Carter exerted personal influence to get the proposed Equal Rights Amendment ratified.

80. For the text of amendments proposed by Congress but not adopted by the states, see George Anastaplo, *The Constitution of 1787* (Baltimore, MD: Johns Hopkins University Press, 1989), pp. 298–99.

81. Consistent with his theory that a constitutional transformation requires a certain breadth of citizen support, it would seem that Ackerman should mandate, as a number of progressives proposing similar schemes once did, that a certain percentage of the people be voting.

82. For sensible reflections on this subject, see Maurice Cranston, *What Are Human Rights?* (New York: Taplinger Publishing, 1973), pp. 65–71.

83. The author is not completely clear about which rights would be entrenched in Ackerman's scheme, but it appears that he plans to entrench both the new social and economic rights which he hopes to introduce as well as more traditional political rights such as freedom of speech. See Ackerman, *We the People,* pp. 320–21.

84. It might further be argued that to entrench such a Bill of Rights is in fact to engage in the kind of rights foundationalism which Ackerman criticizes through much of his book. Certainly, there is something extremely problematical about one generation attempting not only to tell future generations what is morally right but also dictating forever what is legally right. For some particularly interesting reflections on this point, see Noah Webster's, "Government," *American Magazine* 1 (1787–88), pp. 137–45. This article was written under the pen name of Giles Hickory and will be included in John R. Vile, *The Theory and Practice of Constitutional Change in America: A Collection of Original Source Materials* (New York: Peter Lang, 1993). Also see Vile, *The Amending Process in American Political Thought,* Chapter 4, on Thomas Jefferson.

85. Lipkin, "The Anatomy," pp. 701–806.

86. Thomas Kuhn, *The Structure of Scientific Revolutions,* 2d ed. (Chicago: University of Chicago Press, 1970).

87. Lipkin, "The Anatomy," pp. 742–43.

88. Ibid., pp. 752–57. 5 U.S. 137 (1803).

89. Ibid., pp. 757–63. 14 U.S. 304 (1816).

90. Ibid., pp. 763–68. 17 U.S. 316 (1819). It is interesting that in "Accounting for Constitutional Change," Levinson, pp. 418–21, acknowledges that some considered this case to be revolutionary, but does not stop with this single interpretation. On the broader issue, Levinson, p. 428, identifies "constitutional faith" as that process "by which 'best constitutional analysis' is subtly transformed by the passage of time so that a given legal doctrine . . . becomes radically transformed without formal amendment ever being deemed necessary."

91. Ibid., pp. 768–71. 22 U.S. 1 (1824).

92. Ibid., pp. 771–73. 32 U.S. 243 (1833).

93. Ibid., pp. 775–77. 347 U.S. 483 (1954).

94. Ibid., pp. 777–80. 381 U.S. 479 (1965).

95. Levinson, "Accounting for Constitutional Change," p. 522.

96. Lipkin, "The Anatomy," p. 775.

97. See, generally, Goldstein, *In Defense of the Text: Democracy and Constitutional Theory*.

98. Levinson, "Accounting for Constitutional Change," pp. 428–29.

Chapter 6

The Question of Exclusivity—The Arguments of Akil Reed Amar

The previous chapter has examined a number of theories about the legitimacy of constitutional changes effected outside the constitutional amending process. This focus on whether Article V is the exclusive means of amending the Constitution continues in this chapter with attention to the provocative thesis by Akil Reed Amar that the Constitution provides for popular sovereignty and that such sovereignty can be used as a means of proposing and ratifying amendments to the Constitution outside normal Article V processes.

Amar has argued that, while empowering and limiting the government, the Constitution "neither limits nor empowers the People themselves."[1] Specifically, Amar argues that amendments proposed by an Article V convention might, if a convention so specified, be ratified by a majority of the people.[2] Alternatively, he argues that two-thirds majorities in Congress could submit amendments to a direct popular vote and that Congress is "*constitutionally obliged* to convene a proposing convention," if petitioned to do so by "a bare majority of American voters."[3] Amar's thesis deserves particular attention because, like Ackerman's in the previous chapter, it is linked to basic questions involving the very philosophical basis of the American regime.

This writer will argue that Amar's view, provocative though it is, is fundamentally flawed. Specifically, Amar's theory conflates the traditional understanding between revolutionary actions and constitutional actions and cannot be justified by reference to the Founding Fathers or by the best interpretation of the Constitution. Moreover, by attempting to open another door to constitutional amendment, Amar's interpretation would unwisely subject constitutional protections for minorities to erosion and the amending process to undue confusion.

THE PRECEDENT OF 1787

The very novelty of Amar's arguments suggests that his ideas should be greeted cautiously. Surely, it stands to reason that if the doctrine of popular sovereignty made it possible to propose or ratify changes in the national constitution by a simple majority vote, such a mode of constitutional change would have been attempted, or suggested, before now. Yet Amar shows only one person (Edmund Pendleton, whose ambiguous comments are analyzed later) who may have previously suggested this possibility and no example of an attempted exercise of this power in the last 200 years.[4] Moreover, if Amar's understanding is correct, numerous proposals which have sought to liberalize the amending process by mandating some form of popular approval[5] have all rested upon a misunderstanding of the Constitution.

Excluding the Constitution of the Confederate States of America, intended to govern only a part of what is now the United States, the last occasion that the nation operated on the assumption that the constitution could be formally changed in a way other than that specified in the instrument, namely the transition from the Articles of Confederation to the Constitution of 1787 is, in fact, Amar's sole illustration to show that such an option is still viable. There are reasons to suggest, however, that this precedent is less than instructive in current circumstances.

First, it is doubtful that the action can be fully classified as a constitutional action as Amar tries so ardently to do. Certainly, violations of the Articles of Confederation furnished a justification when states decided that they wanted to form a new government.[6] Moreover, the transition from one governmental form to another was effected without the kind of bloodshed that so frequently is associated with revolutionary change. Proponents of the new government, however, argued less on the basis of constitutionality than on grounds of necessity.[7] The Constitutional Convention of 1787 might thus set an example for future revolutionary, or extralegal, changes in governmental forms, but it hardly serves as a model for the kinds of constitutional changes which Amar claims to be advocating.

Given Amar's concern for the doctrine of popular sovereignty, a second difference should also be noted. The current Constitution could be justified by an appeal to popular sovereignty precisely because the Articles of Confederation could not be so defended. After citing "the absolute necessity of the case," "the great principle of self-preservation," and "the transcendent law of nature and of nature's God," James Madison thus observed:

It has been heretofore noted among the defects of the Confederation that in many of the States it had received no higher sanction than a mere legislative ratification.

The principle of reciprocality seems to require that its obligation on the other States should be reduced to the same standard.[8]

Any new proposals for constitutional change would face a Constitution not ratified, like the Articles of Confederation, by mere legislative approval, but by the people themselves, insofar as this was then possible, and arguably accepted by them ever since.

A third difference is also fundamental. However else it may be characterized, the new Constitution was far more than the revision of the confederation for which Congress had originally summoned delegates to Philadelphia.[9] Amar himself argues that the transition from the Articles of Confederation to the Constitution of 1787 marked a change from state sovereignty to popular sovereignty.[10] Without necessarily accepting the full implications of this view (Amar's conceptions of federalism seem at odds with Madison's analysis in *Federalist* No. 39 while his comments on popular sovereignty are criticized below),[11] the example of 1787 is surely not an example of a constitution merely being amended. Rather, 1787–89 marks the transition to a new government. However this government might have borrowed some principles from the old,[12] it was significantly different. One key difference involved the transition from a mode of amendment requiring the unanimous consent of the state legislatures to one permitting amendments to be proposed by two-thirds majorities of both Houses of Congress and ratified by three-fourths of the states. In the words of one scholar, "they [the Framers of the Constitution] knew they were laying the foundation of a new legal system. They were consciously setting out what they hoped would be a new preconstitutional rule."[13]

To advocate bypassing a provision of an older constitution to usher in a new one is much different from ignoring a provision within a constitution so that the same constitution may be amended. In the first case, constitutional inadequacy having already been recognized in issuing a call for a new document, there is little to be lost from suggesting that the amending process of the previous constitution was also defective. In the second case, the resort to an extraconstitutional mode of amendment suggests that proposed revisions do not go far enough, and this resort therefore undermines confidence in the very document that is being revised. Amar's argument is, of course, that his proposed method of amendment is not in violation of the Constitution because Article V is not intended to be exclusive. Even if this dubious assertion were to be conceded, a constitution which fails to mention that the only procedures it outlines for amendments are not exclusive would be, on the order of many state constitutions which seem in part to have inspired Amar, so radically defective that there would still be strong reason to disregard it.[14]

THE INADEQUACY OF COMPARISONS WITH THE STATES

Because no decision in the U.S. federal courts sustains Amar's view that Article V is nonexclusive, he looks for precedents at the state level.[15] While such legal precedents are conflicting, there are indeed some examples of state constitutions which have been amended or superseded after the actions of conventions unauthorized by the preexisting constitution.[16] Again, however, a number of arguments suggest that such precedents should be interpreted carefully.

In the first place, one of the most notable such events in American history—Dorr's Rebellion[17]—was not successful. It encountered opposition by both state and national authorities, opposition clearly legitimated by the Supreme Court.[18] Thinkers as diverse as Daniel Webster and John C. Calhoun agreed that popular sovereignty was not an invitation to "tumultuous assemblages" to write new constitutions as they pleased,[19] but for the people to proceed according to the forms by which they had previously bound themselves.[20]

Second, a number of state constitutions which have been reformed and/ or superseded have, unlike the United States Constitution, contained no formal mechanisms for constitutional amendment and/or conventions.[21] The justification for acting in the absence of any language regarding amendments is surely stronger than the argument for acting in a fashion other than a constitution, which so provides an amending process, directs.

Third, the traditions of state and national constitutional reform are so different that it is precarious to apply lessons from the former to the latter.[22] States have frequently been swept by waves of constitutional reforms, while the national constitution has been amended only twenty-seven times and never completely revised or replaced.[23] In contrast to the United States Constitution, state constitutions have further incorporated all kinds of policy judgments that are generally considered more appropriate for legislative actions.[24]

Fourth, the extent to which state constitutional change has been acceptable may have rested largely on the stability of the national Constitution. State reformers have been able to proceed knowing that this national Constitution, declared to be the supreme law of the land,[25] would set outer limits— the equal protection clause and the guarantee clause being perhaps the most notable examples—beyond which the people could not trespass.[26] Lacking an equivalent security, it might be wise to restrain national constitution changing within explicit constitutional language even more than equivalent state processes.

Fifth, many states have experience, albeit not always positive, with referenda upon which to draw in ratifying changes in the fundamental law.[27] By contrast, there has never been provision for a national referendum of any type. The sheer size and diversity of the nation, in comparison to most states, as well as the lack of a supervising government as described earlier, surely suggests that a national referendum could, despite Amar's assurances, pose peculiar problems for the national government which the states might not face.

HYPOTHETICALLY SPEAKING

Near the beginning of Amar's article, he poses a hypothetical case in which Congress calls a convention at the request of two-thirds of the states. The convention, in turn, proposes an amendment and specifies that this amendment will become law when ratified by a special national referendum called by Congress.[28] Congress then calls an election; a majority of voters ratify the amendment; Congress helps to implement it; and the issue is posed as to whether this amendment is effective.[29] Similarly, in the case he poses where a majority of voters call for a convention, Congress complies and, again, there is no hint of opposition by the other two branches. Amar concludes that amendments proposed or ratified by such extraconstitutional methods would be constitutional. He further believes that this putative constitutionality confirms the foundation of American government upon popular sovereignty.

Before looking into the constitutional basis that Amar uses to defend his position, his hypotheticals need to be examined. The issue Amar is addressing is what he calls popular sovereignty, that is, the right of a simple majority of voters (qualified by Amar only by the proviso that such a majority must be deliberative) either to propose a convention and/or ratify an amendment.[30] In Amar's hypothetical cases, however, the people's desires are further approved by Congress. Moreover, there is no hint of opposition by the other two branches.[31] Thus, Amar's hypothetical examples present an action by a majority of the people plus the concurrence, if not indeed the support, of the governmental branches.

If popular sovereignty alone is to be tested, however, the hypothetical examples should be posed differently. To find out whether the majority of the people have a right to propose or ratify an amendment, one must ask whether such a majority can legally do so without the support or concurrence of the three governmental branches. Thus, imagine that a majority of the people petition for a convention and Congress refused to call it, the president concurs in this judgment, and the courts refuse to compel Congress to act. Could Amar still claim that the call for a convention was legal? What if a case were initiated under Article V, the Supreme Court issued a restraining order against a referendum proposed by Congress or by a convention,[32] and the president expressed strong support of the Court's decision?

Possibly, though improbably, the people could in such a case take up arms, but, as soon as they did so, Amar's defense of their actions would have to switch from the realm of legality to that of morality, from law to right. The very point Amar is trying to make, however, is that the right of popular majorities is a legal right.[33]

Moreover, such revised scenarios both suggest the Pandora's box that a doctrine like Amar's might open and recall to mind the precedent of Dorr's Rebellion. One can imagine a bare majority of the people believing that they had ratified a constitutional amendment, or legally called a constitutional convention, only to find that the rest of the people did not agree. One can further imagine the potential for conflict if one branch accepted the constitutionality of a convention, or ratification, and the other two did not. If, as Walter Dellinger sagely suggests, the amending process should be as free as possible from ambiguity,[34] Amar's speculations can hardly help.

LEGITIMATE BUT NOT LEGAL: PHILADELPHIA REVISITED

Hypothetical consequences aside, Amar's evidence for the nonexclusivity of Article V mechanisms is certainly worthy of consideration. Amar's chief argument is almost directly opposed to the view of Bruce Ackerman discussed in the previous chapter. That is, Amar argues that since the new Constitution was ratified legally—but in a manner uncalled for under the preexisting constitution—then the existing constitution can also be. Amar clearly has not come to this opinion lightly. Thus, he cites an important article by Robert Kay that stresses the new Constitution was adopted extralegally, or illegally, rather than through constitutional forms.[35]

This author does not believe that Amar has refuted Kay's contentions. Kay points out that while the scope of their commission gave some ammunition for Federalists to argue that they had no choice but to disregard their instructions, the delegates to the Constitutional Convention had been appointed to revise and enlarge rather than to rewrite the existing constitution.[36] He notes that, while reported out by Congress, the new Constitution was never officially sanctioned by this Congress as the Articles required.[37] He shows that the Articles specified that amendments were to be ratified by all the states, whereas authors of the new Constitution provided that it would go into effect when ratified by only nine.[38] He further notes that the new Constitution was sanctioned not, as the Articles required, by state legislatures, but by conventions called within each of the states.[39] Perhaps most importantly, Kay demonstrates that while pointing to what legal justifications they could, Federalist proponents of the new Constitution recognized that the act they were performing was revolutionary rather than strictly legal.[40] No one appears to have argued that the mode of amendment specified in the Articles of Confederation was nonexclusive, and, indeed,

Amar himself acknowledges that the language of that amendment is not subject to such an interpretation.[41]

The understanding of the Constitutional Convention as a largely extra-legal or revolutionary body which does not establish a precedent for actions in more normal constitutional situations is hardly new. As noted earlier, in one of the greatest nineteenth-century works on constitutional conventions, Judge John Jameson thus observed how most delegates to the Constitutional Convention of 1787 had "admitted implicitly the binding force of those Acts," and "yet . . . felt constrained by necessity to disregard [them]."[42] Such an argument from necessity may be persuasive and may accord with right, but it is not an argument from law and should not be classified as such.

Amar cites two reasons why he believes the Constitution was legally ratified. First, he thinks that only such an interpretation can explain "the immediate and widespread" approval of the new document.[43] A strong belief in the weaknesses of the Articles of Confederation and the necessity of a new government, as well as in the propriety and moral force of ratification by constitutional conventions, could, however, just as easily account for such acceptance, particularly when it is recalled that the Articles had never had such a ratification. Delegates to the Constitutional Convention apparently realized that their actions exceeded their commissions, yet they took them anyway.[44] So too, Americans must have realized that, in ratifying the new Constitution, they were bypassing the Articles, but for good reason. Amar's fallacy is to equate legitimacy with legality, which is not always its prerequisite, especially in times of crisis and/or at times of regime change.

In supporting his view that the Constitution of 1787 was legally adopted, Amar further argued that the Framers channeled "the theretofore supra-legal right of revolution into precise and peaceful legal procedures"[45] and that ratifications were therefore better understood as legal than as illegal. Admittedly, the authors of the Constitution adopted as legitimate a form as was possible under the circumstances, and they did so without renewed resort to arms. They also formulated a new mechanism of change for the future. To praise a constitution for adopting a future mode of amendment which would save the embarrassment caused by a previous constitution with a wooden provision that did not provide adequately for change is hardly to say that the second constitution was thus achieved in a perfectly legal and unexceptional way. Again, the Founders' own understanding that they were, of necessity, bypassing existing legal forms provides the best key. Surely, if they could have shown that their actions were not only desirable and moral but also completely legal, they would have done so.

THE DUBIOUS EVIDENCE FROM THE FOUNDERS: TOO MUCH RELIANCE ON TOO LITTLE

Buttressing his position by reference to the Founders, Amar does cite one seemingly impressive piece of evidence, the speech of Edmund Pen-

dleton before the Virginia Ratifying Convention. In his speech, after referring to Anti-Federalist criticisms that the people's servants might, under
the new Constitution, resist introducing amendments, Pendleton asked:

What then? . . . Who shall dare to resist the people? No we will assemble in Convention; wholly recall our delegated powers, or reform them so as to prevent such
abuse; and punish those servants who have perverted powers, designed for our
happiness, to their own enolument.[46]

Although Amar concedes the possibility that Pendleton may indeed have
been discussing Article V's alternative convention route to constitutional
change, he states that, since this mechanism also depends on the people's
representatives, it does not fully fit what Pendleton seems to be saying.[47]
Rather, Amar believes Pendleton was arguing for the future right of extraconstitutional change by a majority of the people.

Amar may be correct here though the possibility that Pendleton was
referring to the alternate state route is suggested by the fact that the Anti-
Federalists Pendleton was addressing would probably have distinguished
between the responsiveness of state representatives whom they knew from
the probable unresponsiveness of federal officeholders, further removed
from the people, whom they feared.[48] A second possibility is that Pendleton
was indeed saying what Amar believes he is but that Pendleton was simply
mistaken. As one who did not attend the Constitutional Convention, he
certainly was not privy to any extraordinary insights into what the document meant or how it would operate. Even more likely, however, Pendleton
is stating something far more obvious than Amar proposes. As part of a
"revolutionary" or extralegal attempt to supersede the Articles of Confederation by the Constitution, Pendleton may simply have been indicating
that, even with the adoption of a second constitution, the revolution might
not be over. Thus, if this new Constitution also proved ineffective or ty-
rannical, it, too, could be superseded. From this perspective, Pendleton
would not be so much making a legal point as stating a pragmatic fact
which is perhaps the psychological basis of revolution.[49] That is, if power
is abused under the new system, the people will take it back.

One thing seems certain. Whatever point Pendleton was making, it is
unlikely that he was mollifying Anti-Federalist opponents of the new Constitution, who already feared that state powers under the new Constitution
had been unduly eroded and who were supporting a document under which
constitutional changes required the unanimous consent of the states,[50] by
suggesting that a simple majority of the people would at any time be able
to void or amend the new Constitution in a completely legal fashion. This,
it should be remembered, is the point Amar is trying to make.

As further proof for his hypothesis, Amar cites the decision by Congress
to reject an amendment proposed by Madison as part of the Bill of Rights

that would have granted the people "an indubitable, unalienable and indefeasible right to reform or change their government" as proof that such a power was already recognized in the Constitution.[51] It seems more likely that Americans had come more clearly to distinguish those rights revolutionary in nature that needed no constitutional sanction from those legal in nature and appropriate for inclusion in a constitution.[52] Even if it had been ratified, the amendment would not, without more, have sanctioned amendment by a bare majority. Moreover, Amar's interpretation of the amendment is further undercut by his acknowledgment that Madison's arguments in the *Federalist* were predicated upon the exclusivity of Article V mechanisms and by the fact that Madison had already defended these mechanisms as guarding "equally against that extreme facility which would render the Constitution too mutable; and that extreme difficulty, which might perpetuate its discovered faults."[53]

THE DUBIOUS ARGUMENTS FROM ARTICLE VII

As one who argues that the right of a majority of the people to change the Constitution is a legal right, Amar has a variety of constitutional arguments to buttress his arguments from Pendleton and Madison. Amar begins his arguments from the Constitution with Article VII which specified that the new Constitution would go into effect when ratified by nine states[54] rather than by the thirteen required to amend the Articles of Confederation.[55] To Kay, this difference is partial proof of the Constitution's illegality.[56] Agreeing that Article VII is "*inconsistent*" with the Articles,[57] Amar nonetheless argues that it was not illegal because, as an agreement that had been repeatedly violated, the Articles were no longer in force.[58]

If, contrary to Amar, the Articles were in force, Article VII of the new Constitution provided for an illegal means of constitutional ratification. If the Articles were no longer binding, one might think that Article VII was simply extralegal or revolutionary. By analogy to the United Nations, however, Amar argues that "the most relevant pre-existing legal texts, the true prior rules of recognition, are to be found not in the Articles of Confederation, but in the state constitutions."[59] Adoption of the new Constitution would clearly alter state powers under their existing constitutions.[60] No states provided for ratifying constitutional alterations by majority vote of a convention,[61] and yet that is how the new Constitution was confirmed. One could conclude that this but further established the illegality, or revolutionary nature, of the method of adopting the new Constitution. Amar argues instead that it proves that state methods of amendment, like those specified in Article V today, were nonexclusive.

As proof, Amar cites Madison's words at the Constitutional Convention when replying to a Maryland delegate who argued that Article VII would be contrary to that state's amending mechanism:

The people were in fact, the fountain of all power, and by resorting to them, all difficulties were got over. They could alter constitutions as they pleased. It was a principle in the Bill of rights, [of the state of Maryland?] that first principles might be resorted to.[62]

Amar proceeds to cite the Declaration of Independence and a number of state declarations of rights as to the right of "the People," "a majority of the community," "the community," or "the people" to make such alterations.[63] Such declarations established to Amar's satisfaction that state ratifications of the Constitution were legal because state mechanisms of amendment were nonexclusive.[64]

Amar's arguments are not persuasive on this point. First, because the argument proceeds from an internal state perspective, it ignores the interest of the new national government—whatever state constitutions specified— in spelling out how it would come into being. After having seen one government based on state sovereignty prostrated at the feet of the states, the Framers had reason to declare that the new Constitution would go into effect as they specified and not as states—who stood to lose substantial powers—might choose.[65]

On a second and more important point, the statements Amar cites can be interpreted in more than one way. Madison's appeal to "first principles" hardly sounds so much like an appeal to Maryland's state constitution, with which he and most other convention delegates would not be expected to be overly familiar, but to more general "laws" of nature, or moral principles. It is perhaps significant that Amar seeks to explain Madison's references by proceeding to cite the Declaration of Independence, the single most important aim of which was to articulate reasons for revolution to foreign nations who could care less about internal English law.[66] In the period in which the Articles of Confederation were in force, state constitutions were in their infancy, and some admittedly restated the right of revolution, usually in vague terms,[67] in their Declarations of Rights. Stating a natural right as a legal right,[68] without providing any governmental institutions to enforce it, however, does not make it so,[69] and it is indeed difficult to imagine a group of petitioners going to court to enforce a right "to alter or abolish their form of government whenever they pleased." Vague statements as to the right of the people, or even the majority of the people, to alter their governments did not make such rights "legal" in nature but were in the tradition of the natural rights proclamations of the Declaration of Independence itself, justifying a break from old charters as well as constructing new ones.[70] Amar's classification of state ratifications of the Constitution as legal is thus not persuasive.

ADDITIONAL EVIDENCE FROM THE
CONSTITUTION: ALL BUT THE KITCHEN SINK

Amar, however, cites a variety of other constitutional provisions supporting his view that Article V mechanisms are not exclusive. The potpourri of additional provisions he rallies in support of this novel view are the Preamble, the Ninth and Tenth Amendments, and the First Amendment.

One could hardly deny that the words, "We, the People" which begin the Constitution indicated the popular origin of the Constitution. Undoubtedly, the new Constitution came as close to receiving popular approval as any similar document had done before it. It represented a clear repudiation of the doctrine of divine right of kings or of simple appeals to physical might. To extend the words of a section of the Constitution which is not even recognized as legally enforceable, beyond such obvious meaning to argue that any simple deliberate majority can change rules of the governmental scheme which the Constitution created, is, however, to ask the clause to uphold more theoretical weight than it is capable of bearing.[71] Again, it is worth noting that, while Federalists stressed the preeminent importance of representative institutions as a means of filtering the public will,[72] Anti-Federalists were perhaps even more suspicious of mass human behavior and even less likely to trust majorities that were not funnelled through state channels.[73]

A similar point can be made in regard to the Ninth and Tenth Amendments.[74] Both have, by their very generality, been terribly difficult to interpret and enforce in Court,[75] and it is quite difficult to breathe new content into them now.[76] Even more to the point, prior to the Constitution of 1787, neither a majority of the people nor of the states had a legally recognized right (though many people would certainly have recognized a revolutionary right) to alter the government. Amar himself notes that one Anti-Federalist objection to the new Constitution—and it was largely Anti-Federalist objections that led to the Bill of Rights of which these amendments are a part[77]—was that the proposed method for constitutional ratification was bypassing the requirement for state unanimity.[78]

Amar's argument from the First Amendment focuses on the freedom of assembly and his claim that it includes "the *corporate* right of the People to assemble *in convention,* and, by a majority vote, to peaceably exercise their sovereign right to alter or abolish their government."[79] This argument runs directly into Jameson's classic distinction among four types of conventions, the spontaneous convention or assembly being quite different from the constitutional body that meets to revise a document.[80] Moreover, to focus purely on what the words of the First Amendment actually say is to see a great chasm between them and Amar's interpretation of them. To argue that the people have a constitutional right peacefully to assemble is quite

different from saying that a bare majority of the people (or their representatives in a convention) can assemble to write a new constitution, or amendment, which will, by popular referendum, be binding upon all. As noted
earlier, neither Federalists, with their penchant for republican institutions,
nor the Anti-Federalists, with their concern for states' rights, would have
been likely to accept an amendment which upheld such a view.

FEDERALISM AND ITS EMPHASIS ON NATIONALLY DISTRIBUTED MAJORITIES

Amar's arguments about the amending process are based on his analysis
in a previous article in which he argued that the people, rather than the
state governments, are sovereign.[81] Amar's argument that sovereignty cannot be divided is a complex one that need not be treated in its entirety here,
and to the extent that his argument seeks to vindicate national power over
extreme assertions of state sovereignty, it can be said to have been largely
established by the outcome of the Civil War.[82] It should be clear, however,
that Amar's argument attempts to do far more. His willingness to entrust
the amending process to a majority of voters in the nation as a whole, and
not, as in some previous amending proposals, in a majority of voters in a
majority of the states,[83] indicates that his view of federalism is a radical
departure from that of the Constitution's Founders which has previously
been designated in this book as that of a federal contemporary consensus.
Indeed, one of Amar's arguments for the nonexclusivity of Article V is
precisely that, under the majorities established there, a proposal favored by
a majority of the people, but not by the requisite number of states, might
be frustrated.[84]

Amar does believe that majorities must be deliberative,[85] and this would
surely have been considered important by the Framers, but to assume that
they would have wanted any changes favored by such majorities to be
incorporated into the Constitution is to underestimate the regard that both
Federalists and Anti-Federalists had for the states. While Madison argued
that the amending process was "neither wholly *national* nor wholly *federal,*"[86]
by Amar's analysis it is simply the former.[87]

Again, a reference to the time of the Founders shows the implausibility
of Amar's thesis that the Founders intended for simple majorities to amend
the Constitution. The most controversial issue at the Convention centered
on the dispute between the small states and the large ones.[88] This dispute
was not resolved until the famous Connecticut Compromise was adopted
giving smaller states equal representation in the Senate,[89] a compromise
which was one of two made explicitly unamendable under the terms of
Article V.[90] Not only did Article V seemingly guarantee that states would
not, without their consent, be deprived of their equal suffrage in the Senate
but the amending process itself also seemed a further guarantor of state

representation in decisions about further constitutional changes. By the terms of Article V, amendments could be proposed by no less than three-fourths of the membership of both houses of Congress, including the Senate where states would be represented equally. Only the states could themselves bypass this requirement by calling for a convention in requisite numbers. In both cases, amendments would have to be ratified by three-fourths of the states.

Martin Diamond sagely observed that these provisos helped to assure that amendments could not be approved unless they involved "*nationally distributed* majorities."[91] Diamond further tied these provisions to Madison's famous analysis of factions in *Federalist* No. 10: "harkening back to the 'multiplicity of interests,' it was also hoped that a nationally distributed majority, engaged in the solemn process of constitutional amendment, would favor only necessary and useful amendments."[92]

Under Amar's scheme, no such nationally distributed majorities would be needed, and, thus again, it is difficult to believe that those who wrote and ratified the Constitution would have been so careless. Small states would not have accepted a document that could have been amended by a mere majority of the states. They would have been even less likely to accept a document that gave the right to change the Constitution to a mere majority of voters, many of whom would be concentrated in a few of the largest states.

RETRENCHING THE ENTRENCHMENT CLAUSES

In a subject that is given greater attention in the next chapter, Amar does offer a creative explanation of the two unamendable provisions of Article V, but not an explanation that would have consoled those at the Constitutional Convention who thought such protections were offering them real security.[93] Amar regards both entrenchment clauses not as limitations upon amendments per se, but upon the mechanisms specified in Article V.[94] Amar thus argues that states may be deprived of the equal suffrage in the Senate but only by "Ourselves, through Philadelphia II-type procedures."[95]

Here, this author believes, Amar comes close to the truth, but only if, as the preceding analysis was designed to demonstrate, Philadelphia I is understood to have been an extralegal, or revolutionary, gathering. Surely, no mere parchment barrier can prevent the people from exercising the right to write a new constitution if sufficient numbers insist upon doing so and have power to back up their demands. On matters such as this, a constitution must necessarily be silent. Those who wish to write a new document can make up their own rules. As long as the people accept and operate under this Constitution, however, they have to take any provisions with which they may disagree along with those that they support. The Constitution is a seamless contract binding those who want its benefits to its terms.[96] The people can renounce this contract, or gift, but not at the same time they are appropriating it; in popular parlance, the people cannot have their cake and eat it, too! It would be absurd to think that proponents of equal state representation in the Senate closed a more difficult door to their opponents while leaving an easier door open.

On this point, it is important to look at the language of Article V itself. However the amending mechanism and the two amending restrictions are placed together within the same article, the two prohibitions do not say that they may not be changed through Article V mechanisms. Rather, they state:

Provided that *no Amendment* which may be made prior to the Year One thousand eight hundred and eight shall in any Manner affect the first and fourth Clauses in the Ninth Section of the first Article; and that *no State, without its Consent,* shall be deprived of it's equal Suffrage in the Senate.[97]

This language surely suggests that there is no legal way, by Article V, or otherwise, to alter either of these two restrictions under the existing Constitution.

While Amar concludes that, "the substantive constitutional rules adopted by one generation" govern future generations "unless and until amended,"[98] he fears conceding any more to the "dead hand" of the past. But here, again, as members of a social contract, Americans are like recipients of a conditional will. If they want the blessings of constitutional government as outlined in the document of 1787, they must accept its terms, one of which requires supermajorities to propose and ratify amendments. When Americans choose to ignore such requirements, they take the chance of losing the rest of their heritage as well.

THROWING STONES FROM A GLASS HOUSE

After discussing the entrenched provisions of Article V, Amar proceeds to compare his own view of popular sovereignty with the views of John Hart Ely and Alexander Bickel[99] and then with those of Charles Black, Jr., and Bruce Ackerman.[100] In discussing Ely's and Bickel's view that the judicial branch is uniquely anti-majoritarian, Amar questions whether any branch of government can uniquely speak for the people and reasserts the power of the people themselves, especially as this power is asserted in the convention mechanism. Amar's critique of representative governmental institutions is purposely overdrawn, and it might thus be unfair to make too much of it. It is interesting, however, that, while citing almost every possible obstacle to the representativeness of the elected branches of government,[101] Amar readily accepts the easy equation of the people with a convention. Still, whatever theory during the American revolutionary period may have suggested, a deliberative convention is ultimately a representative institution and, as such, is subject to many of the same representational inefficiencies that may plague a Congress and the president.[102] If it is conceded that a nondeliberative convention may be a mirror reflection of the people's wishes, to the same extent it must also be conceded (as Amar is unwilling to do)[103] that elements of deliberation and statesmanship may be lacking. Amar certainly has not objectively evaluated the comparative merits of conventions and more day-to-day legislative bodies.

Black is praised for recognizing the principle of popular sovereignty but criticized for accepting the exclusivity of Article V amending mechanisms.[104] One might accordingly expect Amar to appreciate Ackerman's view that the three branches can effectively enact "structural amendments" without regard to Article V.[105] Instead, Amar is quite critical.

Consistent with his critique of Kay, Amar first accuses Ackerman of misreading the convention of 1787 as a revolutionary body.[106] He argues that this misreading leads Ackerman to sanction structural amendment processes "that are likewise lawless—poorly grounded in constitutional text or structure, and resting largely on a misreading of Philadelphia I history."[107] Second, and perhaps correctly, Amar thinks Ackerman "undervalues the *formal* character of Philadelphia I."[108] Third, he thinks Ackerman "slights the *majoritarian* character of Philadelphia I" by focusing too much on the nine-thirteenths ratio to adopt the Constitution in Article VII versus the majority approval of conventions within each of the states.[109] Fourth, Amar argues that Ackerman understates the "populist" nature of the Constitutional Convention in that he does not indicate how closely the convention mechanism was tied to popular ratification.[110] Fifth, Amar accuses Ackerman of undercutting the federal nature of Article V.[111]

This last argument might seem particularly extraordinary coming from Amar, but, for him, federal concerns are seemingly only important where instrumentalities of the national government team up against instrumentalities of the states or vice versa. For Amar, the problem in Ackerman's scheme is that the three branches of the national government "could collude to aggrandize their own powers unjustly without either *popular* or state governmental approval."[112] By this novel view, federalism is seemingly rejected as a protection for states' rights; it is there merely to assure popular sovereignty. Finally, Amar faults Ackerman for giving insufficient attention "to the textual character of Philadelphia I."[113] By this, Amar correctly points to the value of incorporating constitutional change into clear language.

Constitutional language is, of course, of little or no value if it is ignored, and thus Amar ends his critique of Ackerman with a question that should be posed of Amar himself. That is, does his own scheme have a coherent textual basis? If, as this author believes, Amar's case is as textually weak as Ackerman's own—and, as the previous chapter indicates, Ackerman's justification is stronger as an interpretation of certain periods of constitutional history than as an exegesis of the constitutional text—then it too must fall by this criticism.

SOME HORRIBLES WERE NOT INVITED TO THIS PARADE

Constitutional arguments are crucial because, as the Supreme Law of the land, the Constitution is important and needs to be taken seriously.[114] If arguments from the constitutional text are ambiguous, it is certainly relevant to consider the probable consequences of alternative interpretations. Amar defends his opinion of the nonexclusivity of Article V mechanisms against criticisms that his view might lead to majority tyranny, majority instability, or be frustrated by majority ignorance.

As to majority tyranny, Amar believes that Americans, many of whom are themselves minorities, have a more sympathetic view of minority rights than they are often credited with and that there would be "safety in numbers," in his proposal; that is, in the need for a national majority.[115] However this argument is designed to track arguments in *The Federalist* for a large republic,[116] this argument ignores the very concern that Martin Diamond believed Article V was designed to safeguard, namely the possibility that majorities in populous sections of the country might try to take advantage of those in less populous states. Along these lines, it is useful to recall the tremendously divisive controversies over the tariff question which split the nation in the 1820s and 30s.[117] What if this controversy had been not simply a matter of congressional law but of constitutional enactment? It is noteworthy that, even with the extraordinary majorities required in Article V, a major motivating factor behind the South's eventual decision to secede stemmed from the view that constitutional provisions might one day be used to abolish the South's peculiar institution.[118]

Amar argues that constitutional changes once enacted can be undone, but, in addition to raising genuine concern about constitutional instability, this ignores the possibility that there may be some changes which simply cannot be so easily rescinded. To take a concern of obvious importance to the Founders, could states be abolished and then recreated? Could the electoral college be eliminated in one election and reestablished in the next? The concern with majority tyranny is not simply that today's temporary majority may be venal or mean-spirited but that, in pursuit of one good, the public may fail adequately to consider others. Governmental structures are embodied within a constitutional text precisely because changes in such structures are likely to have such widespread consequences that there is value in shielding them from every passing whim.

Amar says that the possibility of constitutional amendment by majority vote may, by providing a readier means of repeal, deter amendments; there might, under his interpretation, be fewer amendments rather than more.[119] The opposite could well result. Today advocates of amendments have to overcome the public caution which stems from the very fact that, once in the Constitution, provisions are extremely difficult to amend. As was indicated in the first chapter, of the twenty-seven amendments ratified to date only the Eighteenth has been repealed, and it required an alternate ratification route. It is likely that, as in the state experience, a less sober view of new amendments would be taken if yet another easier mode of amendment were recognized. Amar's argument that no more amendments are likely to be adopted using two modes of amendment rather than one simply strains credulity.

Amar argues that, if a new amending mechanism were recognized, it would be not simply an additional route acting in isolation but would rather be in "dynamic interaction" with previously used Article V mechanisms.[120] As Amar sees it, the people could "wield their Philadelphia-II 'sword' of amendments to deter unpopular Article V amendments, and thus preserve the constitutional status quo."[121]

A less enticing possibility is that both sides of given controversies will push ahead simultaneously, one attempting to incorporate its agenda into the Constitution through one mechanism while another tries to enact its own program by the other mechanism. Thus, two-thirds majorities of both houses of Congress and three-fourths of the state legislatures might affirm or attempt to strengthen federalism; for example, at the same time a popular majority called a convention and ratified its proposals that the states be abolished. A balanced budget mechanism might be adopted through one method at the same time a guaranteed national income was adopted by another.[122]

Arguments on such a point are necessarily speculative, but practices under the existing constitutional understanding are not. After 200 years of experience, Americans know that current Article V amending mechanisms are unlikely to lead to great uncertainty or instability. The consequences of Amar's proposal are necessarily unknown. The mere possibility that it may create governmental instability is a key argument against it.

Amar's defense against "majority ignorance" is perhaps best understood as a straw man or woman.[123] In America, the people were invested with the decision as to whether to accept the Constitution that governs them. They elect their most prominent state and federal officials and are granted liberal rights of political expression. The question is whether this constitutional system is to be further subject to emendation by today's majority or whether such changes will continue to require supermajorities distributed through the nation in a fashion designed to limit the provisions in the Constitution only to the nation's most permanent ideals. The survival of the United States Constitution over a 200-year period that has seen similar state and national constitutions come and go suggests that current amending mechanisms are adequate without drawing up new means with their potential for unintended consequences.

Even if Amar's defenses against majority tyranny, majority instability, and majority ignorance are accepted, there may be other valid objections to his proposal which he has not anticipated. Certainly, two substantial arguments which Amar raised against Ackerman—the argument from the constitutional text and the argument from federalism—apply equally as well, if not indeed more strongly, to Amar's own scheme. Yet another possibility is that the Constitution's delicate system of checks and balances will be seriously upset as the two popularly elected branches manipulate the new amending procedure against one another, or, as in a scenario Madison warned against, in the event a Jeffersonian amending mechanism were adopted against the judiciary.[124] Charles De Gaulle certainly used the plebiscite in the French Fifth Republic to magnify the powers of the presidency in ways that were previously unimaginable, and perhaps something similar could happen here.[125]

Another possibility is that the convention mechanism might itself be weakened by more extensive use and thus lose much of its current legitimating power. At the national level, at least, the convention mechanism has only been used to date as a means of rewriting, not amending, the Constitution. Were it to be evoked more frequently as a device for proposing single amendments, it might lose some of its appeal, were it ever to be needed as a means of complete constitutional revision. Again, the consequences of Amar's scheme simply are unpredictable in advance. Any "parade of horribles" must necessarily be somewhat speculative, but such horribles are not therefore irrelevant.[126] In the end, the potentially far-reaching and uncertain consequences of Amar's interpretation may be the strongest arguments against it. Americans would do well to remember that it is, after all, a *Constitution* that they are considering amending.[127]

POPULAR SOVEREIGNTY VERSUS NATURAL RIGHTS

While American government is grounded upon the consent of the governed, American statesmen and thinkers from Jefferson[128] through Lincoln[129] and King[130] have constantly reaffirmed that natural rights should always morally, and often constitutionally, limit popular choice. Thus, rather than simply affirm popular sovereignty, as Amar does, the authors of the Constitution tried to strike a balance. Once the people accepted this Constitution and the principles it embodied, the people were free legally to change the document, but not unless extraordinary majorities could be convinced that such changes were desirable.

Previous commentators on the amending process understood that, when it came to amending the Constitution, sovereignty would not be exercised by any fifty-one percent or more of the voters but only by the people acting through the requisite majorities established in Article V. Such an amending mechanism could, of course, itself be amended and, if it proved so wooden as to result in sufficient discontent, the people could, acting in revolutionary or extralegal fashion, reclaim the power by which they originally established the Constitution. Unless and until such time, the presence of self-imposed limits on the majority will of the moment was not understood to be a repudiation of rule by "We, the People." One scholar thus distinguished, in language that he himself regarded as somewhat awkward, between the people as ultimate "sovereigns" who could exercise their right to begin a new governmental form, from the "pro-Sovereign," the people's will as it was articulated through the amending power.[131] Such earlier thinkers simply saw no contradiction in a constitution whereby a majority of people had, under ordinary circumstances, simply limited the exercise of their own will.

By contrast, Amar equates American constitutionalism with popular sovereignty and popular sovereignty with the immediate, if deliberative, will of the majority. Unlikely as such a scenario may be, under Amar's scheme, it at first appears that fifty-one percent of the people could call for a convention to repeal the Bill of Rights and the same fifty-one percent could ratify this scheme.[132] In a footnote, however, Amar develops an argument that some amendments—like those repealing free speech and those which would deny to the people "certain economic and social prerequisites"—would themselves be unconstitutional.[133] This idea is the subject of the next chapter. It is worth pointing out here, however, that the notion of substantive limits on the amending process is as much, if not more, in conflict with the idea of popular sovereignty as are the majorities required in Article V. If Amar believes that there are some decisions the people absolutely cannot make at all, it seems ironic for him to say that these same people cannot specify that decisions dealing with their form of government may not be effected except by the processes of extraordinary majorities. Such a view further calls into question whether Amar's position is properly labeled that of popular sovereignty.

AMENDING TODAY, LEGISLATING TOMORROW?

There is one final issue to be addressed in assessing Amar's nonexclusivity thesis and this is how it can be applied to the amending process and not at the same time to the process of legislating. If, as American theory has rather consistently held,[134] changes in a constitution are indeed generally more fundamental than changes in ordinary laws, it would seem that the right of the majority to change the former should surely include the latter.[135] One might rightly ask, if amending the Constitution is not exclusively addressed in Article V, why should legislating be exclusively specified in Articles I and II?

This author does not believe that Amar offers a satisfactory answer. Despite his savage, if purposely overdrawn, attack on the representativeness of republican institutions,[136] Amar ultimately gives this system a vote of confidence.[137] Citing a persuasive contemporary article,[138] Amar further points to the "great dangers" of direct initiative while arguing that, when it comes to amendments, "the dangers are smaller, the philosophic justifications stronger, the alternatives less palatable, and the possible rewards greater."[139] Amar offers to provide proof later in his paper.

This "proof" is, however, completely unresponsive to the constitutional issue, that is, why one process should textually be read as nonexclusive and not the other. Amar's argument is quite simply that, "ordinary lawmaking by the People enjoys neither the elaborate procedural protections of the ordinary legislative process nor the self-restraining solemnity of constitutional amendment."[140] This is surely a distinction that does not make a difference. Certainly, one strong argument against popular amendment is that it too will bypass existing procedural protections which protect minority rights against hasty or ill-advised majority actions. Moreover, the process of amending the Constitution may be solemn largely because this process is now so extraordinary and infrequent in nature. Amar's scheme may or may not keep it so, but to rely on the experience of one amending system to argue for another is simply again to try to have one's cake and eat it, too.

In the end, then, the arguments for the nonexclusivity of Article V mechanisms would seem to hinge on arguments for the nonexclusivity of the legislative process or any other specified in the Constitution. Perhaps Amar shies away from this tie for fear that it will undercut his constitutional argument. It certainly appears, to this author at least, that the arguments for both kinds of popular initiative should fall together in preference to more tried and limited forms.

NOTES

1. Akil Reed Amar, "Philadelphia Revisited: Amending the Constitution Outside Article V," *University of Chicago Law Review* 55 (Fall 1988), p. 1055.

2. Ibid., p. 1057n and p. 1061.

3. Ibid., p. 1065. Underlining mine.

4. Amar does not cite the argument by William MacDonald that Congress can call a constitutional convention on its own authority because Article V should be viewed as "permissive and selective, not as exclusive." See William MacDonald, *A New Constitution for a New America* (New York: B. W. Heubsch, 1922). This work is discussed in John R. Vile, *Rewriting the United States Constitution: An Examination of Proposals from Reconstruction to the Present* (New York: Praeger, 1991), pp. 57–59.

5. Herman Ames, *The Proposed Amendments to the Constitution of the United*

States during the First Century of its History (New York: Burt Franklin, 1970. Reprint of 1896 edition) notes, for example, a proposed amendment by Davis of Kentucky that would have permitted ratification of amendments by a majority vote in three-fourths of the states. Similarly, Herbert Croly, *Progressive Democracy* (Indianapolis, IN: Bobbs-Merrill, 1965. Reprint of 1909 edition), p. 231, advocated adoption of an amendment by Senator LaFollette which, in Croly's words, would have provided for ratification of amendments, "by a majority of all the voters voting, provided that the majority is distributed throughout a majority of states."

6. See Madison's argument in *The Federalist*, No. 43, Alexander Hamilton, James Madison, and John Jay, *The Federalist Papers,* ed. Clinton Rossiter (New York: New American Library, 1961), pp. 279–80.

7. Ibid., *The Federalist*, No. 40, pp. 54–55.

8. Ibid., *The Federalist*, No. 43, Madison, p. 279. On a similar note, see *The Federalist*, No. 22, Hamilton, p. 152.

9. Winton Solberg, *The Federal Convention and the Formation of the Union of the American States* (Indianapolis, IN: Bobbs-Merrill, 1958), p. 58, quotes the congressional resolution calling for the Constitutional Convention. Under this resolution, the Philadelphia delegates were convened "for the sole and express purpose of revising the Articles of Confederation and reporting to Congress and the several legislatures such alterations and provisions therein as shall, when agreed to in Congress and confirmed by the states render the federal constitution adequate to the exigencies of Government and the preservation of the Union."

10. See Akil Reed Amar, "Of Sovereignty and Federalism," *Yale Law Journal* (1987), p. 1425.

11. *The Federalist Papers,* pp. 240–46.

12. Ibid., No. 40, *Madison,* pp. 249–51.

13. Richard S. Kay, "The Illegality of the Constitution," *Constitutional Commentary* 4 (Winter 1987), p. 71.

14. Amar, "Philadelphia Revisited," citing Hoar on pp. 1053, 1061, and 1067. In Roger S. Hoar's, *Constitutional Conventions: Their Nature, Powers, and Limitations* (Boston: Little, Brown, 1919), Hoar indicated "that there exists midway between the class of actions prohibited by the constitution and the class of actions authorized by the constitution, a twilight zone consisting of those actions which are neither authorized nor prohibited." Hoar went on, however, to indicate that "[a]s the Federal government has no powers other than those expressly or impliedly given to it by the Constitution, all Federal activities within the twilight zone are just as illegal as those which fall into the expressly prohibited class."

15. Moreover, the courts have voided attempts at the state level to substitute petitions for a convention from the people rather than the state legislature. See *Hawke v. Smith,* 253 U.S. 221 (1920). Also see, Jonathan L. Walroff, "The Unconstitutionality of Voter Initiative Applications for Federal Constitutional Conventions," *Colorado Law Review* 85 (1985), pp. 1525–45.

16. See Hoar, *Constitutional Conventions,* pp. 38–57. Note, however, that most such conventions have been called, not as Amar proposes to do at the national level by popular referenda, but by the state legislatures. See Hoar, p. 52.

17. For perhaps the most complete account of this event, see George Dennison, *The Dorr War: Republicanism on Trial,* 1831–1862 (Lexington: University Press of

Kentucky, 1972). Also see John R. Vile, "John C. Calhoun on the Guarantee Clause," *South Carolina Law Review* 40 (Spring, 1989), pp. 667–92.

18. See *Luther v. Borden*, 48 U.S. 1 (1849).

19. Ibid., Webster's arguments, p. 31.

20. In a letter to the Hon. William Smith dated July 3, 1843, Calhoun thus noted:

> These various provisions clearly indicate the sense of the people of the United States, that the right of altering or changing constitutions is a conventional right, belonging to the body politic and subject to be regulated by it. In not a single instance, is the principle recognized, that a mere numerical majority of the people of a State, or any other number, have the right to convene, of themselves, without the sanction of legal authority,—and to alter or abolish the Constitution of the State.

See John C. Calhoun, *The Works of John C. Calhoun*, vol. 6, ed. Richard K. Cralle (New York: Russell and Russell, 1968. Reprint of 1852–56 edition), p. 223.

21. Hoar, *Constitutional Conventions*, pp. 38–40.

22. Elmer E. Cornwell, Jr., "The American Constitutional Tradition: Its Impact and Development," in *The Constitutional Convention as an Amending Device*, ed. Kermit L. Hall, Harold M. Hyman, and Leon V. Sigal (Washington, DC: American Historical Association and American Political Science Association, 1981), pp. 19–33.

23. For the best historical survey of U.S. constitutional amendments, see Alan P. Grimes, *Democracy and the Amendments to the Constitution* (Lexington, MA: Lexington Books, 1978). Also see John R. Vile, *A Companion to the United States Constitution and Its Amendments* (Westport, CT: Praeger, 1993).

24. Morton Keller, "The Politics of State Constitutional Revision, 1820–1930," in *The Constitutional Convention as an Amending Device*, ed. Kermit L. Hall, Harold M. Hyman, and Leon V. Sigal (Washington, DC: American Historical Association and American Political Science Association, 1981) pp. 67–86.

25. U.S. Constitution, Article VI.

26. U.S. Constitution, Amendment XIV, paragraph 1; U.S. Constitution, Article IV, paragraph 4. Amar, "Philadelphia Revisited," observes that "the People may experiment by amending state laws and state constitutions only because the federal Constitution stands as a secure political safety net—a floor below which state law may not fall."

27. Amar, "Philadelphia Revisited," p. 1100.

28. Ibid., p. 1045.

29. Ibid.

30. Ibid., p. 1066.

31. Ibid., pp. 1045–46. Amar does presuppose for purposes of his hypothetical some opposition to ratification of the amendment by those, perhaps like this author, waving the text of Article V in their hands.

32. It is, of course, possible that the Court would follow the precedent in *Coleman v. Miller*, 307 U.S. 433 (1929) and declare that the issue was a "political question," unsuitable for its judgment. The weaknesses of this precedent are described at greater length in chapter 2.

33. David R. Dow, "When Words Mean What We Believe They Say: The Case

of Article V," *Iowa Law Review* 76 (1990), p. 33, notes Amar's equivocation between the terms *power* and *right*. Dow says that "statements about powers are statements about physics," and that, "the people may well have the power to alter the Constitution, but this does not establish that in exercising that power they have acted lawfully."

34. Walter Dellinger, "The Legitimacy of Constitutional Change: Rethinking the Amending Process," *Harvard Law Review* 97 (December 1983), p. 387.

35. Kay, "The Illegality of the Constitution."

36. Ibid., p. 63.

37. Ibid., p. 67.

38. Ibid.

39. Ibid.

40. Ibid., pp. 68–70.

41. Amar, "Philadelphia Revisited," p. 1054, observes that Article XIII of the Articles of Confederation specified "that 'any alteration' must follow the procedure set forth in the document." Amar does not conclude, as does this author, that this provision calls into question Amar's view that the Constitution was adopted legally.

42. John A. Jameson, *A Treatise on Constitutional Conventions: Their History, Powers, and Modes of Proceeding*. 4th ed. (New York: Da Capo Press, 1972. Reprint of Callaghan and Company, 1887), p. 380.

43. Amar, "Philadelphia Revisited," p. 1052.

44. Federalists did convincingly argue, however, that by choosing to be bound by their objects rather than limited by the methods spelled out in their commissions, delegates to the convention had decided that "the means should be sacrificed to the end, rather than the end to the means." *The Federalist Papers,* No. 40, Madison, p. 248.

45. Amar, "Philadelphia Revisited," p. 1053.

46. Ibid., p. 1056. Quoted from Jonathan Elliot, *The Debates in State Conventions on the Adoption of the Federal Constitution* (New York: Burt Franklin, 1888), vol. 3, p. 37. The section where Amar uses ellipses reads: "What then: We shall resist did my friend say? conveying an idea of force." This suggests that Pendleton was replying to an earlier speaker, probably Patrick Henry, but this writer cannot identify the specific statement Pendleton was addressing. This ambiguity makes Pendleton's statement especially difficult to interpret and further points to the value of drawing cautious inferences from it.

47. Amar, "Philadelphia Revisited," p. 1057.

48. Gordon S. Wood, *The Creation of the American Republic 1776–1787* (New York: W. W. Norton, 1969), pp. 514–16.

49. John Locke, *Two Treatises of Government,* ed. Peter Laslett (New York: New American Library, 1965), pp. 463–64, thus notes in a theme later repeated in the Declaration of Independence that

> if a long train of Abuses, Prevarications, and Artifices, all tending the same way, make the design visible to the People, and they cannot but feel, what they lie under, and see, whither they are going; 'tis not to be wonder'd, that they should then rouze themselves, and endeavor to put the rule into such hands, which may secure to them the ends for which Government was first erected.

These and other views which influenced the American Founders are discussed in Chapter 1 of Vile, *The Constitutional Amending Process in American Political Thought*.

50. See Kay, "The Illegality of the Constitution."

51. Amar, "Philadelphia Revisited," p. 1057. Amar notes that the decision to append the Bill of Rights to the end of the Constitution rather than weave new provisions into the text may also have accounted for the rejection of Madison's proposed emendation.

52. It may, however, also have been that this decision was "more as a matter of literary than of political judgment." This, at least, is the opinion of William Lee Miller, *The Business of May Next: James Madison & the Founding* (Charlottesville: University Press of Virginia, 1992), p. 253.

53. For Amar's acknowledgment that Madison viewed Article V mechanisms as exclusive, see "Philadelphia Revisited," p. 1063, citing *The Federalist*, Nos. 39 and 43. For the quotation, see *The Federalist Papers*, p. 278.

54. Article VII of the U.S. Constitution, thus specified: "The Ratification of the Conventions of nine States, shall be sufficient for the Establishment of this Constitution between the States so ratifying the same."

55. See Article XIII of the Confederation Constitution, Solberg, *The Federal Convention*, p. 51.

56. See Kay, "The Illegality of the Constitution."

57. Amar, "Philadelphia Revisited," p. 1048.

58. Ibid. However plausible it is to suggest, as Amar does, that violations of the Articles freed the members to "disregard the pact," and this argument was certainly made by the Federalists themselves, there seems some difficulty in allowing the states to disregard the amending clause of the Articles while accepting, in the meantime, the government of these same Articles.

59. Amar, "Philadelphia Revisited," p. 1049.

60. Ibid., p. 1094n.

61. Ibid., p. 1050, citing Max Farrand, ed., *The Records of the Federal Convention of 1787*, vol. 2 (New Haven, CT: Yale University Press, 1966), p. 760.

62. Ibid.

63. Ibid., pp. 1050–51.

64. Ibid., p. 1052.

65. See Article II of the Articles of Confederation, Solberg, *The Federal Convention*, p. 42.

66. Solberg, *The Federal Convention*, p. 34 (Declaration of Independence, paragraph 1) thus notes that, "a decent respect to the opinions of mankind requires that they [people of America] should declare the causes which impel them to the separation."

67. Of the three state constitutions Amar cited at p. 1051, only one (that of Massachusetts) refers specifically to the right of "a majority of the community," the other two constitutions referring simply to the "community" or, like the Preamble to the U.S. Constitution, to the "people."

68. Irving Brant, *The Bill of Rights: Its Origin and Meaning* (Indianapolis, IN: Bobbs-Merrill, 1965), p. 11, thus refers to the right of revolution as "a natural, not a legal right."

69. On a related point, it is worth noting that Massachusetts and New Hampshire both required that amendments and new constitutions would have to be ratified by

two-thirds of the voters. George W. Carey, "Popular Consent and Popular Control, 1776–1789," in *Founding Principles of American Government: Two Hundred Years of Democracy on Trial,* ed. George J. Graham, Jr., and Scarlett G. Graham (Chatham, NJ: Chatham House Publishers, 1984), p. 80. Surely, a constitution would not specify, *at one and the same time,* that it could be amended either by a mere majority of the people or by a two-thirds vote of them. In such circumstances, the first provision would make the second into a nullity. What incentive would there be, in such circumstances, ever to use the two-thirds route?

70. The Preamble to the Virginia Constitution, for example, actually served as one of the models for the Declaration of Independence. See Garry Wills, *Inventing America: Jefferson's Declaration of Independence* (Garden City, NY: Doubleday, 1984).

71. Lester B. Orfield, *The Amending of the Federal Constitution* (Ann Arbor: University of Michigan Press, 1942), p. 144.

72. See especially *The Federalist Papers,* No. 10, pp. 81–82. Madison noted that in a republic, "it may well happen that the public view, pronounced by the representatives of the people, will be more consonant to the public good than if pronounced by the people themselves, convened for the purpose." Madison went on to argue that such a possibility was greater in a larger republic than in a small one.

73. Here, as elsewhere, the Anti-Federalists were the "men of little faith." See Cecelia Kenyon, "The Political Thought of the Anti-Federalists," in *The Anti-Federalists,* ed. Cecelia Kenyon (Indianapolis, IN: Bobbs-Merrill, 1966), pp. xxi-cxix. Also see, Herbert J. Storing, *What the Anti-Federalists Were For* (Chicago: University of Chicago Press, 1981), pp. 15–23.

74. U.S. Constitution, Amendment 9 reads: "The enumeration in the Constitution of certain rights shall not be construed to deny or disparage others retained by the people." U.S. Constitution, Amendment 10 states: "The powers not delegated to the United States by the Constitution, nor prohibited by it to the States, are reserved to the States respectively, or to the people."

75. An earlier authority on the amending process, Orfield, *The Amending of the Federal Constitution,* p. 144, wrote: "Neither amendment confers any affirmative powers in the people, nor clarifies the meaning of the word. Sovereignty or the power to amend can scarcely be derived from them." Moreover, while not all would accept Justice Stone's view that the Tenth Amendment "states but a truism that all is retained which has not been surrendered," *United States v. Darby,* 312 U.S. 100, 124 (1941), the amendment is certainly quite vague. See Sotirios Barber, *On What the Constitution Means* (Baltimore, MD: Johns Hopkins University Press, 1984), p. 64.

76. A notable exception has been in the area of personal privacy. Here, however, reliance on the Ninth Amendment has been but one of a possible battery of amendments upon which the justices have relied. See *Griswold v. Connecticut,* 381 U.S. 479 (1965). Also see, *Roe v. Wade,* 410 U.S. 113 (1973).

77. Grimes, *Democracy and the Amendments to the Constitution,* pp. 6–9.

78. Amar, "Philadelphia Revisited," p. 1049.

79. Ibid., p. 1058. The U.S. Constitution, Amendment 1 reads in relevant part, "Congress shall make no law . . . abridging . . . the right of the people peaceably to assemble, and to petition the Government for a redress of grievances."

80. Jameson, *A Treatise on Constitutional Conventions,* pp. 3–16. For more specific criticism of Amar's interpretation of the First Amendment, see Robert C. Palmer,

"Akil Amar: Elitist Populist and Anti-Textual Textualist," *Southern Illinois Law Journal* 16 (Winter 1992), pp. 403–05.

81. Amar, "Of Sovereignty and Federalism," *Yale Law Journal* 96 (1987) pp. 1425–1520.

82. See *Texas v. White*, 74 U.S. (7 Wall.) 700 (1869).

83. Croly, *Progressive Democracy*. In "Philadelphia Revisited," Amar at p. 1071 further notes that, "[w]e the People can—and perhaps should—abolish the archaic apportionment rules of the Senate."

84. Amar, "Philadelphia Revisited," p. 1060. By contrast, and in line with this author's view, William S. Livingston, *Federalism and Constitutional Change* (Oxford: Clarenden Press, 1956) notes that "as it is implemented in the United States, the federal principle refutes the principle of majority rule as applied to the problem of constitutional amendment." Similarly, at pp. 310–11, Livingston argues that "[b]y its very nature federalism is anti-majoritarian," and that "[i]t is a technique for the protection of a minority within one state or several states against the majority in the rest of the states." See also Palmer, "Akil Amar," pp. 414–16.

85. Amar, "Philadelphia Revisited," p. 1066.

86. *The Federalist Papers*, No. 39, Madison, p. 246.

87. Dow, "When Words Mean What We Believe They Say," also notes that Amar's analysis slights federal values. See pp. 56–61. On p. 58, Dow thus notes that, "In light of the constitutional structure of sovereignty, relying on a national majority to ratify proposed amendments rather than on majorities in discrete states is unconstitutional in the truest sense: It departs from the unmistakable language of the text as well as the concerns underlying the choice of such language."

88. Clinton Rossiter, *1787: The Grand Convention* (New York: W. W. Norton, 1966), pp. 185–96.

89. A solution embodied in U.S. Constitution, Article I, Section 3, paragraph 1.

90. The last provision of U.S. Constitution, Article V, supra, note 1 contains this entrenchment provision.

91. Martin Diamond, Winston Fisk, and Herbert Garfinkel, *The Democratic Republic: An Introduction to American National Government* (Chicago: Rand McNally, 1966), p. 98. By contrast, Amar, "Philadelphia Revisited," p. 1073, says that once it is recognized that the Founders could not have required amending majorities of 99.9 percent, "then there is no principled way to stop short of 50 percent plus one. Any other rule impermissibly entrenches the status quo."

92. Diamond et al., *The Democratic Republic*, p. 99.

93. Note on this point that the slave importation provision was added to the Constitution after Rutledge observed, "that he never could agree to give a power by which the articles relating to slaves might be altered by the States not interested in that property and prejudiced against it." See Farrand, *Records*, vol. 2, p. 559. Similarly, at page 629 Farrand's record indicates that the provision for equal state suffrage was adopted after Sherman noted "that three fourths of the States might be brought to do things fatal to particular States, as abolishing them altogether or depriving them of their equality in the Senate."

94. Amar, "Philadelphia Revisited," p. 1068 and p. 1070.

95. Ibid., p. 1071.

96. This point is elaborated further in the next chapter. Amar, "Philadelphia

Revisited," p. 1057, himself notes the danger of declaring any part of the Constitution to be nonbinding but goes on to make the argument that this issue does not come into play with the entrenchment clauses because he is not arguing that they are nonbinding, but only that they are nonexclusive.

97. U.S. Constitution, Article V. Underlining mine. Amar argues in "Philadelphia Revisited," p. 1069n, that the phrase "provided that" appears "to confine the scope of this later clause of Article V amendment." This interpretation seems overly clever and would hardly have satisfied those who insisted on these entrenchment clauses as a condition of national union.

98. Amar, "Philadelphia Revisited," p. 1074.

99. Amar cites Ely's *Democracy and Distrust: A Theory of Judicial Review* (Cambridge: Harvard University Press, 1980) and Alexander Bickel's, *The Least Dangerous Branch* (Indianapolis, IN: Bobbs-Merrill, 1962).

100. Amar cites Black's, *The People and the Court* (Englewood Cliffs, NJ: Prentice Hall, 1960) and Bruce Ackerman's, "The Storrs Lectures: Discovering the Constitution," *Yale Law Journal* 93 (May 1984), pp. 1013–72.

101. Amar, "Philadelphia Revisited," pp. 1080–85.

102. While problems such as seniority cited in the footnote above may be unique to the legislatures, such problems as the occupation and status of conventioneers (and their effects upon representativeness), public misinformation, the costs of electioneering, and districting might equally plague a convention. Even the problem of "tied goods" which Amar cites might develop if a convention were to consider a package of proposals rather than a single amendment. Amar at p. 1094 disguises these problems, especially the latter, by assuming that a convention would necessarily be limited as the Convention in Philadelphia in 1787 was not, to one issue and one issue only. Such an assumption would appear to be a serious limit on the notion of "popular sovereignty" that Amar is advancing.

103. Amar, "Philadelphia Revisited," pp. 1096–1102.

104. Ibid., p. 1088.

105. Ibid., p. 1091.

106. Ibid.

107. Ibid., p. 1092.

108. Ibid.

109. Ibid., p. 1093.

110. Ibid., p. 1094.

111. Ibid., p. 1095.

112. Ibid. Underlining mine.

113. Ibid. In a similar vein, but from someone with a much different perspective than Amar, see Stephen Markman, "The Amendment Process of Article V: A Microcosm of the Constitution," *Harvard Journal of Law & Public Policy* 12 (1989), pp. 113–32.

114. A thought suggested by Gary L. McDowell's, *Taking the Constitution Seriously* (Dubuque, IA: Kendall/Hunt, 1981).

115. Amar, "Philadelphia Revisited," p. 1097.

116. Ibid. thus cites *The Federalist Papers,* Nos. 9 and 10.

117. Glyndon G. VanDeusen, *The Jacksonian Era, 1828–1848* (New York: Harper & Row, 1959), pp. 39–91.

118. See Vile, *The Constitutional Amending Process in American Political Thought*, p. 86.

119. Amar, "Philadelphia Revisited," p. 1099.

120. Ibid., p. 1100.

121. Ibid., p. 1100–1101.

122. This possibility suggests that Amar might be creating potentially rival sovereigns. Even though Article V currently provides a separate convention mechanism, possible conflict with the method of congressional proposal is reduced to almost nothing by the fact that both methods require ratification by three-fourths of the states that are unlikely to ratify two contradictory amendments at the same time. Amar's scheme provides no such comparable safety.

123. Amar, "Philadelphia Revisited," pp. 1101–02.

124. *The Federalist Papers*, No. 49, Madison, pp. 313–17. Jefferson's proposal, quoted at p. 313, was "that whenever any two of the three branches of government shall concur in opinion, each by the voices of two thirds of their whole number, that a convention is necessary for altering the Constitution, or *correcting breaches of it,* a convention shall be called for the purpose."

125. Suzanne Berger, *The French Political System* (New York: Random House, 1974), pp. 53–54.

126. By so classifying objections to his scheme, Amar, "Philadelphia Revisited," p. 1096, puts one who questions at a rhetorical disadvantage. Still, horribles are no less horrible because they are on parade, and Amar's own list of parade participants is self-chosen and incomplete.

127. Suggested both by John Marshall's statement in *McCulloch v. Maryland,* 17 U.S. (4 Wheat) 316, 407 (1819) and by Laurence Tribe, "A *Constitution* We Are Amending: In Defense of a Restrained Judicial Role," *Harvard Law Review* 97 (December 1983), pp. 433–45.

128. In the Declaration of Independence, paragraph 1, Solberg, *The Federal Convention,* p. 34, Jefferson thus referred to the "self-evident" truths, "that all men are created equal, that they are endowed by their Creator with certain unalienable Rights, that among these are Life, Liberty and the pursuit of Happiness."

129. See Lincoln's comments in Harry V. Jaffa, "Abraham Lincoln," in *American Political Thought,* ed. Morton J. Frisch and Richard G. Stevens (Dubuque, IA: Kendall/Hunt, 1976), p. 136.

130. Thus in Martin Luther King, Jr.'s "Letter from Birmingham Jail," in *Free Government in the Making,* 4th ed., ed. Alpheus T. Mason and Gordon E. Baker (New York: Oxford University Press, 1985), p. 743, he followed Thomas Aquinas in distinguishing just from unjust laws. Also see Taylor Branch, *Parting the Waters: America in the King Years, 1954–63* (New York: Simon & Schuster, 1988), p. 740.

131. Max Radin, "The Intermittent Sovereign," *Yale Law Journal* 39 (1930), p. 526.

132. The possibility that Amar's two examples of permissible popular sovereignty (first calling for a convention and second ratifying its results) might be combined adds further concern about how deliberative his amending mechanisms might ultimately prove to be.

133. Amar, "Philadelphia Revisited," p. 1045. Amar goes beyond the negative to assert a more positive view that he grants is "controversial." Amar suggests at pp. 1044–45 that his view of popular sovereignty might compel the view that every

American is constitutionally entitled, "to minimal entitlements of food, shelter and education." However desirable, these were not the kinds of rights, and surely not the kinds of *legal* rights, championed by the American Revolutionaries. See Maurice Cranston, *What Are Human Rights?* (New York: Taplinger Publishing, Inc., 1973), pp. 65–71.

134. In the United States, the Constitution is spoken of as fundamental and is regarded as superior to other laws. See Howard L. McBain, *The Living Constitution* (New York: Macmillan, 1928), p. 10. Thus, American revolutionaries rejected Blackstone's doctrine of parliamentary sovereignty in preference for the view attributed to Sir Edward Coke that even the lawmaker could be bound by the law. Edward S. Corwin, *The 'Higher Law' Background of American Constitutional Law* (Ithaca, NY: Cornell University Press, 1965), pp. 49–50, 87. Amar's view would appear closer to the British model of government on this point than the American, though it is doubtful that even the British, with their elaborate system of governmental institutions, would permit changes in their unwritten "constitution" by mere majorities of fifty percent plus one.

135. By contrast, Amar, "Philadelphia Revisited," p. 1078, seems to suggest that the Constitution should be more easily changed than ordinary acts of legislation.

136. Ibid., pp. 1080–85.

137. Ibid., p. 1085.

138. Charles L. Black, Jr., "National Lawmaking by Initiative? Let's Think Twice," *Human Rights* 8 (Fall 1979), pp. 28–31, 49.

139. Amar, "Philadelphia Revisited," p. 1085.

140. Ibid., p. 1100.

Chapter 7

The Question of Limitations—Are There Implicit Restraints on the Constitutional Amending Process?

Given the Founders' desires to accommodate change, the Article V provisions protecting slave importation for twenty years, and guaranteeing that states would not be deprived of their equal suffrage in the Senate without their consent are somewhat anomalous. Why did the Framers, otherwise so cognizant of the need for change, make these exceptions? What would happen if an amendment were adopted to repeal the equal suffrage provision and the states involved did not, at least not unanimously, give their consent? Should an unamendable provision in an otherwise amendable constitution be ignored or disregarded like past unamendable Constitutions, or is it enforceable in the courts?

THE CONSTITUTIONAL CONVENTION AGREES TO TWO ENTRENCHMENT CLAUSES

In addressing these questions, the records of the Constitutional Convention offer at least some guidance. As has been noted earlier, the major debates on the amending process came in the closing week of deliberations. By September 10, the amending provision provided for Congress to call a convention "on the application of the Legislatures of two thirds of the States."[1] Elbridge Gerry, Alexander Hamilton, and James Madison criticized this proposal. Gerry feared that two-thirds of the states might agree to a convention that would propose amendments "that may subvert the State-Constitutions altogether."[2] Hamilton argued that the state legislatures would not request a convention except "to increase their own powers,"[3] and that ills would be better perceived by the national legislature. Madison objected to the vagueness of the Convention provision,[4] and subsequently proposed that Congress would introduce amendments after two-thirds of the members agreed to do so or after petitions from two-thirds of the state legislatures.[5] John Rutledge, a delegate from South Carolina, almost immediately amended this proposal to include the slave importation reservation, noting that he could never approve alterations of current slave relations by nonslave states.[6]

The amendment issue reemerged on September 15, when the present method of constitutional amendment was finalized. The provision requiring a constitutional convention upon the request of two-thirds of the states was adopted after George Mason expressed fears that otherwise Congress would have too much control.[7] More to the point, the provision for equal suffrage in the Senate was also accepted after Roger Sherman expressed fears that the required majority of states might otherwise "do things fatal to particular States, as abolishing them altogether or depriving them of their equality in the Senate."[8] He proposed that the restriction on altering slavery should be broadened to specify "that no State should be affected in its internal police, or deprived of its equality in the Senate."[9] Madison feared that the floodgates were about to be opened. "Begin with these special provisos," he noted, "and every State will insist on them, for their boundaries, exports &c."[10] While enough delegates shared Madison's sentiments to narrow the range of Sherman's reservations, after rejecting a series of amendments proposed by Sherman,[11] the Convention adopted Morris's proposal to protect states from being deprived of their equal vote in the Senate without their consent.[12] Madison attributed this unanimous action to "the circulating murmurs of the small States."[13]

THE STATUS OF THE ENTRENCHMENT CLAUSES

Thus, the two limitations in Article V were no mere accidents. While accepting proposals essential to pacifying the small states and those with slaves, the Convention rejected more radical proposals to void any interference in state police powers or to omit an amending process altogether. In effect, the Founders delineated four categories of rights and activities: those believed to need no specific constitutional protection; those thought to be protected by such mechanisms as bicameralism, the separation of powers, and judicial review; those considered sufficiently necessary, important, or endangered to be included in the Constitution subject to amendment; and those guarantees thought to need additional security even against the amendment process.[14]

In writing the Constitution, the Framers were in a sense establishing the rules of a game governed by an association, similar in certain respects to that governing college basketball. Those desiring the advantages of the Constitution must abide by its provisions, just as those wanting the thrill of playing basketball must abide by basketball rules. The nation is no more permanently bound to this Constitution than a player is prevented from trying his luck at another game. Just as a person cannot, however, share the joys of one game while following the rules of another, so too, one cannot reap the rewards of the Constitution while ignoring its rules, one of which specifies an unamendable provision.[15]

Nonetheless, some have argued that the equal suffrage provision is not legally binding. Such a view was advanced by congressmen who opposed passage of the Corwin Amendment, an amendment proposed as part of the Crittenden Compromise introduced just prior to the Civil War with the intention of safeguarding slavery against further constitutional change.[16] These congressmen argued that the equal suffrage provision, like the proposed compromise, was "a mere declaration."[17] More recently, Edward S. Corwin and Mary L. Ramsey argued that the equal suffrage provision "has the moral force of a promise given more than one hundred sixty years ago."[18] While justifications for this view vary, it appears largely based on notions of popular sovereignty.[19] For example, Corwin and Ramsey argued that "if the amending power is the same power which ordained and established the original Charter, any limitation on it must be considered as having only such force and validity as the amending power itself may at any time choose to accord it."[20]

This writer believes that this view, which seems to suggest that the entrenchment provision cannot be enforced in the courts, is profoundly mistaken. By accepting the Constitution and its strictures on the amending process (and every state joining the Union has given such assent), the nation has already accepted certain restraints on the momentary popular will. There is no reason why the United States should be bound by one such restraint, the supermajorities required for most amendments, and not another, the unanimous state consent required for altering a state's equal suffrage in the Senate. Acceptance of an unamendable provision in an otherwise amendable constitution is not a denial of sovereignty. The nation may indeed exercise its sovereignty by changing the equal suffrage provision but only by paying a price. That is, the nation may choose—to revert to the earlier analogy— a new constitutional game, presumably through means of a revolution or a revolutionary convention. A nation might even choose in writing a new constitution to keep most of the old rules but, if it is proceeding under the auspices of the existing constitutional scheme, it must follow that scheme or jeopardize the entire constitutional framework:[21]

We are free to touch the Constitution, to shape it to fit current needs, even, if necessary, to tear it up and write a new one. What we are not free to do is to ignore it, and that is precisely what those who urge the invalidity of the article five proviso would have us do.[22]

EARLY DEBATES ABOUT IMPLICIT CONSTITUTIONAL RESTRAINTS ON THE CONSTITUTIONAL AMENDING PROCESS—JOHN C. CALHOUN AND THOMAS COOLEY

The question of explicit restraints leads logically to the question of whether there are any implicit limitations on Article V. The argument for such restraints was advanced early in the nineteenth century by one-time vice-president and later South Carolina Senator John C. Calhoun as part of his scheme of nullification. Under this scheme, if states believed that the national government was exercising powers which had not been entrusted to it, these states could nullify the law, requiring its suspension until the states could adopt an amendment to grant this power to the national government. Even where states adopted such an amendment, however, Calhoun argued that states could secede in cases where such an amendment "would radically change the character of the constitution, or the nature of the system; or if the former should fail to fulfill the ends for which it was established."[23] Calhoun's arguments for secession were, of course, resoundingly rejected by the outcome of the Civil War as were later arguments that the Thirteenth Amendment would be unconstitutional.[24]

Arguments from states' rights, however, continued to be popular. These arguments were specifically applied to the amending process by Thomas Cooley, one of the most influential legal commentators of his day, in an article published in 1893. Reviewing the two entrenchment clauses within the Constitution, Cooley argued that they were not exclusive but that "there are limitations that are far more important than this, that stand unquestionably as restrictions upon the power to amend."[25] In an argument which was apparently not directed to any specific amendment, Cooley formulated four examples of unconstitutional amendments. These were an amendment that attempted to detach a certain part of the Union, an amendment that applied different taxing rules to some states, an amendment that established a nobility, or an amendment that attempted to create a monarchy.[26] Arguing that the first fifteen amendments had all "been in the direction of further extending the democratic principles which underlie our constitution," Cooley contended that amendments "must be in harmony with the thing amended," and he distinguished that which amends a constitution from that which "overthrows or revolutionizes it."[27] Cooley also attempted to offer a credible reason why the Founders did not include other stated restrictions on the amending process:

If the makers of the constitution, in limiting this provision [Article V] stopped short of forbidding such changes as would be inharmonious, they did so because it was not in their thought that any such changes could for a moment be considered by congress or by the states as admissible, since in the completed instrument no place could possibly be found for them, however formal might be the process of adoption; and as foreign matter, they would just as certainly be declared inadmissible and therefore invalid without an express inhibition as with it.[28]

Cooley proposed an analogy based on the notion of higher law.

The fruit grower does not forbid his servants engrafting the witch-hazel or the poisonous sumac on his apple trees; the process is forbidden by a law higher and more imperative than any he could declare, and to which no additional force could possibly be given by re-enactment under his orders.[29]

ARGUMENTS FROM IMPLIED RESTRAINTS APPLIED TO PROGRESSIVE ERA AMENDMENTS— WILLIAM MARBURY AND SELDEN BACON

Cooley's arguments, which do not appear to have been directed to any particular amendment, were appropriated and expanded by numerous conservative commentators who subsequently hoped to persuade the courts to invalidate the Fifteenth, Eighteenth, and Nineteenth Amendments.[30] The arguments are too numerous and detailed to treat them in full here, although two representatives may be taken as examples of how the arguments typically proceeded. Thus, in an article challenging the national prohibition and women's suffrage amendments, attorney William Marbury contended "that the power to 'amend' the Constitution was not intended to include the power to *destroy* it," but only to "*carry out the purpose for which it was framed.*"[31] More specifically:

the power to amend the Constitution cannot be deemed to have been intended to confer the right upon Congress . . . to adopt any amendment . . . which would have the same tendency . . . to destroy the states, by taking from them, directly, any branch of their legislative powers.[32]

Marbury further argued that Prohibition deprived each state of its equality in the Senate by opening the door to a destruction of "those functions which are essential 'to its separate and independent' existence as a state."[33] Finally, distinguishing constitutional matters from matters of ordinary legislation, Marbury argued that it was unwise to lay down conditions which might prove ultimately unsuited to the future.

In a similar vein, law professor Selden Bacon relied on an ambiguous letter sent by James Winthrop to the Massachusetts Constitutional Ratifying Convention to argue that the Bill of Rights was designed to limit the scope of future constitutional amendments.[34] While the first nine amendments protected personal rights, the Tenth Amendment addressed itself to limiting governmental powers. Moreover, by the subtle maneuver of Roger Sherman,[35] who had argued for a restriction at the Philadelphia Convention limiting the scope of amendments, those powers reserved to the states and the people were those "not delegated to the United States"[36] But, asked Bacon, what power could this be other than the power of amendment? Thus viewing the Tenth Amendment as a specific limit on the amending power, Bacon concluded that only conventions had the power to ratify amendments infringing state police powers. In Bacon's paraphrase of the Tenth Amendment:

If the Federal Government wants added direct powers over the people or the in- dividual rights of the people, it must go to the people to get them; the power to confer any such added direct powers over the people and their individual rights is reserved to the people; and the right, at the option of Congress, to get such added powers from any other source, is wiped out.[37]

Arguments like those of Marbury and Bacon were rejected in a series of court decisions[38] that culminated in the Court's almost complete hands-off approach to the amending process in *Coleman v. Miller*.[39]

WALTER MURPHY'S ARGUMENTS FOR IMPLICIT CONSTITUTIONAL RESTRAINTS ON THE CONSTITUTIONAL AMENDING PROCESS

Nonetheless, many of the same arguments made earlier in this century for implicit limits on the amending process are relevant to Walter Murphy's recent attempts to breathe new life into the notion of implied limits on the amending process. Murphy has argued that certain provisions of the Con- stitution are so fundamental, and so essential to human dignity, that an amendment repealing them should be voided by the courts.

Murphy offered two examples of unconstitutional amendments.[40] The first involved restriction of the First Amendment. Murphy reasoned as follows:

1. Incorporation of the First Amendment into the Fourteenth means that the op- erative constitutional provision effectively reads: 'Neither Congress nor the states, singly or together, can make a law abridging freedom of speech, press, assembly, or religion.
2. Constitutional amendments are law.
3. Therefore it is outside the scope of state and legislative powers to amend the Constitution to restrict the First Amendment's protections.[41]

In a second example, Murphy imagined that an "ideology of repressive racism sweeps the country."[42] Its proponents muster the requisite majorities in Congress and in the states to ratify a constitutional amendment endorsing racial discrimination. If such an amendment were challenged in court, Murphy did "not see how the Justices, as officials of a constitutional democracy, could avoid holding the amendment invalid."[43]

Murphy outlined three arguments. The first, borrowed from the Federal Constitutional Court of West Germany, suggested that the Constitution is a unit with "an inner unity" and a commitment to "certain overarching principles and fundamental decisions to which individual provisions are subordinate."[44] In this case, he argued, the "protection of human dignity," as a core constitutional value, would take precedence over the racist amendment. Murphy adopted a second argument from a court decision in India. He reasoned that Americans have chosen "a constitutional democracy which enshrines certain values, paramount among which is human dignity."[45] This value is even more important than the democratic procedures by which it was intended to be secured. "By adopting and maintaining such a system of values, the American people have surrendered their authority, *under that system,* to abridge human dignity by any procedure whatever."[46] Since this Constitution makes "no provision for destroying the old polity and creating a new one . . . its terms cannot supply legitimate procedures for such a sweeping change."[47] Murphy further noted that "constitutional tradition establishes a legitimate process for establishing a totally new system through a convention chosen from the *entire polity.*"[48] Murphy's third argument was similar to the previous two. Since "there are principles above the literal terms of the constitutional document," Murphy argued, the racist amendment would be invalid as a denial of "the right to respect and dignity," because it sought to "contradict the basic purpose of the whole constitutional system."[49]

PROBLEMS WITH MURPHY'S ANALYSIS

Despite Murphy's appealing objectives, this writer believes that courts should steer clear of imposing implicit limits on the substance of amendments, even in the extreme circumstances Murphy mentions. From the standpoint of constitutional interpretation and the Framers' intent, the presence of two explicit limits within Article V, and the Constitutional Convention's deliberate rejection of two others, seems to argue against the existence of still more. As Chief Justice John Marshall wrote in regard to provisions in Article III: "Affirmative words are often, in their operations, negative of other objects than those affirmed; and in this case, a negative or exclusive sense must be given to them or they have no operation at all."[50]

An additional objection to judicially recognized limits on the amending process stems from what such a notion might do to the delicate balance which has been worked out during the last 200 years between the judicial branch and the people. However one might stress the "constitutional" as opposed to the "democratic" aspects of the American government,[51] the exercise of judicial power by an unelected branch of government whose members serve for life has always been in tension with popular rule.[52] One reason that judicial review is accepted is that judgments of the courts can be reversed through the amending process. Moreover, the potential impact of the amendment process on the courts cannot be measured merely by counting those few occasions when it has been directly utilized,[53] since the possibility may have deterred court decisions in other areas as well. To empower the courts not simply to review the procedures whereby amendments were adopted but also to void amendments on the basis of their substantive content would surely threaten the notion of a government founded on the consent of the governed.[54]

Recognition of the right of the judiciary to invalidate amendments might also upset the delicate balance that has been worked out among the three branches of government. There is certainly merit in the notion that while the judicial branch may interpret the Constitution, the Constitution is created by other hands, that is, by the Congress, the state legislatures, and/or a constitutional convention. Murphy notes the possibility, albeit arguably a fairly remote one, that the people or their agents could adopt measures that would undermine human dignity. What should also be noted, however, is that, if the judiciary took upon itself the power to void the very substance of amendments, this branch of government could itself end up undermining such dignity. Indeed, attention to American history would suggest that such dangers of judicial usurpation would be far more likely than the dangers that Murphy cites. Surely, for example, it would not have been preposterous (along lines Taney developed in *Dred Scott*) to argue that the Constitution was adopted by whites and could not be extended to others, the Civil War amendments to the contrary notwithstanding.[55] As noted earlier, almost all the Progressive Era amendments were met with similar challenges.

Under the U.S. constitutional system, it is clear that the solution to a bad or unworkable amendment, the Eighteenth for example, is another one repealing it. Similarly, undesirable judicial decisions can be overturned by amendments. But what would the people or the other branches do if the courts, relying on the idea of implicit limits on the amending power, adamantly rejected all attempts at reform?

Here the role of the amending process as a "safety-valve" or alternative to revolution needs to be appreciated.[56] When popular sentiment has reached the boiling point, it is unlikely to be calmed by plugging the stopper. Even if the courts had the courage to oppose the raging tides of opinion in such contingencies—and cases such as *Dred Scott*,[57] *Plessy*,[58] *Gobitis*,[59] *Korematsu*,[60] and *Yamashita*[61] show that they have often failed in similar circumstances—there is little reason to believe they would be successful in doing anything other than sparking revolution. It is far more likely that courts accepting Murphy's invitation to judge the validity of the Constitution itself would intervene on those more problematic occasions where they could enhance their own institutional powers or their own view of what is best at the expense of the people and/or the elected branches of government.

These arguments notwithstanding, one must still meet Murphy's own positive examples and arguments. His argument against restrictions on the First Amendment has the advantage of resting on a seemingly explicit, rather than an implicit, constitutional limit, but it has problems. While an amendment may indeed be a form of law, it is unlikely to be the form referred to in the First Amendment; the two would rarely be equated in ordinary discourse. If the Founders meant no law or amendment, surely they would have been explicit, as they were in establishing limits in Article V.[62] Moreover, the language of the supremacy clause seems to indicate that the terms *law* and *amendment* are not used synonymously elsewhere in the Constitution.[63] Finally, Murphy's argument is inconsistent with existing constitutional interpretation under which presidents and governors can veto laws but not amendments.[64]

As to Murphy's example of a racist amendment, he first argues that unifying constitutional principles should take precedence over contrary provisions. This argument would be more compelling if one could assume that the Constitution expressed a single set of coherent principles, laid down once and for all by divine decree. Not only is the Constitution an imperfect document, however, but it is also evolutionary; amendments and changes in interpretations are designed to reflect the development of refined public opinion.[65] In such a constitution, more recent constitutional provisions are presumptively in closer accord with the consent of the governed than conflicting earlier provisions.[66] Thus, today's justices do not ask whether blacks should be counted as three-fifths of a person or whether senators should be elected by state legislatures. Moreover, a court proceeding from Murphy's assumptions might have heeded past requests to void several amendments whose commitment to human dignity Murphy now heralds.

Murphy's second argument is that the nation has opted for a system in which the people "have surrendered their authority, *under that system,* to abridge human dignity by any procedure," short of "a convention chosen from the *entire polity*."[67] It is doubtful that the existing Constitution was itself written and adopted in such a convention.[68] Surely, the Constitution permitted a number of practices—including slavery and the disenfranchisement of women—that are today clearly recognized as violations of such human dignity. More important, Murphy's proposal is dangerously close to that of Calhoun's concurrent majority and could just as easily be applied not to enhance human dignity, but—to cite some plausible historical examples—as a means of protecting the South's "peculiar institution," the all-white or all-male suffrage, or the election of senators by state legislatures.[69]

To turn, finally, to Murphy's contention that there are "principles above the literal terms of the constitutional document," is to enter a constitutional morass.[70] This writer accepts the notion that such natural law principles exist, but he believes it would be dangerous to enthrone the judiciary as the guardian of such principles in such circumstances. It would be particularly difficult to reverse decisions which misinterpreted or misapplied natural law principles. Clearly, not every moral wrong has a constitutional or judicial remedy. Prudence dictates that popular rule and national union may sometimes, at least in the short term, have to take priority over the protection of a specific conception of human dignity. Ultimately, the best haven for human dignity is the cleft of a constitution changeable by a populace that is, over time, subject to enlightenment and improvement.

APPLICATION OF IMPLICIT LIMITS TO THE FLAG-BURNING CONTROVERSY

The virtue of Murphy's arguments for limits on the amending process is that they are, like similar reflections by Sanford Levinson,[71] Sotorios Barber,[72] and William Harris III,[73] designed as much to promote scholarly reflection as to address any specific controversies. These arguments, however, have been applied to a specific controversy which may further illuminate the strengths and weaknesses of this view.

The precipitate for follow-up arguments was provided by the Supreme Court's rulings in *Texas v. Johnson* and *United States v. Eichman* voiding the application of state legislation designed to prohibit the burning of the American flag.[74] Amendments were quickly introduced in Congress and supported by President George Bush to reverse these judgments. A popular version of this proposal would have provided that, "The Congress and the States shall have power to prohibit the physical desecration of the flag of the United States."[75] This proposed amendment was defeated by congressional votes in 1989 and 1990.[76]

This author believes that a flag-burning amendment would be unwise and contrary to the wide protection typically given to free speech in America. If proposed and ratified according to the procedures specified in Article V of the U.S. Constitution, however, he believes that an amendment protecting the flag, or even restricting freedom of speech more generally, would be as valid as any other.

ERIC ISAACSON'S ARGUMENTS

The authors of the two recent articles specifically addressing the flag-burning amendment, however, while taking different approaches,[77] both argue that such an amendment would be unconstitutional. Eric Isaacson, whose argument consciously or unconsciously tracked that of Walter Murphy, focused primarily on the language of the First Amendment, and he ultimately concluded that there was a limit not so much on the substance of amendments restricting speech as on the procedures by which they may be adopted. Jeff Rosen, whose argument is on this point somewhat akin to Selden Bacon's, focused more on the issue of natural rights and on the role of the Ninth Amendment, but he also concluded that there is an important unstated limit on the amending power.

Isaacson began from the premise that constitutional amendments are a form of law.[78] The language of the First Amendment, however, provides that Congress "shall make no law" limiting freedom of speech.[79] Isaacson portrayed the language of the First Amendment as unique:

It is far more restrictive than any other limitation contained in the Bill of Rights. No other provision in the Bill of Rights operates by withdrawing from Congress the *power to make any law*. Thus, the first amendment is radically different from the rest of the Bill of Rights; its only analogue may be found in the absolute disabilities to act imposed by article V.[80]

Isaacson believes that the language of the First Amendment was designed specifically *"to disable the Congress,"* language subsequently extended through the doctrine of incorporation to state legislation as well.[81] As such, Isaacson suggested that alteration of the First Amendment by a flag-burning exception or any other could only be made by a method of amendment that bypassed Congress and the state legislatures, that is, by amendments proposed by the people in an Article V convention and subsequently ratified by special conventions within three-fourths of the states.[82]

PROBLEMS WITH ISAACSON'S ANALYSIS

This author believes that Isaacson's arguments are flawed. In the first place, whatever the words of the First Amendment appear to say, the Court has not as yet interpreted these words to have the blanket meaning that Isaacson has attributed to them. Especially at the state level, laws prohibiting obscenity, libel, false advertising, perjury, fighting words, and other forms of speech continue to be upheld by the courts. Even the most liberal advocates of free speech seem to have been convinced by Oliver Wendell Holmes's example of the illegality of falsely shouting fire in a crowded theater and causing a panic.[83] As commentators have noted, at least since incorporation, "the Supreme Court's interpretation of these guarantees has been both broader [applying, for example, to executive as well as legislative actions] and narrower than a literal reading of the amendment might suggest."[84] It would therefore be inconsistent to use Isaacson's approach only in the area of constitutional amendments.

One could, of course, argue that Justice Hugo Black and other absolutists, although never commanding a majority of the Court, were nonetheless correct and that the First Amendment provision for "no law" means precisely "no law."[85] If this position is accepted, however, Isaacson would have to show that "law" not only "may" be interpreted but should be interpreted to include constitutional amendments.[86] For reasons suggested when criticizing Murphy's arguments on this point, however, this is a dubious argument. Despite his analysis of the purposeful nature of the language of the First Amendment,[87] Isaacson presents no direct evidence that one of the intentions of those who proposed or ratified the First Amendment was to limit the amending process (which was already far more difficult than the normal law-making procedures) as opposed to the ordinary law-making process. Second, Isaacson offers no reason to suggest why, if freedom of speech was of such concern, it would be any less permissible for conventions to limit this right than for legislatures. Third, the language of Article V where the amending power is specified does not refer to amendments as laws but as amendments. Similarly, although the language is not necessarily conclusive, the wording of the Supremacy Clause in Article VI of the Constitution suggests that the Constitution (and presumably the amendments added to it) should be distinguished from "the Laws of the United States which shall be made in Pursuance thereof."[88] By the same token, the provisions of the Bill of Rights are called "amendments" or "articles" rather than "laws,"[89] and it would be quite awkward, and even inaccurate, to refer to them as the first ten "laws."[90] Surely, if the Framers of the First Amendment intended to limit amendments, as well as laws, or even in addition to them, they picked some circuitous language to fulfill their purpose.

As the provisions of Article V reveal, Congress has no authority "to make" any amendment. It can, of course, override a presidential veto and thus make a law, as it were, on its own authority; it has, however, no authority to make an amendment absent consent on the part of three-fourths of the states. It would seem that if it was the purpose of the First Amendment specifically to limit Article V, it should either have directly said so or at least prohibited Congress and the states (as it now effectively does through the doctrine of incorporation, albeit not with any specific design that Isaacson or anyone else has shown thereby specifically to restrict the amending process) from passing such "laws" jointly. If Isaacson is correct, by his own analysis, the First Amendment would be the only one of the first ten amendments to carry such a meaning, again suggesting that the First Amendment (not originally, it should be remembered, designated as the First but as the Third Amendment) may have a more extraordinary place in American history than we have as yet come to realize.[91] To this writer, at least, Isaacson's arguments are not convincing.

To these arguments must be added the fact that the language of Article V does not appear, as Isaacson seeks to do, to designate one type of ratification for one class of amendments and a second type of ratification for others. To the contrary, this language clearly leaves this decision to Congress, specifying that amendments become valid "when ratified by the

Legislatures of three fourths of the several States, or by Conventions in three fourths thereof, as the one or the other Mode of Ratification may be proposed by the Congress."[92]

JEFF ROSEN'S ARGUMENTS

Jeff Rosen's arguments are even more revolutionary than Isaacson's and would overturn many existing understandings of the workings of Article V and the amending process. Like Isaacson, Rosen ultimately concludes not that amendments restricting freedom of speech are impossible but rather that they can only be adopted by a special process and by employing specific language. He bases his arguments, however, not simply on the First Amendment but on his understanding of Article V and the more elusive Ninth Amendment.

Rosen argued that the right of speech was one of the unalienable natural rights retained by the people and therefore subject to judicial protection, even against the amending process, under the Ninth Amendment. The primary obstacle to using the Ninth Amendment has been, of course, the problem of defining what particular rights it was designed to secure.[93] For Rosen, such rights can be identified by reading sources at the time of the American Founding, particularly state constitutions. Although Rosen acknowledges some difficulty in deciding which such rights were alienable— that is, which could be exchanged for some kind of societal guarantees— and which were unalienable, he included "rights of religious conscience and the right of revolution" in addition to freedom of speech in the latter category.[94] Rosen also believes that each generation has the right to add or subtract from the list of what they consider to be natural rights, and he suggested that state constitutions are once again the place to turn for such determinations.[95]

Almost by definition, natural rights that are unalienable may not be surrendered by the people. If the people cannot surrender them, then, arguably, neither can their representatives.[96] While some, including this author, would agree that this would give the people the moral right to disobey unjust laws which sought to deprive them of their natural rights, Rosen would go much further, arguing that such rights are "judicially enforceable" under the Ninth Amendment,[97] and that to withhold judicial protection from such rights would be to "deny or disparage" the very rights the Ninth Amendment was designed to protect.[98] Acknowledging special problems in protecting natural rights against constitutional amendments, Rosen nonetheless argued that the Court has a special responsibility to do so

by striking down an amendment that appears to violate a right "retained by the people," the Supreme Court, in effect, would "remand" the amendment back to the people or to their Article V delegates and ask them if they really believe the right to be natural and retained.[99]

Rosen continued:

If the proposers and ratifiers, on remand, *are* determined to overrule the Supreme Court, they may not merely express their legislative *will* (we believe Congress should have the power to regulate flag burning); they must also provide a clear statement of their judicial *reason* (because we no longer believe the rights of speech to be natural). In this way, judicial review of the substance of an amendment does not thwart popular sovereignty, but merely ensures that it is deliberately exercised as the Founders intended—within the boundaries of natural law, as defined by the people themselves.[100]

Rosen concluded that, to be accepted by the Supreme Court, an amendment would have to say "something like" the following: "Freedom of speech shall not be construed as a natural right retained by the people and protected by the First and Ninth Amendments."[101] Rosen repeats his view that in voiding amendments which fell short of expressing such sentiments, the Court "would defer to, rather than thwart, the sovereignty of the people."[102]

PROBLEMS WITH ROSEN'S ARGUMENTS

   This author believes, however, that Rosen's arguments are seriously flawed. To begin with a minor point, Rosen seeks to ascertain the content of natural rights by looking at statements of the Founders and provisions in contemporary state constitutions, but it is far from clear that either support his view that freedom of speech (particularly the kind of symbolic speech represented by flag-burning) was and is recognized as such a natural right. While Rosen has a fairly convincing quotation indicating that Madison accepted free speech (albeit not necessarily symbolic speech) as a natural right, his quotation from Roger Sherman refers specifically to "writing and publishing" within restraints of "decency and freedom."[103] Moreover, as far as this writer can ascertain, Rosen identifies only two contemporary state constitutions—Kentucky's and Utah's—which specifically identify speech as such a right, quite far indeed from a majority.[104] If the courts were permitted to identify a right as natural on the basis of statements in two or more constitutions, many of which are quite prolix, it is doubtful that there would be any effective limit on its authority to overturn both laws and amendments.
   There is, in Rosen's analysis, a more significant problem which has generally plagued those who have attempted to enforce the Ninth Amendment, namely, how to make a positive, judicially enforceable obligation, from language which appears, like the language in that of the Tenth Amendment which follows it, to be a simple declaration. The Bill of Rights, it will be

recalled, was adopted when fears were expressed by Anti-Federalists that the national government might exercise powers over speech, press, and other important rights whose protection was not specifically enumerated in the Constitution. In originally arguing against the adoption of such amendments, leading Federalists argued that a Bill of Rights might not only be unnecessary but could also be dangerous.[105] What if, in listing rights, the Constitution did not include a person's right to refrain from tipping a hat to a governmental official? Would such an omission indicate that governors could therefore adopt such an absurd requirement?[106] The most obvious reason to suggest that the Ninth Amendment was included in the Bill of Rights was to answer this question in the negative. The people need not worry that just because they forgot to list a right, the government therefore had power to take it away. While such issues have more frequently been adjudicated under the due process clauses of the Fifth and Fourteenth Amendments, if there is any occasion when reliance on the Ninth Amendment might be justified, this is it.

Rosen seeks, however, to do more. While the Ninth Amendment is worded to protect rights *not enumerated* in the Constitution, Rosen attempts to interpret this amendment to protect the right of free speech which clearly *is so enumerated* against the possibility that such protection could be withdrawn or limited.[107] This not only fills in the meaning of an already elusive amendment but also seems to do so in direct contradiction to what the amendment says. Incidentally, if Rosen's interpretation is accurate, it would also oblige the Supreme Court to recognize, and presumably enforce other unalienable natural rights, including the right of revolution—which is clearly not a legally enforceable conventional right.[108]

Another way to see the flaw in Rosen's scheme is to ask what would have happened had the Supreme Court decided differently in *Texas v. Johnson* and *United States v. Eichman*. The possibility that the Court could easily have done so (and, indeed, could still do so) is heightened by the five to four votes in these decisions and by the vigorous language used by the dissenting justices.[109] In short, a change in a single vote of a single justice would have altered the outcome. In such a case, the presumed natural right to burn the American flag would have had no national constitutional protection, and, indeed, absent a change of mind on the part of the Court itself, an amendment would have been required to afford such protection. In such a plausible case, the putative purpose of the Ninth Amendment, as envisioned by Rosen, would have been defeated, and that would have been the end of the matter.

Rosen argued, however, that once five or more justices of the Supreme Court decided that flag-burning was a right protected by the First Amendment, even an amendment could not overturn this decision, short of language specifically indicating an intent to restrict the scope of the First and Ninth Amendments. Rosen justified this stance, not as a way of thwarting popular will but giving it, as it were, a second chance. What Rosen seemingly forgets in formulating this scheme, however, is that this would not be a second chance but a third—one in which the people might well conclude that the idea of popular sovereignty had struck out.[110]

Under existing state and national constitutions and perhaps by the principle of the Ninth Amendment itself, no act is illegal unless and until there is a law against it.[111] Thus, the people, through their representatives, make a decision about the status of certain activities when they first pass laws prohibiting them. Because of the separation of powers in both the national and state governments and the presence of bicameral legislatures at the national level and in all but one state, there is indeed a strong inertia against the passage of most legislation. In most state legislatures, there are a variety of structural and constitutional hurdles to the passage of legislation as well as the threat of executive veto.[112] There are similar and perhaps even greater obstacles to the passage of legislation in Congress.[113]

Once legislation has emerged from the state legislatures or from Congress, however, the matter of constitutionality is hardly over. Because of the acceptance of judicial review in America, such legislation may then, if it is challenged before the courts in a given case or controversy,[114] still be declared unconstitutional, as were the flag-burning statutes at issue in *Texas v. Johnson* and *United States v. Eichman*. This is the mechanism that already provides for the second look which Rosen thinks is so important.

Faced with judicial invalidation of a law, the people have three options—disobedience, acquiescence, or adoption of a constitutional amendment. As indicated earlier, this latter process is so difficult[115] that only four decisions of the U.S. Supreme Court have been overturned in all American history.[116] In more than 200 years of such history, only thirty-three amendments have been proposed by the necessary congressional majorities,[117] and, of these, only twenty-seven have subsequently been ratified by the necessary three-fourths of the states.

Under Rosen's scheme, however, an amendment which attempted to limit flag desecration or alter unalienable rights should be struck down by the Court unless it says it is specifically aimed at modifying the First and Ninth Amendments, in which case it would have to go once again through the awesome amending hurdles before being valid. Not surprisingly, Rosen finds no evidence for this view in the language of Article V itself which does not specify that some amendments must be adopted twice or that they must evoke the kind of talismanic language that Rosen advocates.

Indeed, it would be difficult to think of a parallel understanding of the amending process that has been expressed in American history without going back to the view of another Connecticut law student, John C. Calhoun, whose views were outlined briefly above. By Rosen's analysis, if a majority of justices on the Supreme Court thought that there was a natural right to own slaves (and Southern defenses of slavery as a positive good for both master and slave, as well as recognitions in previous state consti-tutions of the rights of slave-owners, do not make this proposition appear as ludicrous as it might first appear), then the Fourteenth Amendment would not have been sufficient but would have required a specific follow-up to amend the Ninth Amendment.[118]

FLAWS IN THE NOTION OF INHERENT LIMITS ON THE AMENDING PROCESS

This illustration may further point to the whole problem with interpre-tations that attempt to read implicit limits into Article V. To guard against fairly unlikely scenarios, proponents of such limits have urged the Court, as Calhoun once urged the states, effectively to usurp the sovereignty of the people as it is expressed in the amending process.[119]

It can surely be argued that the people are not always right and that popular sovereignty is therefore no guarantee of justice, but the invitation to increased judicial activism ignores the already fine balance that has been developed among the three branches of government to preserve liberty and justice.[120] Today, charges that the judiciary is a counter-majoritarian institution[121] can be cogently met by the argument that in exercising judicial review, the Court is merely enforcing the people's will as this will is ex-pressed in the Constitution.[122] This claim is strained the further judges stray from the constitutional text[123] (so-called noninterpretative review).[124] What-ever difficulty judges may now face in invalidating laws in the absence of clear constitutional language would be geometrically compounded if courts sought to invalidate validly ratified parts of the Constitution itself. A Court seeking to invalidate an amendment adopted through Article V procedures would risk a serious backlash that might cripple all its authority. Perhaps more importantly, there is the distinct possibility that the courts would use their power to undermine core constitutional values. It is also possible that talk of judicially invalidated amendments could encourage a certain reck-lessness and lack of concern among amendment advocates, allowing them to take the same position regarding amendments that some now take in regard to laws—that is, deferring questions of wisdom and constitutionality to the courts.

DOUGLAS LINDER DENIES THE POSSIBILITY OF ADDITIONAL ENTRENCHMENT CLAUSES

In changing the Constitution, do the people have the right to pass una-mendable amendments? In raising this question, Douglas Linder reminds us that it was a living issue at least once in the nation's history, on the occasion of the pre-Civil War Corwin Amendment.[125]

Linder's judgment that the Corwin Amendment, and others similar to it, would be unconstitutional is worthy of attention, not only because Linder reasoned that only such amendments are unconstitutional but also because he recognized that the existence of explicit limits in Article V undercuts his position.[126] Linder nonetheless opposed unamendable amendments:

> The prohibition of amendments that would dismantle certain fundamental institutions and arrangements established by the Constitution, including the states themselves, was a topic specifically debated by delegates to the Philadelphia Convention; the question of amendments that would alter the nature of the Constitution itself was not discussed. The debates indicate that the framers wanted the principles and institutions established in the Constitution to be open to evaluation and change. What is not clear is whether they intended their *conception of a Constitution* to be similarly subject to modification.[127]

Citing evidence that the Founders regarded the Constitution as "a vehicle through which change could peaceably occur," Linder added that "nothing could be more inconsistent with the conception of the living Constitution than an unamendable amendment or an amendment authorizing unamendable amendments and which by its own terms is unamendable."[128] Such amendments posed the "risk of violence and revolutionary change" and "the risk that people will grow to disrespect the source of the institutions and arrangements that are forced on them."[129] Apart from these risks, Linder also suggests that one generation should not be allowed to prevent succeeding generations from making fundamental moral and political choices.[130] He concluded that "article V itself cannot be amended so as to create any new limitations on the amending power."[131]

CRITIQUE OF LINDER'S VIEW

Presumably, Linder does not think that the precise formula mentioned in Article V is somehow sacrosanct and inviolable. Surely, there is nothing talismanic about the consent of two-thirds of both Houses of Congress and three-fourths of the states (as opposed, for example, to three-fifths and seven-sixteenths or four-fifths and seven-eighths). By Linder's own reasoning, the provisions of Article V should, upon experience, be subject to the same modifications as any other constitutional provision. Presumably, Linder must consider that an unamendable amendment is distinguishable from a mere change or procedure.

What then of Linder's question, "Is it moral or consistent with democratic theory to allow one generation to prevent succeeding generations from making certain fundamental moral and political choices?" The apparent negative answer does not, in fact, settle the controversy. In the first place, such a response calls into question the whole notion of a constitution whereby one generation decrees that succeeding generations may not change the Framers' constitutional handiwork without the concurrence of extraordinary majorities. Beyond this is Linder's own willingness to allow the Founders to bind subsequent generations on the issue of equal state suffrage. To Linder's question may thus be posed the following counterquestions: What gives the current generation less sovereignty than that exercised by the Founders? If they could enact an unamendable provision, why cannot the present generation? Has the sovereignty involved in writing constitutional documents somehow vanished?

If the answer to this last question is negative, a generation creating or modifying a given constitutional system has the right, within the rules of that system, to set whatever conditions it thinks are necessary to its preservation. Arguably, no generation can reasonably claim authority irrevocably to bind the future; by the same token, one generation should have the right to say that the next generation must choose to follow the forms it has specified or choose another system.[132] To return to an earlier analogy, a constitution is like a conditional gift or will. To enjoy it, one must accept its stipulations. A nation can free itself of the gift or inheritance and its conditions (particularly if they are such as to make the gift into a curse) by renouncing it altogether, but the nation may not enjoy it without abiding by its terms.

This analysis certainly casts doubt on Linder's argument that, had they thought about it, the Founders would not have intended that "their conception of a Constitution" allowing for change could be altered. As statesmen who recognized that at least two limits on the amending process were necessary to institute the Union, the Founders probably would not have been shocked to discover that similar compromises might be utilized to preserve the Union. Moreover, arguments like Linder's were rejected by the courts when faced with attempts to void the expanded suffrage amendments and the prohibition amendment. The latter amendment almost surely grafted a sumptuary regulation that the Founders would have thought inappropriate in a constitution, but the Court wisely refused to declare it unconstitutional.[133] A contrary ruling would have subjected all future amendments to a judicial hurdle unlikely to have been intended by the Founding Fathers.

This, of course, speaks only to the constitutional and theoretical, and not to the prudential, issues. On the latter ground, Linder's caution is well taken. As a rule, unamendable amendments are surely not good public policy; extensive resort to such amendments might indeed spark revolution or instill disrespect for the Constitution. Only perhaps as a means of saving the Union, or as a means of guaranteeing the most fundamental rights, should they be utilized. To argue that such amendments are generally unwise, however, is not necessarily to say they are unconstitutional.

ARE FURTHER REMEDIES NEEDED?

In concluding, it seems appropriate to consider possible remedies. As a guard against projected worst-case scenarios, one might propose that no amendment could be ratified by the states until first approved by two or three successive Congresses, or until states conducted hearings on the subject of ratification.[134] This, or some similar measure, would expose new amendments to increased publicity and reflection before they could be incorporated into the Constitution. Such worst-case scenarios seem far too unlikely, however, to justify such a change in an already difficult amending process.[135]

It is even less likely that the popular conscience could be sufficiently aroused to ratify an amendment to prevent future unamendable amendments. The irony of such a proviso—which, to be effective, would have to be unamendable—would itself be enough to argue against such a change. Moreover, the need for such a change seems dubious, as unamendable amendments do not seem imminent and have never been adopted in more than 200 years of practice.

In the end, then, the arguments surrounding Article V do not so much point to the need for future constitutional reform, as illuminate the nature and wisdom of the existing constitutional document. The Constitution—and, more specifically, the amending clause—wisely protects liberty by guarding against the transient whims of the majority, while placing its ultimate faith in the consent of the governed. To date, at least, this faith does not appear to have been misplaced.

NOTES

1. Max Farrand, ed., *The Records of the Federal Convention of 1787* (New Haven, CT: Yale University Press, 1966), vol. 2, p. 557.
2. Ibid., vol. 2, pp. 557–58.
3. Ibid., vol. 2, p. 558.
4. Ibid.
5. Ibid., p. 559.
6. Ibid.
7. Ibid., pp. 629–33.
8. Ibid., p. 629.
9. Ibid.
10. Ibid., p. 630.
11. Ibid. These included a proposal to omit the three-fourths requirement for state ratification and leave this to the discretion of future conventions; the proposal "that no State shall without its consent be affected in its internal police, or deprived of its equal suffrage in the Senate"; and the proposal "to strike out art. V together."
12. Ibid., p. 631.
13. Ibid.
14. The first two categories, to any meaningful extent, are indistinct. Clearly,

however, mechanisms such as bicameralism and the separation of powers are means to an end rather than ends in themselves. To quote Walter Murphy,

> The Constitution does not divide authority between federal and state governments so that Americans can boast that they have federalism. Nor does the Constitution create a network of shared powers at the national level so that citizens can take to the street celebrating a trifurcated institutional system.

Murphy, "An Ordering of Constitutional Values," *Southern California Law Review* 53 (1980), pp. 748–49.

15. There are, of course, constitutional guarantees that are not enforceable in courts. For example, in *United States v. Richardson*, 418 U.S. 166 (1974), the Court has ruled that parties who have challenged the provision whereby CIA budgets are secret do not have standing. Chapter 2 presents the view that issues surrounding the amending process are justiciable.

16. For a discussion of this proposal, see Douglas Linder, "What in the Constitution Cannot Be Amended?" *Arizona Law Review* 23 (1981), pp. 728–30.

17. The language is that of Bigler. Ibid. at p. 729, n. 67.

18. Edward S. Corwin and Mary L. Ramsey, "The Constitutional Law of Constitutional Amendment," *Notre Dame Lawyer* 26 (Winter 1951), p. 188.

19. Douglas Linder, for example, cites, but does not accept, three such justifications: one based on popular sovereignty, one based on enforcement difficulties, and one based on natural law. See Linder, "What in the Constitution Cannot Be Amended?" pp. 722–35.

20. Corwin and Ramsey, "The Constitutional Law," p. 188.

21. I do not accept the notion advanced by Walter Berns that the equal state suffrage proviso would have voided the amendment proposing that the District of Columbia be treated as a state, and my reservations should be clear after examining this paper. See Berns, "The Forms of Article V," *Harvard Journal of Law & Public Policy* 6 (1982), pp. 76–77.

22. Linder, p. 725.

23. Found in John C. Calhoun, *The Works of John C. Calhoun*, vol. 1, ed. Richard K. Cralle (New York: Russell and Russell, 1968. Reprint of 1851–56 edition), p. 301. The quotation is from Calhoun's *Discourse on the Constitution and Government of the United States*. Calhoun's views on the amending process are analyzed in greater detail in John R. Vile, *The Constitutional Amending Process in American Political Thought* (New York: Praeger, 1992), pp. 79–94.

24. See Sanford Levinson, "Accounting for Constitutional Change (Or How Many Times Has the United States Constitution Been Amended? (A) < 26; (B) 26 (C) > 26 (D) All of the Above," *Constitutional Commentary* 8 (1991), p. 414.

25. Thomas M. Cooley, "The Power to Amend the Federal Constitution," *Michigan Law Journal* 2 (April 1893), p. 117.

26. Ibid., pp. 117–18. Lester B. Orfield lists more than twenty-five differing subjects that have been offered as implicit limits on the amending process. See *The Amending of the Federal Constitution* (Ann Arbor: University of Michigan, 1942), pp. 87–88, n. 12.

27. Cooley, "The Power to Amend the Federal Constitution," p. 118.

28. Ibid., p. 119.

29. Ibid., p. 119–20.

30. This controversy is covered in much greater detail in Vile, *The Constitutional Amending Process*, pp. 157–82.

31. William Marbury, "The Limitations upon the Amending Power," *Harvard Law Review* 33 (December 1919), p. 225. Marbury is quoting from a contemporary decision, *Livermore v. Waite*, 102 Cal. 113, 119, 36 Pac. 424 (1894). For further analysis of Marbury's views, see Peter Suber, *The Paradox of Self-Amendment* (New York: Peter Lang, 1990), pp. 95–97. For another article by Marbury, see "The Nineteenth and After," *Virginia Law Review* 7 (October 1920), pp. 1–29.

32. Marbury, "The Limitations upon the Amending Power," p. 228.

33. Ibid., p. 229.

34. Selden Bacon, "How the Tenth Amendment Affected the Fifth Article of the Constitution," *Virginia Law Review* 16 (June 1930), pp. 775.

35. Ibid., p. 778, n. 19.

36. Ibid., p. 777.

37. Ibid., p. 782.

38. See especially, *The National Prohibition* cases, 253 U.S. 350 (1920); and *Leser v. Garnett*, 258 U.S. 130 (1922).

39. 397 U.S. 433 (1939).

40. In "The Right to Privacy and Legitimate Constitutional Change," in *The Constitutional Bases of Social and Political Change in the United States*, ed. Shlomo Slonin (New York: Praeger, 1990), Walter Murphy uses the example of privacy as another right that cannot be radically abridged under the current constitutional system.

41. Walter Murphy, "The Art of Constitutional Interpretation: A Preliminary Showing, in *Essays on the Constitution of the United States,* ed. M. Harmon (Port Washington, NY: Kennikat, 1978), p. 151.

42. Murphy, "An Ordering of Constitutional Values," p. 755.

43. Ibid.

44. Ibid. The material cited is quoted directly from the German court decision.

45. Ibid., p. 756.

46. Ibid., emphasis in original.

47. Ibid., p. 757.

48. Ibid., emphasis in original. This reservation suggests that Murphy's argument is more limited than it may first appear—not that certain changes simply cannot be made but rather that to make them special procedures must be utilized.

49. Ibid.

50. *Marbury v. Madison*, 5 U.S. (1 Cranch) 137, 174 (1803).

51. The distinction is Murphy's. Murphy argues that "democracy stresses equality and popular rule" while "constitutionalism emphasizes that certain rights of the individual citizen are protected against government, even against popular government and majority rule." Ibid., pp. 707–8.

52. Alexander Bickel, *The Least Dangerous Branch* (Indianapolis, IN: Bobbs-Merrill, 1962), pp. 16–23. Also see Henry Abraham, "The Judicial Function under the Constitution: Theory and Practice," *NEWS for Teachers of Political Science*, Spring 1984, p. 12.

53. The threat of using the untried convention mechanism, for example, has been linked to the passage of at least four amendments. Dwight W. Connelly,

"Amending the Constitution: Is This Any Way to Call for a Constitutional Convention?" *Arizona Law Review* 22 (1980), p. 1016.

54. Laurence Tribe, "A *Constitution* We Are Amending: In Defense of a Restrained Judicial Role," *Harvard Law Review* 97 (1983), pp. 435–36.

In Walter Murphy's "Consent and Constitutional Change," in *Human Rights and Constitutional Law: Essays in Honour of Brian Walsh*, ed. James O'Reilly (Dublin: The Round Hall Press, 1992), Murphy defers treating the "fear of judicial oligarchy" (p. 124, also see p. 145) but essentially argues that the virtue of government by consent is subordinate to higher constitutional notions of human dignity. To this writer, the simple fact that both notions are embodied in the same constitution and are in potential conflict shows the danger of allowing courts to choose one or the other principle to void new amendments which may be added to the document.

55. *Scott v. Sandford,* 60 U.S. (19 How.) 393 (1857).

56. This specific analogy is found in many places. It may have been coined by Joseph Story. See Vile, *The Constitutional Amending Process in American Political Thought,* p. 79. A recent study suggests that, among thirty nations surveyed, only one nation has a more difficult amending process than the U.S. Such a study would further point to the undesirability of adding yet another obstacle to constitutional amendment. Donald S. Lutz, "Toward a Theory of Constitutional Amendment" (Paper presented at the American Political Science Convention, Chicago, IL, September 1992), pp. 32–33.

57. *Scott v. Sandford,* 60 U.S. (19 How.) 393 (1857).

58. *Plessy v. Ferguson,* 163 U.S. 537 (1896).

59. *Minersville School District v. Gobitis,* 310 U.S. 586 (1940).

60. *Korematsu v. United States,* 323 U.S. 214 (1944).

61. *In Re Yamashita,* 327 U.S. 1 (1946).

62. Addressing a related issue, Francis H. Heller observes that

> A Constitution viewed as a political document, is a framework for the exercise of power in the polity. Legal rules, by contrast, purport to determine the broad range of societal relationships. When a constitution is treated as just another form of law, there results an ambiguity of thought that tends to overshadow significant functional differences.

Heller, "Article V: Changing Dimensions in Constitutional Change," *University of Michigan Journal of Law Reform* 7 (1973), pp. 71–72.

63. The language is not conclusive, but it would appear that a proper reading would place amendments under the heading of "Constitution" rather than "the Laws of the United States." The supremacy clause, found in Article VI, reads as follows:

> This Constitution, and the Laws of the United States which shall be made in Pursuance thereof; and all Treaties made, or which shall be made, under the Authority of the United States, shall be the supreme law of the Land; and the Judges in every State shall be bound thereby, any Thing in the Constitution or Laws of any State to the Contrary notwithstanding.

64. *Hawke v. Smith,* No. 2, 253 U.S. 231 (1920); *Hollingsworth v. Virginia,* 3 U.S. (3 Dall.) 378 (1798).

65. Mark A. Grabner, "Our (Im)Perfect Constitution," *Review of Politics* 51 (Winter 1989), pp. 86–106.

66. This is the principle that Peter Suber labels the "*ex posterior* principle." See *The Paradox of Self-Amendment,* (New York: Peter Lang, 1990), pp. 207–8.

67. Murphy, "An Ordering of Constitutional Values," p. 756–57. Emphasis in original.

68. The state of Rhode Island did not send delegates to the Constitutional Convention, and delegates to the Convention were appointed by state legislatures rather than elected by conventions. Each state delegation had a single vote.

69. Murphy himself indicates that such arguments could have been plausibly raised by those on the Supreme Court seeking to restrict the application of the Thirteenth and Fourteenth Amendments. See Walter Murphy, "Slaughterhouse, Civil Rights, and Limits on Constitutional Change," *American Journal of Jurisprudence* 32 (1987), pp. 8–17.

70. Murphy, "An Ordering of Constitutional Values," p. 757.

71. Sanford Levinson, *A Constitutional Faith* (Princeton, NJ: Princeton University Press, 1988).

72. Sotorios Barber, *On What the Constitution Means* (Baltimore, MD: Johns Hopkins University Press, 1984), p. 43.

73. William F. Harris, "The Interpretable Constitution." (Ph.D. diss., Princeton University, 1985).

74. *Texas v. Johnson,* 109 S. Ct 2533 (1989); and *United States v. Eichman,* 110 S. Ct. 2404 (1990).

75. Jeff Rosen, "Was the Flag Burning Amendment Unconstitutional?" *Yale Law Journal* 100 (1992), p. 1073.

76. Ibid. For the most comprehensive treatment of the flag-burning issue, see Robert J. Goldstein, "The Great 1989–1990 Flag Flap: An Historical, Political, and Legal Analysis," *University of Miami Law Review* 45 (September 1990), pp. 19–106. Also see Murray Dry, "Flag Burning and the Constitution," in *The Supreme Court Review,* ed. Gerhard Casper, Dennis J. Hutchinson, and David A. Strauss (Chicago: University of Chicago Press, 1991), pp. 69–103.

77. Another article, James McBride's, "Is Nothing Sacred?: Flag Desecration, the Constitution, and the Establishment of Religion," *St. John's Law Review* 65 (1991), p. 322, indicates on the basis of arguments advanced by Emile Durkheim, that

> if the [flag-burning] amendment were passed, its imposition on the Bill of Rights would introduce irreconcilable tensions into the Constitution: freedom of religion would be encroached upon by the establishment of an American civil religion, identified with the nation-state.

If McBride therefore intends to argue that such an amendment would be legally unconstitutional, however, he does not elaborate this argument any further.

78. Eric A. Isaacson, "The Flag Burning Issue: A Legal Analysis and Comment," *Loyola of Los Angeles Law Review* 23 (January 1992), p. 591.

79. U.S. Constitution, Amendment 1.

80. Isaacson, "The Flag Burning Issue," p. 593. This author does not see how the language of the First Amendment is any more prohibitive than that of the language restricting Congress in Article I, Section 9 of the Constitution or restricting

the states in Article I, Section 10. The second clause of Article I, Section 9, for example, says that, "No Bill of Attainder or ex post facto Laws shall be passed."

81. Isaacson, "The Flag Burning Issue," p. 595.

82. Ibid., p. 599.

83. See *Schenck v. United States,* 249 U.S. 47 (1919).

84. Ralph A. Rossum and G. Alan Tarr, *American Constitutional Law,* 3d ed. (New York: St. Martin's Press, Inc., 1991), p. 343.

85. See Hugo L. Black's, *A Constitutional Faith* (New York: Alfred A. Knopf, 1969), pp. 43–66. Black's authority would not on this point help Isaacson, however, because Black did not believe that the First Amendment extended protection to symbolic speech. See his dissent in *Tinker v. Des Moines School District,* 393 U.S. 503 (1969).

86. Isaacson, "The Flag Burning Issue," p. 591.

87. Ibid., pp. 593–95.

88. U.S. Constitution, Article VI.

89. In proposing the Bill of Rights to the states, the first Congress used the following terminology:

> *Resolved, by the Senate and House of Representatives of the United States of America, in Congress assembled,* two thirds of both houses concurring, that the following articles be proposed to the legislatures of the several states, as amendments to the Constitution of the United States, all or any of which articles, when ratified by three fourths of the said legislatures, to be valid, to all intents and purposes, as part of the said Constitution, namely—

This language is followed by another statement, often still recorded in prefaces to the Bill of Rights, which refers to "Articles in Addition to, and Amendment of, the Constitution of the United States of America, proposed by Congress, and ratified by the Legislatures of the several States, pursuant to the Fifth Article of the original Constitution." See, *The Founders' Constitution,* vol. 5, ed. Philip B. Kurland and Ralph Lerner (Chicago: University of Chicago Press, 1987), p. 40.

90. When other amendments in the Constitution refer to themselves, they use the terminology of *article, amendment, article of amendment,* or *article . . . as an amendment.* See U.S. Constitution, amendments 13, 14, 15, 17, 18, 19, 20, 21, 22, 23, 24, and 26. Amendments, such as the 13th, 14th, and 15th, which have specific enforcement clauses, clearly appear to distinguish the articles of amendment from other *legislation* adopted under their authority.

91. Akil R. Amar, "The Bill of Rights as a Constitution," *Yale Law Journal* 100 (Winter 1992), pp. 1137–43. I raise this point to indicate that, originally the First Amendment had no special physical placement within the Bill of Rights that might have indicated its function was significantly different from other provisions in the Bill of Rights.

92. U.S. Constitution, Article V.

93. This amendment provides that "The enumeration in the Constitution of certain rights shall not be construed to deny or disparage others retained by the people." U.S. Constitution, Amendment 9. This amendment is discussed at length in Randy Barnette, ed., *The Rights Retained by the People: The History and Meaning of the Ninth Amendment* (Fairfax, VA: George Mason University Press, 1989). For

further discussion, see John H. Ely, *Democracy and Distrust: A Theory of Judicial Review* (Cambridge, MA: Harvard University Press, 1980), pp. 34–40.

94. Rosen, "Was the Flag Burning Amendment Unconstitutional?" p. 1079.

95. Ibid., p. 1082.

96. Ibid., p. 1086.

97. Ibid.

98. Ibid., p. 1087. Rosen is obviously "tracking" the language of the Ninth Amendment.

99. Ibid., pp. 1088–89.

100. Ibid., p. 1089.

101. Ibid., p. 1092. By Rosen's analysis, it would appear that his model amendment should also include reference to the Fourteenth Amendment.

102. Ibid.

103. Ibid., p. 1073, n. 5.

104. Ibid., p. 1074, n. 6.

105. Herbert Storing, *What the Anti-Federalists Were For* (Chicago: University of Chicago Press, 1981), p. 67.

106. The author believes he remembers seeing this precise illustration used but is not sure where he has seen it. For indications that these were the kinds of concerns influencing those who introduced the Ninth Amendment, however, see Barnette, *The Rights Retained by the People*. This author has treated the Ninth Amendment in *A Companion to the United States Constitution and Its Amendments* (Westport, CT: Praeger, 1993), Chapter 9.

107. The amendment reads, "The enumeration in the Constitution of certain rights shall not be construed to deny or disparage others retained by the people." U.S. Constitution, Amendment 9.

108. Abraham Lincoln thus noted that "the right of revolution, is never a legal right. . . . At most, it is but a moral right, when exercised for a morally justifiable cause. When exercised without such a cause revolution is no right, but simply a wicked exercise of physical power." Quoted by James M. McPherson, *Abraham Lincoln and the Second American Revolution* (New York: Oxford University Press, 1990), p. 28. The analysis in *Luther v. Borden*, 7 Howard 1 (1849) suggests some of the difficulties with the view that the right of revolution may be enforced by the courts. For further analysis, see John R. Vile, "John C. Calhoun on the Guarantee Clause," *South Carolina Law Review* 40 (1989), pp. 669–82.

109. Goldstein, "The Great 1989–1990 Flag Flap," p. 98, notes, however, that dissenting opinions were more moderate in the second opinion.

110. It is worth noting that were a flag-burning amendment to be adopted, it would be after two clear Supreme Court decisions on the subject, making the notion of a "second chance" especially problematic.

111. This author has not seen the Ninth Amendment explained in this fashion, but he believes this is a plausible interpretation. This would arguably make the Ninth Amendment somewhat redundant with the due process clauses of the Fifth and Fourteenth Amendments, but not significantly more so than a number of other possible interpretations.

112. Charles Press and Kenneth VerBurg, *State and Community Governments in a Dynamic Federal System,* 3d ed. (New York: Harper Collins, 1991), pp. 266–68.

113. A persistent criticism that has been made of American government, partic-

ularly by those who would prefer a different constitution, is that it fails to provide the same vigor and accountability as rival parliamentary models. For an examination of these and other such criticisms, see John R. Vile, *Rewriting the United States Constitution: An Examination of Proposals from Reconstruction to the Present* (New York: Praeger, 1991). For a particularly vivid description of some of the obstacles to effective and representative lawmaking in Congress, see Amar, "Philadelphia Revisited," pp. 1080–85.

114. For questions about the usefulness of this maxim of judicial restraint, see Martin H. Redish, *The Federal Courts in the Political Order: Judicial Jurisdiction and American Political Theory* (Durham, NC: Carolina Academic Press, 1991), pp. 87–109.

115. See Mary F. Berry, "How Hard It Is to Change," *New York Times Magazine* (September 13, 1987), pp. 93–98. Also see Peter Suber, "Population Changes and Constitutional Amendments: Federalism versus Democracy," *Journal of Law Reform* 20 (Winter 1987), pp. 409–36; and William Van Alstyne, "Interpreting This Constitution: The Unhelpful Contributions of Special Theories of Judicial Review," *University of Florida Law Review* 35 (1983), p. 218.

116. The Eleventh Amendment reversed the Court's opinion in *Chisholm v. Georgia,* 2 U.S. 419 (1793); the Fourteenth Amendment overturned the *Dred Scott* decision, 60 U.S. 393 (1857); the Sixteenth Amendment overturned *Pollock v. Farmers' Loan & Trust Company,* 158 U.S. 601 (1895); and the Twenty-Sixth Amendment modified the result which would have otherwise prevailed in *Oregon v. Mitchell,* 400 U.S. 112 (1970).

117. For texts of those amendments not ratified, see George Anastaplo, *The Constitution of 1787* (Baltimore, MD: Johns Hopkins University Press, 1989), pp. 298–99.

118. See, for example, Harvey Wish, ed., *Ante-Bellum: Writings of George Fitzhugh and Hinton Rowan Helper on Slavery* (New York: Capricorn Books, 1960).

119. For identification of the amending process with popular sovereignty, see Lester Orfield, *The Amending of the Federal Constitution* (Ann Arbor: University of Michigan Press, 1942); and Max Radin, "The Intermittant Sovereign," *Yale Law Journal* 39 (1930).

120. Murphy, "Consent and Constitutional Change." Also see Lawrence G. Sager, "The Incorrigible Constitution," *New York University Law Review* 65 (October 1990), pp. 893–961.

121. Alexander Bickel, *The Least Dangerous Branch* (Indianapolis, IN: Bobbs-Merrill, 1962), p. 16.

122. In justifying judicial review, Alexander Hamilton argued that such review did not assume the superiority of the judicial branch but rather:

> It only supposes that the power of the people is superior to both, and that where the will of the legislature, declared in its statutes, stands in opposition to that of the people, declared in the Constitution, the judges ought to be governed by the latter rather than the former. They ought to regulate their decisions by the fundamental laws rather than by those which are not fundamental.

Alexander Hamilton, James Madison, and John Jay, *The Federalist Papers,* ed. Clinton Rossiter (New York: New American Library, 1961), p. 468.

123. Justice White thus noted in *Bowers v. Hardwick,* 478 U.S. 186 (1986) that, "The Court is most vulnerable and comes nearest to illegitimacy when it deals with judge-made constitutional law having little or no cognizable roots in the language or design of the Constitution." Quoted in Robert Bork, *The Tempting of America* (New York: Free Press, 1990), p. 119.

124. See Eulis Simien, "It Is a Constitution We Are Expounding," *Hastings Constitutional Law Quarterly* 18 (1990), pp. 67–123.

125. Linder, "What in the Constitution Cannot Be Amended," pp. 728–30.

126. Ibid., p. 730.

127. Ibid., pp. 730–31 (emphasis in original).

128. Ibid., p. 731.

129. Ibid.

130. Ibid., p. 732.

131. Ibid., p. 733.

132. See Walter Berns's comment: "What we were not permitted to do in 1787–88 was to deprive—or pretend to deprive—our posterity of their natural right to do in the future what we did in 1776." Berns, "Do We Have a Living Constitution?" *National Forum* (Fall 1984), p. 31.

133. The *National Prohibition* cases, 253 U.S. 350 (1920).

134. Alternatively, Clement Vose has proposed that Congress conduct a three-day conference after proposing amendments to consist of delegates from the fifty states who would learn of arguments for and against the proposal. See *Constitutional Change: Amendment Politics and Supreme Court Litigation Since 1900* (Lexington, MA: D.C. Heath and Company, 1972), p. 371.

135. Writing about the electoral college, Saul Brenner notes, "But the Constitution should not be amended to guard against remote possibilities." Brenner, "Should the Electoral College Be Replaced by the Direct Election of the President?" *PS* 17 (Spring 1984), p. 247.

Selected Bibliography

BOOKS

Ackerman, Bruce. *We the People: Foundations*. Cambridge, MA: Belknap, 1992.

Alderman, Allen, and Caroline Kennedy. *In Our Defense: The Bill of Rights in Action*. New York: William Morrow, 1991.

American Bar Association, Special Constitutional Convention Study Committee. *Amendment of the Constitution by the Convention Method under Article V*. Chicago: American Bar Association, Public Service Activities Division, 1979.

Ames, Herman. *The Proposed Amendments of the Constitution of the United States during the First Century of Its History*. New York: Burt Franklin, 1970. Reprint of 1896 edition.

Anastaplo, George. *The Constitution of 1787: A Commentary*. Baltimore, MD: Johns Hopkins University Press, 1989.

Arendt, Hannah. *On Revolution*. New York: Viking Press, 1963.

Barber, Sotirios. *On What the Constitution Means*. Baltimore, MD: The Johns Hopkins University Press, 1984.

Barnette, Randy, ed. *The Rights Retained by the People: The History and Meaning of the Ninth Amendment*. Fairfax, VA: George Mason University Press, 1989.

Barron, Dennis. *The English-Only Question*. New Haven, CT: Yale University Press, 1990.

Beatty, Edward C. *William Penn as Social Philosopher*. New York: Octagon Books of Farrar, Strauss and Giroux, 1975.

Berger, Suzanne. *The French Political System*. New York: Random House, 1974.

Berns, Walter, ed. *After the People Vote: A Guide to the Electoral College*. Rev. ed. Washington, DC: American Enterprise Institute, 1992.

Berry, Mary F. *Why ERA Failed*. Bloomington: Indiana University Press, 1986.

Best, Judith. *The Case Against Direct Election of the President: A Defense of the Electoral College*. Ithaca, NY: Cornell University Press, 1975.

Bickel, Alexander. *The Least Dangerous Branch*. Indianapolis, IN: Bobbs-Merrill, 1962.

Black, Hugo L. *A Constitutional Faith*. New York: Alfred A. Knopf, 1969.

Blitzer, Charles, ed. *The Political Writings of James Harrington*. Indianapolis, IN: Bobbs-Merrill, 1955.

Bork, Robert. *The Tempting of America*. New York: Free Press, 1990.

Bowen, Catherine D. *Miracle at Philadelphia*. Boston: Little, Brown, 1966.

Boyd, Steven R. *Alternative Constitutions for the United States: A Documentary History*. Westport, CT: Greenwood Press, 1992.

Brown, Everett S., ed. *Ratification of the Twenty-First Amendment to the Constitution of the United States: State Convention Records and Laws*. Ann Arbor: University of Michigan Press, 1938.

Bryant, Irving. *The Bill of Rights: Its Origin and Meaning*. Indianapolis, IN: Bobbs-Merrill, 1965.

Burnham, Walter. *Critical Elections and the Mainsprings of American Politics*. New York: W. W. Norton, 1970.

Cahn, Edmond. *Supreme Court and Supreme Law*. Bloomington: Indiana University Press, 1954.

Calhoun, John C. *The Works of John C. Calhoun*. Ed. Richard K. Crallé. New York: Russell and Russell, 1968. Reprint of 1852–56 edition.

Caplan, Russell L. *Constitutional Brinkmanship*. New York: Oxford University Press, 1988.

Corwin, Edward S. *The 'Higher Law' Background of American Constitutional Law*. Ithaca, NY: Cornell University Press, 1965.

Cranston, Maurice. *What Are Human Rights?* New York: Taplinger Publishing, 1973.

Croly, Herbert. *Progressive Democracy*. Indianapolis, IN: Bobbs-Merrill, 1965. Reprint of 1909 edition.

Davis, Richard. *Proposed Amendments to the Constitution of the United States of America Introduced in Congress from the 91st Congress 1st Session, through the 98th Congress, 2nd Session, January 1969—December 1984*. Congressional Research Service Report No. 85–36, February 1, 1985.

Dennison, George. *The Dorr War: Republicanism on Trial, 1831–1862*. Lexington: University Press of Kentucky, 1976.

DeRosa, Marshall L. *The Confederate Constitution of 1861*. Columbia: University of Missouri Press, 1991.

Diamond, Martin, Winston M. Fisk, and Herbert Garfinkel. *The Democratic Republic*. Chicago: Rand McNally, 1966.

Edel, William. *A Constitutional Convention: Threat or Challenge?* New York: Praeger, 1981.

Elliot, Jonathan, ed. *The Debates in State Conventions on the Adoption of the Federal Constitution*. 5 vols. New York: Burt Franklin, 1888.

Ely, James W., Jr. *The Guardian of Every Other Right: A Constitutional History of Property Rights*. New York: Oxford University Press, 1992.

Ely, John H. *Democracy and Distrust: A Theory of Judicial Review*. Cambridge, MA: Harvard University Press, 1980.

Epstein, Lee, and Joseph F. Kobylka. *The Supreme Court and Legal Change: Abortion and the Death Penalty*. Durham, NC: University of North Carolina Press, 1992.

Equal Rights Amendment Extension. Hearings before the Subcommittee on Civil and Constitutional Rights of the Committee on the Judiciary, House of Representatives, 95th Congress, 1st and 2d Session on H.J. Res. 638, 1977, 1978.

Equal Rights Amendment Extension. Hearings before the Subcommittee on the Constitution of the Committee on the Judiciary, United States Senate, 95th Congress, 2d Session on S.J. Res. 134, 1978.

Farrand, Max. *The Framing of the Constitution of the United States.* New Haven, CT: Yale University Press, 1913.

————. *The Records of the Federal Convention of 1787.* 5 vols. New Haven, CT: Yale University Press, 1966.

Feerick, John D. *The Twenty-Fifth Amendment: Its Complete History and Earliest Applications.* 2d ed. New York: Fordham University Press, 1992.

Finer, S. E. *Five Constitutions.* Middlesex, England: Penguin Books, 1979.

Fisher, Sidney G. *The Trial of the Constitution.* New York: Da Capo Press, 1972. Reprint of J. P. Lippincott of 1862.

Foley, Michael. *The Silence of Constitutions: Gaps, 'Abeyances' and Political Temperament in the Maintenance of Government.* London: Routledge, 1989.

Frisch, Morton J., and Richard G. Stevens, eds. *American Political Thought.* Dubuque, IA: Kendall/Hunt, 1976.

————. *The Political Thought of American Statesmen.* Dubuque, IA: Kendall/Hunt, 1973.

Gerard, Jules B. *The Proposed Washington D.C. Amendment.* Jefferson City: Missouri Council for Economic Development, 1979.

Gillespie, Michael A., and Michael Lienesch. *Ratifying the Constitution.* Lawrence: University Press of Kansas, 1989.

Goldstein, Joseph. *The Intelligible Constitution.* New York: Oxford University Press, 1992.

Goldstein, Leslie. *In Defense of the Text: Democracy and Constitutional Theory.* Savage, MD: Rowman & Littlefield, 1991.

Goldwin, Robert A., and Art Kaufman. *Separation of Powers—Does It Still Work?* Washington, DC: American Enterprise Institute for Public Policy Research, 1986.

Graham, George J., and Scarlett G. Graham. *Founding Principles of American Government: Two Hundred Years of Democracy on Trial.* Chatham, NJ: Chatham House Publishers, 1984.

Grimes, Alan P. *Democracy and the Amendments to the Constitution.* Lexington, MA: Lexington Books, 1978.

Hall, Kermit L., ed. *By and for the People: Constitutional Rights in American History.* Arlington Heights, IL: Harlan Davidson, 1992.

Hall, Kermit L., Harold M. Hyman, and Leon V. Sigal. *The Constitutional Convention as an Amending Device.* Washington, DC: American Historical Association and American Political Science Association, 1981.

Halpern, Stephen C., and Charles M. Lamb, eds. *Supreme Court Activism and Restraint.* Lexington, MA: Lexington Books, 1982.

Hamilton, Alexander, James Madison, and John Jay. *The Federalist Papers,* ed. Clinton Rossiter. New York: New American Library, 1961.

Harris, William F. "The Interpretable Constitution." Ph.D. diss., Princeton University, 1985.

Hartz, Louis. *The Liberal Tradition in America*. New York: Harcourt, Brace & World, 1955.

Hoar, Roger S. *Constitutional Conventions: Their Nature, Powers, and Limitations*. Boston: Little, Brown, 1919.

Horwill, Herbert. *The Usages of the American Constitution*. London: Oxford University Press, 1925.

Jacobs, Clyde E. *The Eleventh Amendment and Sovereign Immunity*. Westport, CT: Greenwood Press, 1972.

Jacobsohn, Gary J. *The Supreme Court and the Decline of Constitutional Aspiration*. Totowa, NJ: Rowman & Littlefield, 1986.

James, Joseph B. *The Ratification of the Fourteenth Amendment*. Macon, GA: Mercer University Press, 1984.

Jameson, John A. *A Treatise on Constitutional Conventions: Their History, Powers, and Modes of Proceeding*. 4th ed. New York: Da Capo Press, 1972. Reprint of Callaghan and Company, 1887.

Kammen, Michael. *A Machine that Would Go of Itself: The Constitution in American Culture*. New York: Alfred A. Knopf, 1987.

Kaufman, Burton I., ed. *Washington's Farewell Address: The View from the 20th Century*. Chicago: Quadrangle Books, 1969.

Kenyon, Cecelia. *The Anti-Federalists*. Indianapolis, IN: Bobbs-Merrill, 1966.

Keyes, Edward, with Randall K. Miller. *The Court vs. Congress: Prayer, Busing, and Abortion*. Durham, NC: Duke University Press, 1989.

Kuhn, Thomas. *The Structure of Scientific Revolutions*. 2d ed. Chicago: University of Chicago Press, 1970.

Kurland, Philip B., and Ralph Lerner. *The Founders' Constitution*. Chicago: University of Chicago Press, 1987.

Kyvig, David E., ed. *Alcohol and Order: Perspectives on National Prohibition*. Westport, CT: Greenwood Press, 1985.

Kyvig, David E. *Repealing National Prohibition*. Chicago: University of Chicago Press, 1979.

Lee, Charles R., Jr. *The Confederate Constitutions*. Chapel Hill: University of North Carolina Press, 1963.

Levinson, Sanford. *A Constitutional Faith*. Princeton, NJ: Princeton University Press, 1988.

Livingston, William S. *Federalism and Constitutional Change*. Oxford: Clarenden Press, 1956.

Lutz, Donald S. *A Preface to American Political Theory*. Lawrence: University Press of Kansas, 1992.

McBain, Howard L. *The Living Constitution*. New York: Macmillan, 1927.

MacDonald, William. *A New Constitution for a New America*. New York: B. W. Heubsch, 1922.

McDowell, Gary L. *Taking the Constitution Seriously*. Dubuque, IA: Kendall/Hunt, 1981.

McNamara, Joseph S., and Lissa Roche, eds. *Still the Law of the Land?* Hillsdale, MI: Hillsdale College Press, 1987.

McPherson, James M. *Abraham Lincoln and the Second American Revolution*. New York: Oxford University Press, 1990.

Mansbridge, Jane J. *Why We Lost the ERA*. Chicago: University of Chicago Press, 1986.

Mason, Alpheus T. *The Supreme Court from Taft to Warren*. Baton Rouge: Louisiana University Press, 1968.

Mason, Alpheus T., and Gordon E. Baker. *Free Government in the Making*. 4th ed. New York: Oxford University Press, 1985.

Miller, William L. *The Business of May Next: James Madison & the Founding*. Charlottesville: University Press of Virginia, 1992.

Moore, W. S., and Rudolph G. Penner. *The Constitution and the Budget*. Washington, DC: American Enterprise Institute for Public Policy Research, 1980.

Musmanno, M. A. *Proposed Amendments to the Constitution*. Washington, DC: United States Government Printing Office, 1929.

Nelson, William E. *The Fourteenth Amendment: From Political Principle to Judicial Doctrine*. Cambridge, MA: Harvard University Press, 1988.

Orfield, Lester B. *The Amending of the Federal Constitution*. Ann Arbor: University of Michigan Press, 1942.

Orth, John V. *The Judicial Power of the United States: The Eleventh Amendment in American History*. New York: Oxford University Press, 1987.

Patterson, Bennett B. *The Forgotten Ninth Amendment*. Indianapolis, IN: Bobbs-Merrill, 1955.

Peck, Robert S. *The Bill of Rights & the Politics of Interpretation*. St. Paul: West Publishing, 1992.

Peters, William. *A More Perfect Union*. New York: Crown Publishers, 1987.

Peterson, Merrill D., ed. *Democracy, Liberty, and Property: The State Constitutional Conventions of the 1820s*. Indianapolis, IN: Bobbs-Merrill, 1966.

Pocock, J. G. A. *The Machiavellian Moment*. Princeton, NJ: Princeton University Press, 1975.

Press, Charles, and Kenneth VerBurg. *State and Community Governments in a Dynamic Federal System*, 3d ed. New York: Harper Collins Publishers, 1991.

Price, Don K. *America's Unwritten Constitution: Science, Religion and Political Responsibility*. Cambridge, MA: Harvard University Press, 1988.

Proposed Amendments to the Constitution of the United States Introduced in Congress from the 69th Congress, 2d Session through the 85th Congress, 2d Session, December 6, 1926, to January 3, 1957. Washington, DC: U.S. Government Printing Office, 1957.

Proposed Amendments to the Constitution of the United States of America Introduced in Congress from the 88th Congress, 1st Session through the 90th Congress, 2d Session, January 9, 1963, to January 3, 1969. Washington, DC: U.S. Government Printing Office, 1969.

Pullen, William R. "Applications of State Legislatures to Congress for the Call of a National Constitutional Convention, 1788–1867." Master's thesis, University of North Carolina at Chapel Hill, 1948.

Reagan, Ronald et al. *Restoring the Presidency: Reconsidering the Twenty-Second Amendment*. Washington, DC: The National Legal Center for the Public Interest, 1990.

Redish, Martin H. *The Federal Courts in the Political Order: Judicial Jurisdiction and American Political Theory*. Durham, NC: Carolina Academic Press, 1991.

Rossiter, Clinton. *1787: The Grand Convention*. New York: W. W. Norton, 1966.

Rossum, Ralph A., and G. Alan Tarr. *American Constitutional Law, Cases and Interpretation.* 3d ed. New York: St. Martin's Press, 1991.

Rutland, Robert A. *The Birth of the Bill of Rights, 1776–1791.* Chapel Hill: University of North Carolina Press, 1955.

Schwartz, Bernard. *A History of the American Bill of Rights.* New York: Oxford University Press, 1977.

———. *The Roots of the Bill of Rights.* 5 vols. New York: Chelsea House, 1980.

Solberg, Winton. *The Federal Convention and the Formation of the Union of the American States.* Indianapolis, IN: Bobbs-Merrill, 1958.

Storing, Herbert J., ed. *The Complete Anti-Federalist.* 7 vols. Chicago: University of Chicago Press, 1981.

Story, Joseph. *Commentaries on the Constitution of the United States,* ed. Ronald D. Rotunda and John E. Nowak. Durham, NC: Carolina Academic Press, 1987.

Suber, Peter. *The Paradox of Self-Amendment.* New York: Peter Lang, 1990.

Tananbaum, Duane. *The Bricker Amendment Controversy: A Test of Eisenhower's Political Leadership.* Ithaca, NY: Cornell University Press, 1988.

Tansill, Charles C. *Proposed Amendments of the Constitution of the United States Introduced in Congress from December 4, 1889, to July 2, 1926.* Washington, DC: U.S. Government Printing Office, 1926.

Taper, Bernard. *Gomillion v. Lightfoot: Apartheid in Alabama.* New York: McGraw-Hill, 1962.

Tiedeman, Christopher. *The Unwritten Constitution of the United States.* New York: G. P. Putnam's Sons, 1890.

Tocqueville, Alexis de. *Democracy in America.* Trans. George Lawrence. Ed. J. P. Mayer. Garden City, NY: Anchor Books, 1969.

Traynor, Roger J. "The Amending System of the United States Constitution, An Historical and Legal Analysis." Ph.D. diss., University of California, 1927.

Urofsky, Melvin I. *A March of Liberty.* New York: Alfred A. Knopf, 1988.

VanDeusen, Glyndon G. *The Jacksonian Era, 1828–1848.* New York: Harper & Row, 1959.

Veit, Helen, Kenneth Bowling, and Charlene Bickford, eds. *Creating the Bill of Rights: The Documentary Record from the First Federal Congress.* Baltimore, MD: The Johns Hopkins University Press, 1991.

Vile, John R. *A Companion to the United States Constitution and Its Amendments.* Westport, CT: Praeger, 1993.

———. *The Constitutional Amending Process in American Political Thought.* New York: Praeger, 1992.

———. *Rewriting the United States Constitution: An Examination of Proposals from Reconstruction to the Present.* New York: Praeger, 1991.

———. *The Theory and Practice of Constitutional Change in America: A Collection of Original Source Materials.* New York: Peter Lang, 1993.

Vile, M. J. C. *Constitutionalism and the Separation of Powers.* Oxford: Clarendon Press, 1969.

Vose, Clement. *Constitutional Change: Amendment Politics and Supreme Court Litigation since 1900.* Lexington, MA: Lexington Books, 1972.

Weber, Paul J., and Barbara A. Perry. *Unfounded Fears: Myths and Realities of a Constitutional Convention.* New York: Praeger, 1989.

Wiecek, William M. *The Guarantee Clause of the U.S. Constitution*. Ithaca, NY: Cornell University Press, 1972.

Wills, Garry. *Inventing America: Jefferson's Declaration of Independence*. Garden City, NY: Doubleday, 1984.

———. *Lincoln at Gettysburg: The Words that Remade America*. New York: Simon & Schuster, 1992.

Wilson, Woodrow. *Constitutional Government in the United States*. New York: Columbia University Press, 1961. Reprint of 1908 edition.

Wish, Harvey, ed. *Ante-Bellum: Writings of George Fitzhugh and Hinton Rowan Helper on Slavery*. New York: Capricorn Books, 1960.

Wolfe, Christopher. *Judicial Activism: Bulwark of Freedom or Precarious Security?* Pacific Grove, CA: Brooks/ Cole Publishing, 1991.

Wood, Gordon S. *The Creation of the American Republic, 1776–1787*. New York: W. W. Norton, 1969.

Wood, Stephen B. *Constitutional Politics in the Progressive Era: Child Labor and the Law*. Chicago: University of Chicago Press, 1968.

ARTICLES AND ESSAYS

Abraham, Henry J. "The Judicial Function under the Constitution: Theory and Practice." *NEWS for Teachers of Political Science* (Spring 1984), 10–15.

Ackerman, Bruce. "Constitutional Politics/Constitutional Law." *Yale Law Journal* 99 (December 1989), 453–547.

———. "The Storrs Lectures: Discovering the Constitution." *Yale Law Journal* 93 (1984), 1013–72.

———. "Transformative Appointments." *Harvard Law Review* 101 (1988), 1164–84.

———. "Unconstitutional Convention." *The New Republic* 180 (March 3, 1979), 8–9.

Amar, Akil R. "The Bill of Rights as a Constitution." *Yale Law Journal* 100 (Winter 1992), 1131–1210.

———. "The Bill of Rights and the Fourteenth Amendment." *Yale Law Journal* 101 (April 1992), 1193–1284.

———. "The Case of the Missing Amendments: *R.A.V. v. City of St. Paul*." *Harvard Law Review* 106 (November 1992), 124–61.

———. "Philadelphia Revisited: Amending the Constitution Outside Article V." *University of Chicago Law Review* 55 (Fall 1988), 1043–1104.

———. "Of Sovereignty and Federalism." *Yale Law Journal* 96 (1987), 1425–1520.

Amar, Akil R., and Vik Amar. "President Quayle?" *Virginia Law Review* 78 (May 1992), 913–47.

Anastaplo, George. "Amendments to the Constitution of the United States: A Commentary." *Loyola University Law Journal* 23 (Summer 1992), 631–865.

Bacon, Selden. "How the Tenth Amendment Affected the Fifth Article of the Constitution." *Virginia Law Review* 16 (June 1930), 771–91.

Baker, A. Diane. "ERA: The Effect of Extending the Time for Ratification on Attempts to Rescind Prior Ratifications." *Emory Law Journal* 28 (1979), 71–110.

"The Balanced Budget Amendment: An Inquiry Into Appropriateness." *Harvard Law Review* 96 (May 1983), 1600–20.

Barker, William T. "A Status Report on the 'Balanced Budget' Constitutional Convention." *John Marshall Law Review* 20 (1986), 29–96.

Beaney, William M. "Prayer and Politics: The Impact of Engel and Schempp on the Political Process." In *The Impact of Supreme Court Decisions,* 2d ed, ed. Theodore L. Becker and Malcolm M. Feeley. New York: Oxford University Press, 1972, 22–36.

Berke, Richard L. "1789 Amendment Is Ratified but Now the Debate Begins." *New York Times,* May 8, 1991, 1.

Berns, Walter. "Do We Have a Living Constitution?" *National Forum* 64 (Fall 1984), 29–34.

———. "The Forms of Article V." *Harvard Journal of Law & Public Policy* 6 (1982), 73–77.

Bernstein, Richard B. "Fixing the Electoral College." *Constitution* 5 (Winter 1993), 42–48.

Berry, Mary F. "How Hard It Is to Change." *New York Times Magazine* (September 13, 1987), 93–98.

Black, Charles L., Jr. "Amending the Constitution: A Letter to a Congressman." *Yale Law Journal* 83 (December 1972), 189–215.

———. "Amendment by National Constitutional Convention: A Letter to a Senator." *Oklahoma Law Review* 32 (1969), 626–44.

———. "Correspondence: On Article I, Section 7, Clause 3—and the Amendment of the Constitution." *Yale Law Journal* 87 (1978), 896–900.

———. "National Lawmaking by Initiative? Let's Think Twice." *Human Rights* 8 (Fall 1979), 28–31.

———. "The Proposed Amendment of Article V: A Threatened Disaster." *Yale Law Journal* 72 (1963), 957–66.

Bond, James E., and David E. Engdahl. "The Duties and Powers of Congress Regarding Conventions for Proposing Amendments." *The Constitutional Convention: How Is It Formed? How Is It Run? What Are the Guidelines? What Happens Now?* Washington, DC: National Legal Center for the Public Interest, 1987.

Brenner, Saul. "Should the Electoral College Be Replaced by the Direct Election of the President?" *PS: Political Science and Politics* 17 (Spring 1984), 237–50.

Brown, Everett S. "The Ratifications of the Twenty-First Amendment." *American Political Science Review* 29 (December 1935), 1005–17.

Brown, George S. "The People Should be Consulted as to Constitutional Change." *American Bar Association Journal* 16 (1930), 404–6.

Brown, Raymond G. "The Sixteenth Amendment to the United States Constitution." *American Law Review* 54 (1920), 843–54.

Burke, Yvonne B. "Validity of Attempts to Rescind Ratification of the Equal Rights Amendment." *University of Los Angeles Law Review* 8 (1976), 1–22.

"Comments, The Equal Rights Amendment and Article V: A Framework for Analysis of the Extension and Rescission Issues." *University of Pennsylvania Law Review* 127 (1978), 494–532.

Carroll, John. "Constitutional Law: Constitutional Amendment. Rescission of Ratification. Extension of Ratification Period. State of Idaho v. Freeman." *Akron Law Review* 14 (Summer 1982), 151–61.

Connelly, Dwight W. "Amending the Constitution: Is This Any Way to Call for a Constitutional Convention?" *Arizona Law Review* 22 (1980), 1011–36.

Cooley, Thomas M. "The Power to Amend the Federal Constitution." *Michigan Law Journal* 2 (April 1892), 109–20.

Corwin, Edward S., and Mary L. Ramsey. "The Constitutional Law of Constitutional Amendment." *Notre Dame Lawyer* 26 (Winter 1951), 185–213.

Dellinger, Walter. "Another Route to the ERA." *Newsweek* 100 (August 2, 1982), 8.

———. "Constitutional Politics: A Rejoinder." *Harvard Law Review* 97 (December 1983), 446–50.

———. "The Legitimacy of Constitutional Change: Rethinking the Amending Process." *Harvard Law Review* 97 (December 1983), 380–432.

———. "The Recurring Question of the 'Limited' Constitutional Convention." *Yale Law Journal* 88 (1979), 1623–40.

Diamond, Ann S. "A Convention for Proposing Amendments: The Constitution's Other Method." *Publius: The Journal of Federalism* 11 (Summer 1981), 113–46.

Dow, David R. "When Words Mean What We Believe They Say: The Case of Article V." *Iowa Law Review* 76 (October 1990), 1–66.

Dry, Murray. "Flag Burning and the Constitution." *Supreme Court Review 1990.* Ed. Gerhard Casper, Dennis J. Hutchinson, and David A. Strauss. Chicago: University of Chicago Press, 1991, 69–103.

Ervin, Sam, Jr. "Proposed Legislation to Implement the Convention Mechanism of Amending the Constitution." *Michigan Law Review* 66 (March 1968), 875–902.

Gaugush, Bill. "Principles Governing the Interpretation and Exercise of Article V Powers." *The Western Political Quarterly* 35 (June 1982), 212–21.

Gely, Rafael, and Palbo T. Spiller. "The Political Economy of Supreme Court Constitutional Decisions: The Case of Roosevelt's Court-Packing Plan." *International Review of Law and Economics* 12 (1991), 45–67.

Gerhardt, Michael J. "The Role of Precedent in Constitutional Decisionmaking and Theory." *George Washington Law Review* 60 (November 1991), 68–159.

Ginsberg, Ruth B. "Ratification of the Equal Rights Amendment: A Question of Time." *Texas Law Review* 57 (1969), 919–45.

Goldberg, Arthur J. "The Proposed Constitutional Convention." *Hastings Constitutional Law Quarterly* 11 (Fall 1983), 1–4.

Goldstein, Robert J. "The Great 1989–1990 Flag Flap: An Historical, Political and Legal Analysis." *University of Miami Law Review* 45 (September 1990), 19–106.

Grabner, Mark A. "Our (Im)Perfect Constitution." *Review of Politics* 51 (Winter 1989), 86–106.

Graham, Fred P. "The Role of the States in Proposing Constitutional Amendments." *American Bar Association Journal* 49 (December 1963), 1175–83.

Green, Steven K. "The Blaine Amendment Reconsidered." *The American Journal of Legal History* 36 (January 1992), 38–69.

Hamburger, Philip A. "The Constitution's Accommodation of Social Change." *Michigan Law Review* 88 (November 1989), 239–327.

Heard, Thomas E. "Proposed Constitutional Amendments as a Research Tool: The Example of Prohibition." *Law Library Journal* 84 (Summer 1992), 499–508.

Heller, Francis H. "Article V: Changing Dimensions in Constitutional Change." *University of Michigan Journal of Law Reform* 7 (Fall 1973), 71–89.

———. "Limiting a Constitutional Convention: The State Precedents." *Cardozo Law Review* 3 (1982), 563–79.

Herrmann, Mark E. "Looking Down from the Hill: Factors Determining the Success of Congressional Efforts to Reverse Supreme Court Interpretations of the Constitution." *William and Mary Law Review* 33 (Winter 1992), 543–610.

Horn, Dottie. "Another Star for the Stripes?" *Endeavors* 8 (Fall 1990), 4–6.

Hutson, James H. "The Birth of the Bill of Rights: The State of Current Scholarship." *Prologue* 20 (Fall 1988), 143–61.

Hyman, Harold M. "The Narrow Escape from a 'Compromise of 1860': Secession and the Constitution." In *Freedom and Reform: Essays in Honor of Henry Steele Commanger,* ed. Harold M. Hyman and Leonard S. Levy. New York: Harper & Row, 1967, 149–66.

Isaacson, Eric A. "The Flag Burning Issue: A Legal Analysis and Comment." *Loyola of Los Angeles Law Review* 23 (January 1992), 535–600.

Kanowitz, Leo, and Marilyn Klinger. "Can a State Rescind Its Equal Rights Amendment Ratification: Who Decides and How?" *Hastings Law Journal* 28 (March 1978), 969–1009.

Kay, Richard S. "The Illegality of the Constitution." *Constitutional Commentary* 4 (Winter 1987), pp. 57–80.

Kean, Thomas H. "A Constitutional Convention Would Threaten Rights We Have Cherished for 200 Years." *Detroit College Law Review* 4 (Winter 1986), 1087–91.

Keller, Morton. "Failed Amendments to the Constitution." *The World & I* 2 (September 1987), 87–93.

Keough, Stephen. "Formal & Informal Constitutional Lawmaking in the United States in the Winter of 1860–1861." *Journal of Legal History* 8 (1987), 275–99.

Klarman, Michael J. "Constitutional Fact/Constitutional Fiction: A Critique of Bruce Ackerman's Theory of Constitutional Moments." *Stanford Law Review* 44 (February 1992), 759–97.

Kyvig, David E. "Alternative to Revolution: Two Hundred Years of Constitutional Amending." In *The Embattled Constitution: Vital Framework or Convenient Symbol,* ed. Adolph H. Grundman. Malabar, FL: Robert E. Krieger Publishing, 1986, 136–48.

———. "Can the Constitution Be Amended? The Battle Over the Income Tax, 1895–1913." *Prologue* 20 (Fall 1988), 181–200.

———. "The Road Not Taken: FDR, the Supreme Court and Constitutional Amendment." *Political Science Quarterly* 104 (Fall 1989), 463–81.

Labbé, Ronald M. "New Light on the Slaughterhouse Monopoly Act of 1869." In *Louisiana's Legal Heritage,* ed. Edward F. Hass. Pensacola, FL: Perdido Bay Press, 1983, 143–62.

LaJoie, Andree, and Henry Quillian. "Emerging Constitutional Norms: Continuous Judicial Amendment of the Constitution—The Proportionality Test as a Moving Target." *Law and Contemporary Problems* 55 (Winter 1992), 285–302.

Lawrence, Z. Melissa. "Constitutional Revision by Amendment—A Louisiana Tradition." *Louisiana Law Review* 51 (March 1991), 849–60.

Lee, R. Alton. "The Corwin Amendment in the Secession Crisis." *Ohio Historical Quarterly* 70 (January 1961), 1–26.

Leepson, Marc. "Calls for Constitutional Conventions." *Editorial Research Reports* 1 (March 16, 1979), 187–204.

Leuchenburg, William E. "The Origins of Franklin D. Roosevelt's 'Court-Packing' Plan." *Supreme Court Review,* ed. Philip Kurland. Chicago: University of Chicago Press, 1966, 347–400.

Levinson, Sanford. "Accounting for Constitutional Change: (Or, How Many Times Has the United States Constitution Been Amended? (A) <26; (B) 26 (C) >26 (D) All of the Above)." *Constitutional Commentary* 8 (Summer 1991), 409–31.

———. "On the Notion of Amendment, Reflections on David Daube's 'Jehovah the Good.' " *S'Vara: A Journal of Philosophy and Judaism* 1 (Winter 1990), 25–31.

———. " 'Veneration' and Constitutional Change: James Madison Confronts the Possibility of Constitutional Change." *Texas Tech Law Review* 21 (1990), 2443–61.

Linder, Douglas. "What in the Constitution Cannot Be Amended?" *Arizona Law Review* 23 (1981), 717–31.

Lipkin, Robert J. "The Anatomy of Constitutional Revolutions." *Nebraska Law Review* 68 (1989), 701–806.

Little, Laura E. "An Excursion into the Uncharted Waters of the Seventeenth Amendment." *Temple Law Review* 64 (Fall 1991), 629–58.

Lutz, Donald S. "Toward a Theory of Constitutional Amendment." Paper presented at the American Political Science Convention, Chicago, IL, September 1992.

McAllister, Bill. "Congress Backs Madison, But Does It Really Matter?" *Washington Post,* May 21, 1991, A23.

McBride, James. "Is Nothing Sacred?: Flag Desecration, the Constitution, and the Establishment of Religion." *St. John's Law Review* 65 (1991), 297–324.

Manne, Neal S. "Good Intentions, New Inventions, and Article V Constitutional Conventions." *Texas Law Review* 58 (December 1979), 131–70.

Marbury, William. "The Limitations upon the Amending Power." *Harvard Law Review* 33 (December 1919), 223–35.

———. "The Nineteenth and After." *Virginia Law Review* 7 (October 1920), 1–29.

Markman, Stephen. "The Amendment Process of Article V: A Microcosm of the Constitution." *Harvard Journal of Law & Public Policy* 12 (1989), 113–32.

———. "The Jurisprudence of Constitutional Amendments." In *Still the Law of the Land?* Ed. Joseph S. McNamara and Lissa Roche. Hillsdale, MI: Hillsdale College Press, 1987, 79–96.

———. "A Poor Choice of Words: Careless Rhetoric about the Constitution." *Detroit College of Law Review* 1991 (Fall), 1325–47.

Martin, Philip L. "Madison's Precedent of Legislative Ratification for Constitutional Amendments." *Proceedings of the American Philosophical Society* 109 (February 1965), 47–52.

Meador, Lewis A. "The Council of Censors." *The Pennsylvania Magazine of History and Biography* 22 (1898), 265–300.

Miller, Robert S., and Donald O. Dewey. "The Congressional Salary Amendment: 200 Years Later." *Glendale Law Review* (1991), 92–109.

Moses, Jonathan M. "Statehood for Washington Faces Hurdle." *Wall Street Journal* (December 9, 1992), B14.

Moyer, Thomas J. "The Bill of Rights—Its Origins and Its Keepers." *Judicature* 75 (August–September 1991), 57–61.

Murphy, Walter. "The Art of Constitutional Interpretation: A Preliminary Showing." In *Essays on the Constitution of the United States,* ed. M. Harmon. Port Washington, NY: Kennikat, 1978, 130–59.

———. "Consent and Constitutional Change." In *Human Rights and Constitutional Law: Essays in Honour of Brian Walsh,* ed. James O'Reilly. Dublin: Round Hall Press, 1992, 123–46.

———. "An Ordering of Constitutional Values." *Southern California Law Review* 53 (January 1980), 703–60.

———. "The Right to Privacy and Legitimate Constitutional Change." In *Constitutional Bases of Political and Social Change in the United States,* ed. Shlomo Slonim. New York: Praeger, 1990, 213–35.

———. "*Slaughterhouse, Civil Rights,* and Limits on Constitutional Change." *American Journal of Jurisprudence* 32 (1987), 1–22.

Palmer, Robert C. "Akil Amar: Elitist Populist and Anti-Textual Textualist." *Southern Illinois Law* 16 (Winter 1992), 397–419.

Pedrick, William H., and Richard C. Dahl. "Let the People Vote! Ratification of Constitutional Amendments by Convention." *Arizona Law Review* 30 (1988), 243–56.

Peters, Ronald M., Jr. "Repeal the Seventeenth!" *Extensions* (Spring 1990), 2, 16–17.

Planell, Raymond M. "The Equal Rights Amendment: Will States Be Allowed to Change Their Minds?" *Notre Dame Lawyer* 49 (February 1974), 657–70.

Pope, James G. "Republican Moments: The Role of Direct Popular Power in the American Constitutional Order." *University of Pennsylvania Law Review* 139 (December 1990), 287–368.

"Proposed Legislation on the Convention Method of Amending the United States Constitution." *Harvard Law Review* 85 (June 1992), 1612–48.

Radin, Max. "The Intermittent Sovereign." *Yale Law Journal* 39 (1930), 514–31.

Raven-Hansen, Peter. "The Constitutionality of D.C. Statehood." *George Washington Law Review* 60 (November 1991), 160–93.

Rees, Grover III. "The Amendment Process and Limited Constitutional Conventions." *Benchmark* 2 (1986), 67–108.

———. "Throwing Away the Key: The Unconstitutionality of the Equal Rights Amendment Extension." *Texas Law Review* 58 (May 1980), 875–932.

Rhodes, Robert M. "A Limited Federal Constitutional Convention." *University of Florida Law Review* 26 (Fall 1973), 1–18.

Robinson, Donald L. "The Comparative Study of Constitutions: Suggestions for Organizing the Inquiry." *PS: Political Science and Politics* 25 (June 1991), 272–80.

Rosen, Jeff. "Was the Flag Burning Amendment Unconstitutional?" *Yale Law Journal* 100 (1991), 1073–92.

Sager, Lawrence G. "The Incorrigible Constitution." *New York Law Review* 65 (October 1990), 893–961.

"Sawing a Justice in Half." *Yale Law Journal* 48 (1939), 1455–58.

Scharpf, Fritz W. "Judicial Review and the Political Question: A Functional Analysis." *Yale Law Journal* (March 1966), 517–97.

Sherry, Suzanna. "Book Review, The Ghost of Liberalism Past." *Harvard Law Review* 105 (February 1992), 918–34.

Simien, Eulis. "It Is a Constitution We Are Expounding." *Hastings Constitutional Law Quarterly* 18 (Fall 1990), 67–123.

Smith, Edward P. "The Movement Towards a Second Constitutional Convention in 1788." In *Essays in the Constitutional History of the United States in the Formative Period, 1775–1789,* ed. John F. Jameson. Boston: Houghton, Mifflin, 1909, 49–115.

Smith, Goldwin. "Is the Constitution Outworn?" *North American Review* 166 (March 1898), 257–67.

Sorenson, Theodore. "The Quiet Campaign to Rewrite the Constitution." *Saturday Review* (July 15, 1967), 17–20.

Stathis, Stephen. "The Twenty-Second Amendment: A Practical Remedy or Partisan Maneuver?" *Constitutional Commentary* 7 (Winter 1991), 61–68.

Suber, Peter. "Population Changes and Constitutional Amendments: Federalism versus Democracy." *Journal of Law Reform* 20 (Winter 1987), 409–90.

Swindler, William F. "The Current Challenge to Federalism: The Confederating Proposals." *The Georgetown Law Review* 52 (Fall 1963), 1–41.

"Symposium on the Article V Convention Process." *Michigan Law Review* 66 (March 1968), 837–1017.

Tribe, Laurence. "A *Constitution* We Are Amending: In Defense of a Restrained Judicial Role." *Harvard Law Review* 97 (December 1983), 433–45.

———. "Issues Raised by Requesting Congress to Call a Constitutional Convention to Propose a Balanced Budget Amendment." *Pacific Law Journal* 10 (1979), 627–39.

Turner, John J., Jr. "The Twelfth Amendment and the First American Party System." *Historian* 35 (1973), 221–37.

Tushnet, Mark. "The Flag-Burning Episode: An Essay on the Constitution." *University of Colorado Law Review* 61 (1990), 39–53.

Van Alstyne, William W. "Does Article V Restrict the States to Calling Unlimited Conventions Only?—A Letter to a Colleague." *Duke Law Journal* (January 1978), 1295–1306.

———. "Interpreting the Constitution: The Unhelpful Contributions of Special Theories of Judicial Review." *University of Florida Law Review* 35 (Spring 1983), 209–35.

———. "The Limited Constitutional Convention—The Recurring Answer." *Duke Law Journal* (September 1979), 985–1001.

———. "Notes on a Bicentennial Constitution: Part I, Processes of Change." *University of Illinois Law Review,* 1984, 933–58.

Van Sickle, Bruce M., and Lynn M. Boughey. "Lawful and Peaceful Revolution: Article V and Congress' Present Duty to Call a Convention for Proposing Amendments." *Hamline Law Review* 14 (Fall 1990), 1–115.

Vieira, Norman. "The Equal Rights Amendment: Rescission, Extension and Jus-
    ticiability." *Southern Illinois Law Journal* (1981), 1–29.
Vile, John R. "The Amending Process: The Alternative to Revolution." *Southeastern
    Political Review* 99 (Fall 1983), 49–95.
———. "American Views of the Constitutional Amending Process: An Intellectual
    History of Article V." *American Journal of Legal History* 35 (January 1991),
    44–69.
———. "Ann Diamond on an Unlimited Constitutional Convention." *Publius: The
    Journal of Federalism* 19 (Winter 1989), 177–83.
———. "Book Review: Filling a Void in Scholarship: Russell L. Caplan on Con-
    stitutional Conventions." *Journal of Law & Politics* 6 (Fall 1989), 125–34.
———. "Constitutional Interpretation and Constitutional Amendment: Alternative
    Means of Constitutional Change." *Research in Law and Policy Studies*. Vol.
    3. Ed. Stuart Nagel. Greenwich, CT: JAI Press, 1992.
———. "How a Constitutional Amendment Protecting the Flag Might Widen Pro-
    tection of Symbolic Expression." *Louisiana Bar Journal* 37 (October 1989),
    169–72.
———. "John C. Calhoun on the Guarantee Clause." *South Carolina Law Review*
    40 (Spring 1989), 667–92.
———. "Judicial Review of the Amending Process: The Dellinger-Tribe Debate."
    Journal of Law & Politics 3 (Winter 1986), 21–50.
———. "Just Say No to 'Stealth' Amendment." *National Law Journal* 14 (June 22,
    1991), 15–16.
———. "Legally Amending the United States Constitution: The Exclusivity of
    Article V's Mechanisms." *Cumberland Law Review* 21 (1990–1991), 271–307.
———. "Limitations on the Constitutional Amending Process." *Constitutional Com-
    mentary* 2 (Summer 1985), 373–88.
———. "Permitting States to Rescind Ratifications of Pending Amendments to the
    U.S. Constitution." *Publius: The Journal of Federalism* 20 (Spring 1990), 109–
    22.
———. "Proposals to Amend the Bill of Rights: Are Fundamental Rights in Jeop-
    ardy?" *Judicature* 75 (August–September 1991), 62–67.
———. "The Supreme Court and the Amending Process." *Georgia Political Science
    Association Journal* 8 (Fall 1980), 33–66.
———. "Three Kinds of Constitutional Founding and Change: The Convention
    Model and Its Alternatives." Forthcoming in *Political Research Quarterly*, 1993.
Vose, Clement. "When District of Columbia Representation Collides with the
    Constitutional Amendment Institution." *Publius: The Journal of Federalism* 9
    (Winter 1979), 105–25.
Walroff, Jonathan L. "The Unconstitutionality of Voter Initiative Applications for
    Federal Constitutional Conventions." *Colorado Law Review* 85 (1985), 1525–
    45.
Weber, Paul. "The Constitutional Convention: A Safe Political Option." *Journal of
    Law & Politics* 3 (Winter 1986), 51–70.
———. "Madison's Opposition to a Second Convention." *Polity* 20 (Spring 1988),
    498–517.
Webster, Noah. "Government." *American Magazine* 2 (1787–88), 137–45.

Zuchert, Michael P. "Completing the Constitution, The Thirteenth Amendment." *Constitutional Commentary* 4 (1987), 259–83.

CASES

Abington School District v. Schempp, 374 U.S. 203 (1963).
Bailey v. Drexel Furniture Company, 259 U.S. 20 (1922).
Baker v. Carr, 369 U.S. 186 (1962).
Barron v. Baltimore, 32 U.S. 243 (1833).
Bolling v. Sharpe, 347 U.S. 397 (1954).
Bowers v. Hardwick, 478 U.S. 186 (1986).
Brown v. Board of Education, 347 U.S. 483 (1954).
Chandler v. Wise, 307 U.S. 474 (1939).
Chisholm v. Georgia, 2 U.S. (2 Dall.) 419 (1793).
Civil Rights cases, 109 U.S. 3 (1883).
Coleman v. Miller, 307 U.S. 433 (1939).
Colegrove v. Green, 328 U.S. 549 (1946).
Dillon v. Gloss, 256 U.S. 368 (1921).
Dred Scott v. Sandford, 19 Howard 393 (1857).
Dyer v. Blair, 390 F. Supp. 1291 (1975).
Engel v. Vitale, 379 U.S. 421 (1962).
Frontiero v. Richardson, 411 U.S. 677 (1973).
Gibbons v. Ogden, 22 U.S. 1 (1824).
Goldwater v. Carter, 444 U.S. 996 (1979).
Griswold v. Connecticut, 381 U.S. 479 (1965).
Frontiero v. Richardson, 411 U.S. 677 (1973).
Hammer v. Dagenhart, 247 U.S. 251 (1918).
Harper v. Virginia Board of Elections, 383 U.S. 663 (1966).
Hawke v. Smith (No. 1), 253 U.S. 221 (1920).
Hawke v. Smith (No. 2), 253 U.S. 231 (1920).
Hollingsworth v. Virginia, 3 U.S. (3 Dall.) 378 (1798).
Home Building & Loan Association v. Blaisdell, 290 U.S. 398 (1934).
Idaho v. Freeman, 529 F. Supp. 1107 (1981).
In Re Yamashita, 327 U.S. 1 (1946).
Katzenbach v. Morgan, 384 U.S. 641 (1966).
Korematsu v. United States, 323 U.S. 214 (1944).
Lee v. Weisman, 112 S. Ct. 2649 (1992).
Leser v. Garnett, 258 U.S. 130 (1922).
Livermore v. Waite, 102 Cal. 113, 36 Pac. 424 (1894).
Luther v. Borden, 48 U.S. 1 (1849).
Marbury v. Madison, 5 U.S. 137 (1803).
Martin v. Hunter's Lessee, 14 U.S. 304 (1816).
McCulloch v. Maryland, 17 U.S. 316 (1819).
Minersville School District v. Gobitis, 310 U.S. 586 (1940).
National Prohibition Cases, 253 U.S. 350 (1920).
N.L.R.B. v. Jones & Laughlin Steel Corporation, 301 U.S. 1 (1937).
Oregon v. Mitchell, 400 U.S. 112 (1970).
Plessy v. Ferguson, 163 U.S. 537 (1896).

Pollock v. Farmers' Loan & Trust Company, 158 U.S. 601 (1895).

Powell v. McCormack, 395 U.S. 486 (1969).

Reynolds v. Sims, 377 U.S. 523 (1964).

Rhode Island v. Palmer, 253 U.S. 386 (1920).

Roe v. Wade, 410 U.S. 113 (1973).

Schenck v. United States, 249 U.S. 47 (1919).

Slaughterhouse cases, 83 U.S. 36 (1873).

Smith v. Directors of Union Bank of Georgetown, 30 U.S. (5 Pet.) 518 (1831).

Springer v. United States, 102 U.S. 586 (1881).

Texas v. Johnson, 109 S. Ct. 2533 (1989).

Texas v. White, 74 U.S. (7 Wall.) 700 (1869).

Trimble v. Gordon, 430 U.S. 762 (1977).

Trinsey v. Pennsylvania, 766 F. Supp. 1338; 941 F. 2d 224 (1991).

United States v. Carolene Products, 304 U.S. 149 (1938).

United States v. Darby, 312 U.S. 100 (1941).

United States v. Eichman, 110 S. Ct. 2404 (1990).

United States v. Richardson, 418 U.S. 166 (1974).

United States v. Sprague, 282 U.S. 716 (1931).

Ware v. Hylton, 3 Dall. 199 (1796).

Index

About the Author

JOHN R. VILE is Professor and Chair in the Department of Political Science at Middle Tennessee State University. His many articles have appeared in journals such as *The Journal of Law & Politics, The American Journal of Legal History*, and *The National Law Journal*. In addition, he is the author of three books on the U.S. Constitution: *Rewriting the United States Constitution* (Praeger, 1991), *The Constitutional Amending Process in American Political Thought* (Praeger, 1992), and *A Companion to the United States Constitution* (Praeger, 1993).